D1686450

September 11, Terrorist Attacks, and U.S. Foreign Policy

Edited by

DEMETRIOS JAMES CARALEY

THE ACADEMY OF POLITICAL SCIENCE
NEW YORK

Copyright © 2002 by The Academy of Political Science

All rights reserved. No part of this publication may be reproduced, stored in a retrieval system, or transmitted in any form or by any means, electronic, mechanical, photocopying, recording, or otherwise, without the prior written permission of the publisher.

Published by
The Academy of Political Science
475 Riverside Drive, Suite 1274
New York, NY 10115

Cover design: Loren Morales

Cover credits: Department of Defense and spaceimaging.com

Library of Congress Cataloging-in-Publication Data

September 11, terrorist attacks, and U.S. foreign policy/edited by Demetrios James Caraley.
    p. cm.
  Includes bibliographical references.
  ISBN 1-884853-01-3 (alk. paper)
  1. United States—Foreign relations—2001– . 2. United States—Foreign relations—1989– . 3. Terrorism—Political aspects. 4. September 11 Terrorist Attacks, 2001—Causes. 5. September 11 Terrorist Attacks, 2001—Influence. I. Caraley, Demetrios.
E902.S47 2002
327.73'009'0511—dc21

                                                                                2002010120

Printed in the United States of America
p 5 4 3 2 1

In memory of
Steven B. Paterson
and the other innocent dead
of September 11, 2001

Contents

Foreword from the Editor of Political Science Quarterly
        DEMETRIOS JAMES CARALEY vii

PART I: INTRODUCTION

September 11: An Overview
        DEMETRIOS JAMES CARALEY
        ALEXANDER A. COOLEY 1

PART II: THE ATTACKS

The Post September 11 Debate Over Empire, Globalization, and Fragmentation
        WALTER LAFEBER 15

The Soft Underbelly of American Primacy: Tactical Advantages of Terror
        RICHARD K. BETTS 33

The Pragmatic Fanaticism of al Qaeda: An Anatomy of Extremism in Middle Eastern Politics
        MICHAEL DORAN 51

PART III: THE AXIS OF EVIL

North Korea's Weapons of Mass Destruction: Badges, Shields or Swords?
        VICTOR D. CHA 65

U.S. Policy Toward Iraq Since Desert Storm
        DANIEL BYMAN 87

CIA's Strategic Intelligence in Iraq
        RICHARD L. RUSSELL 111

Contradictions in Iranian and Indonesian Politics
        DANIEL BRUMBERG 129

PART IV: LOOKING TO THE FUTURE

Al Qaeda, Military Commissions, and American Self-Defense
        RUTH WEDGWOOD 161

An Interim Assessment of September 11: What Has Changed and What Has Not?
        ROBERT JERVIS 179

Foreword from the Editor of *Political Science Quarterly*

DEMETRIOS JAMES CARALEY

September 11, 2001, is, as President Franklin Roosevelt said about December 7, 1941, "a date which will live in infamy." As with analysis of the 1941 surprise attack on Pearl Harbor, political scientists and others will examine for generations why and how Muslim extremists mounted a surprise attack during peacetime by crashing hijacked American airliners into the World Trade Center and the Pentagon, causing some 3,000 deaths, mostly of civilians. What the articles in this book attempt to do is to disseminate the first considered thoughts of leading scholars on the implications of the September 11 attacks for American foreign and military policy. While this book is not an integrated analysis of every relevant topic, the collection as a whole does hit all of the major ones. Six of the articles were commissioned by the editor and were completed from four to eight months after the attacks. The other four came from unsolicited submissions to *Political Science Quarterly*.

The United States has shown in the Gulf War, Kosovo, and Afghanistan that it is militarily more powerful by many orders of magnitude than any other state or any terrorist organization. By common agreement, the United States is "the world's only remaining superpower." But as great as U.S. military power is, it has not been able to compel states or terrorist groups to comply with its policy preferences; nor, indeed, could it even stop terrorists from attacking the United States homeland itself. Further, America's superior military power cannot guarantee protection to the American people against future terrorist attacks, even though shielding the civilian population has been the central mission of military forces throughout history.

U.S. military power is essentially the power to destroy. It can destroy the noncompliant if they can be found, and if the United States is willing to pay the political price. Finding the Serb army in Kosovo or Serbia and the Iraqi army in Kuwait was simple. Finding terrorist cells based all over the globe including within the United States will be difficult and might even prove impossible. There is simply no geographical area where the United States and its allies can force a series of major battles against the terrorists and, if successful, have the terrorists' defeated leaders sign surrender documents and totally end further attacks.[1] It is thus not more military power that the United States needs, rather it is strengthened intelligence and security forces and more efficient diplomacy with the intelligence and security forces of allies that will count most in reducing and possibly stopping new terrorist attacks.

But the war against terrorism also poses a different danger to the United States—legitimating unilateral presidential warmaking in violation of the constitutional system of checks and balances. After September 11, President Bush received congressional authority to use military force in Afghanistan. With respect to the future, the president's Article II designation as "commander in chief" gives him authority to use the military to repel attacks on the United States. Furthermore, as President Bush announced in his June 2002 commencement speech at West Point, the president as commander in chief can launch "preemptive attacks" based on secret intelligence and does not have to wait until the last minute before acting to destroy the would-be attackers. The nature of this kind of operation is to be swift and secret, and therefore it is not conducive to congressional debate before the fact.

The constitutional problem arises from President Bush's repeated threats of going to war against Iraq to topple Saddam Hussein and his regime. Here no secrecy or swiftness is required. President Bush talked about it in his 2000 election campaign, formally in his 2002 "axis of evil" speech, and in many other speeches and press conferences. In July 2002, a plan for attacking Iraq from three directions was leaked to the press.[2] A new war against Iraq will be difficult, especially if the Israeli-Palestinian conflict is still highly volatile and al Qaeda leaders and cells are still at large. Such a war would probably bring high casualties and alienate many European and Arab allies who do not see Saddam Hussein as posing the kind of danger the United States sees.

Yet President Bush has never said that he would seek congressional authority to start a war against Iraq, even though Article I of the Constitution gives the power to declare war to Congress, not to the president.[3] In December 1990, some five months after huge American military forces had already been de-

---

[1] This is of course what happened in 1945 when, three-and-one-half years after Pearl Harbor and after much bitter fighting across island chains in the Pacific and in bombing the Japanese home islands, the Japanese leaders signed surrender documents on the deck of an American battleship anchored in Tokyo bay.

[2] Eric Schmitt, "U.S. Plan For Iraq Is Said to Include Attack on 3 Sides," *New York Times*, 5 July 2002.

[3] See Alexander Hamilton, *The Federalist*, No. 69. "The President is to be commander-in-chief of the army and navy of the United States.... In this respect his authority would be nominally the same with that of the king of Great Britain, but in substance much inferior to it. It would amount to nothing more than the supreme command and direction of the military and naval forces, as first General and admiral of the Confederacy; while that of the British king extends to the DECLARING of war and to the RAISING and REGULATING of fleets and armies, all which, by the Constitution under consideration, would appertain to the legislature."

ployed at positions from which they could strike immediately against Iraq and roll back its occupation of Kuwait, the first President George Bush did finally ask for and receive congressional authority to use American force in the Gulf War. A war against Iraq in 2002 or 2003 would not have the relatively simple task of driving Iraqi troops out of Kuwait but would require mass destruction of Iraq's core and possibly cause the disintegration of the Iraqi state, which the United States would then be responsible for reintegrating. The short- and long-term benefits and costs would be major and thus especially relevant for discussion by the people's elected representatives in Congress, not just by policy wonks in the secrecy of the defense department, the national security council, and the White House.

Americans live in the most open society in the world. Given the vulnerabilities such an open society presents, Americans should take for granted that terrorist groups will develop or steal biological, chemical, and nuclear weapons or use existing technology such as blockbuster truck bombs against the United States and its allies. Because no shields exist to deploy against such weapons, about the only card the United States has to play is to harden the most lucrative targets and greatly strengthen intelligence efforts with the help of allies. The allies should understand that while the United States became the prime target for large-scale terrorist attacks in the last decade, unforeseeable events may put other nations in the crosshairs at another time. There is, therefore, a common interest in foreign policies and intelligence efforts to destroy terrorist groups that can move across national borders. If pooled intelligence forces can find and infiltrate terrorist groups either at home or overseas, then American military power and police can be used to destroy or abort attacks already planned, whether with precision bombing and special forces or with more conventional military techniques.

Acknowledgements

I thank two sets of authors of the articles in this collection: Richard Betts, Michael Doran, Bob Jervis, Walter LaFeber, and Ruth Wedgwood wrote articles specifically for this book at my request with a short deadline. Daniel Brumberg, Daniel Byman, Victor Cha, and Richard Russell wrote for publication in *Political Science Quarterly* and then gave permission for their articles also to appear here. I thank Alex Cooley for coauthoring with me the introductory overview. I am especially grateful to three members of the PSQ editorial advisory board who are also my colleagues and friends—Robert Jervis, Richard Pious, and Robert Shapiro; they not only helped with this book, but have over the years always provided assistance, advice, and performed chores above and beyond the call of duty. I thank my wife, Vilma Caraley, who reads, edits, and therefore improves everything I write and did so again while nursing a new left knee. I want especially to acknowledge the great enthusiasm and assistance given at the earliest stages of this project by the late Joseph Lepgold of Georgetown University, who in December of 2001 met an untimely and tragic death in a Paris hotel fire. Others who warrant my thanks are Elena Rigacci Hay and Kristin Zellmer, my research assistants; Abigail Moses, *PSQ*'s managing editor; Jean Highland, *PSQ*'s manuscript editor; and Loren Morales, who as business manager, production manager, and vice president for operations of the Academy of Political Science does everything she can to make my job easier and allow me to still function as a professor. Ms. Morales also designed the book's cover.

A Personal Note

In judging my objectivity, the reader is entitled to know that the September 11 attack inflicted on my family one of the greatest sadnesses of our lives. Steven Bennett Paterson, my son-in-law in title but in fact a beloved and loving son to my wife and myself, was killed on the 105th floor of the north tower of the World Trade Center, leaving our daughter Lisa a widow at age 40 and our twin grandchildren, Wyatt James and Lucy Belle, fatherless at the tender age of four-and-one-half. None of us will ever live this tragedy down or forget Wyatt's and Lucy's reactions when we had to tell them that their adored Daddy was never again coming home. May he and the other innocent dead of September 11 not have died in vain.

Part I:
INTRODUCTION

September 11: An Overview

DEMETRIOS JAMES CARALEY
ALEXANDER A. COOLEY

   This collection of articles by a distinguished group of scholars represents a significant first step in explaining the causes and consequences of the September 11 terrorist attacks. Each article differs in its exact theoretical concern and empirical focus; yet all our authors are concerned with understanding the broader implications of recent events. In the first article, Walter LaFeber places the recent attacks and subsequent U.S. military response within an historical process of imperial consolidation and fragmentation and examines how the institutions of globalization that helped to bolster American imperial power are now aiding anti-American movements such as al Qaeda. Richard K. Betts argues that the September 11 attacks were a response to American primacy and then applies offense-defense theory to explain the intense advantages that terrorist offensive strikes have in exploiting state defenses in this era of asymmetric warfare. Michael Doran overviews the rise of al Qaeda as a political organization in Middle Eastern and international politics, challenging us to go beyond its public images of irrational Islamic fanaticism to consider the set of shrewd political calculations that inform the group's strategy and tactics.

 The second set of articles addresses aspects of the geopolitical challenges left in the wake of the successful military campaign in Afghanistan. In his 30 January 2002 State of the Union address, President George W. Bush denounced regimes in North Korea, Iraq, and Iran as constituting an "axis of evil" that threatens the interests and security of the international community. While this denouncement of "rogue states" provides some guidance for current American grand strategy, it is also a characterization that warrants further re-

---

DEMETRIOS JAMES CARALEY is the Janet Robb Professor of the Social Sciences at Barnard College and professor of international and public affairs at Columbia University. He has published numerous books and articles on national security policy including *The Politics of Military Unification* and *The New American Interventionism*.
ALEXANDER A. COOLEY is assistant professor of political science at Barnard College and a member of Columbia University's Harriman Institute.

flection and debate. Two of our authors place U.S.–Iraqi relations in historical and analytical perspective. Victor D. Cha writes about North Korean foreign policy and reactions to the axis of evil speech by examining the origins and rationale behind the regime's attempts to develop nuclear and missile weaponry. Daniel Byman details the evolution of U.S. policy toward Iraq after the Gulf War and assesses the effectiveness of the sanctions regime, UN weapons inspections, and the sporadic military strikes of the Clinton administration. Richard L. Russell considers the role of American strategic intelligence in the conduct of the Gulf War and looks at the critical role human intelligence might play in a future military campaign to oust Saddam Hussein. Daniel Brumberg explores the dissonant politics that has characterized domestic politics in Iran and Indonesia. Far from acting as a monolithic fundamentalist regime, Brumberg observes how Iranian leaders have pragmatically drawn upon elements of leftist ideology and symbolism in attempts to institutionalize competing visions of political community. He goes on to explain the political and social underpinnings of the strong support currently enjoyed by the reformist Khatami regime over more conservative elements in the clergy.

In the concluding section, Ruth Wedgwood critically examines the U.S. detainment of al Qaeda prisoners and others accused of visa violations or of being enemy combatants and explains why such detentions as of the date of her writing, are in conformity with the Constitution, legislation, and historical precedent. But as she explains: "In a world where terrorist action flirts with catastrophic weapons, the competing paradigms of crime and war may provide no more than analogies. Fitting the law to this unwanted new world thus will require tact, judgment, and the weight of a heavy heart."

In the final article, Robert Jervis systematically confronts and debunks much of the conventional wisdom that has emerged about the post-September 11 world and questions what exactly has changed in the international system and why.

We provide in the rest of this introductory essay, an overview of the main themes and arguments that our authors advance. In particular, we ask four questions: First, what exactly is distinctive about the September 11 terrorist attacks? Second, how have international relations changed as a result of September 11? Third, what policies should the United States adopt to deal most effectively with the global terror threat? Fourth, what is the likely future of Islamic fundamentalist movements? We end with a short analysis of what the United States can do to cope with the threat of terrorist attacks. Our goal is to identify both agreements and differences among our authors in the hope of stimulating discussion and debate among academics and policy makers alike.

TERRORISM AND SEPTEMBER 11: WHAT EXACTLY IS NEW?

As many of our authors remark, terrorism itself is not a new phenomenon in international politics. Terrorist tactics have been used by a number of antistate movements of all political orientations throughout the developing world and the West. Numerous anticolonial movements used terrorist tactics as part of their campaign of decolonization, as have numerous guerrilla and insurgent movements in Latin America, Africa, and Southeast Asia. Terrorism also has a long history within the West. In Europe, the Irish Republican Army (IRA) has repeatedly struck at British civilian targets, the Basque separatist organization ETA has killed over 800 Spanish civilians since 1968, and the French have coped with terrorist acts by a number of independence seekers from Algeria to, most recently, Corsica. Terrorist groups have also successfully attacked a wide variety of American targets overseas including the hijackings by pro-Palestinian militant groups in the 1970s and 1980s, Libyan-sponsored acts in the 1980s, the Hezbollah bombing of the U.S. Marines in Beirut in 1982, and the sporadic targeting of American and British officials by the Greek organization November 17. The World Trade Center bombing of 1993 and al Qaeda's attacks on the Khobar Towers (1996), the American embassies in Kenya and Tanzania (1998), and the USS Cole in Yemen (2000) represented the major terrorist strikes against U.S. targets in the last decade. Clearly, terrorism in and of itself has been an enduring feature of international relations.

What differentiated the attacks of September 11 from previous terror campaigns was the enormous scale of destruction, especially in the killing of civilians and the use of modern technologies in an act of "geopolitical jujitsu," as LaFeber and Betts describe. Modern airliners were turned into weapons, wreaking havoc on a relatively small area of Manhattan that served as a hub of global technological and financial interdependence and on the Pentagon, the nation's military command center. The fourth hijacked airliner that was made to crash in Pennsylvania was almost certainly headed for the Capitol, the White House, or CIA headquarters. The sheer magnitude and spectacle of these events were almost instantaneously transmitted across the world via satellite TV, radio, and international news agencies such as CNN and al Jazeera. The resulting damage was unprecedented in terms of both human lives and material losses. The hijacking of four planes by a small number of well-trained terrorists killed over 3,000 people, and its ripple effects, according to Betts, may have inflicted over $100 billion worth of damages on the United States.

The greatest consequence of the acts of September 11 has been to instill a sense of fear and vulnerability into a population that had grown accustomed to ignoring routine issues of safety and national security. There is an irony here, as Jervis points out. For at a time when the United States enjoys unrivalled military superiority throughout the world, the U.S. population now sees itself as more vulnerable to injury or death from an attack than at any other time in modern history. Although the American military can still protect itself very robustly, it cannot shield the American civilian population from surprise terrorist attacks.

From a military perspective, these acts of terror emphasize the enormous advantage that offensive terrorist acts can now inflict on ill-prepared societies.

As Betts points out, the costs of adopting effective defensive measures in the wake of September 11 have been large, estimated by Betts as $2 billion per month beyond the regular defense budget and at a cost to the U.S. economy of 1.8 million jobs. From sterilizing mail to halting shipments of goods at customs warehouses and increasing security at airports, the implementing of defensive countermeasures against potential terrorist action has proven costly and has added significant transaction costs to a system of commerce that was the symbol of global liberalization and governmental noninterference. Betts estimates the number of "high-value potential targets" in the United States for potential terrorist acts such as bridges, power plants, airports, and public arenas to be in the hundreds of thousands.

The psychological effects of this new sense of vulnerability have also been reflected in the actions and statements of the administration. For several months government officials assured citizens that the best way to combat terrorism was to go about their daily lives and routine business while at the same time the Justice Department issued alerts warning of further terrorist activities. But if, as our authors argue, combating terrorism is as much about soothing psychological fears as achieving discernible military victories, then the successful campaign in Afghanistan is likely to be forgotten or discounted should al Qaeda launch another successful operation against U.S. targets. By framing the campaign in such explicitly psychological terms while acknowledging the near certainty of additional attacks, the administration risks failure on its own terms.

A Changed World?

While we can identify with some degree of confidence the historical significance and political dynamics of the September 11 acts of terror, assessing the broader changes, both internationally and domestically, is more difficult. Here our authors emphasize different possible aspects of broader political change but also caution against declaring the post-September 11 period the beginning of a definitively new era.

For many commentators, the attacks of al Qaeda signify that states have relinquished their central role in international relations, and the activities of nonstate actors have become the primary security concerns for states. Usually, however, the concept of transnational networks has been employed to explain how Western nongovernmental organizations (NGOs) have created an emergent global civil society that has successfully promoted liberal values and social change on issues like human rights, women's rights, and environmental politics.[1]

But as LaFeber points out, the very features of globalization that enable transnational actions by Western NGOs have also facilitated the networking of

---

[1] For examples, see Jessica Matthews, "Power Shift: The Rise of Global Civil Society," *Foreign Affairs* 76 (January-February 1997): 50-66; Margaret E. Keck and Kathryn Sikkink, *Activists beyond Borders: Advocacy Networks in International Politics* (Ithaca, NY: Cornell University Press, 1998); and P. J. Simmons, "Learning to Live with NGOs," *Foreign Policy* 112 (Fall 1998): 82-96.

terrorist movements like al Qaeda. Just as Western liberal NGOs seek to bypass or circumvent obstructive state institutions, terrorist networks have developed a similar array of strategies to diversify, spread, and finance their cells. LaFeber points out that terrorist groups have seized the opportunities provided by privatization, liberalization, and communication advances in their determination to halt the advance of Western power on a global level. From this perspective, al Qaeda represents the neglected side of globalization. And as the organization regroups from the loss of its Afghan hub, it now appears as if the group is further fragmenting into clusters and networking with other terrorist organizations around the world.[2]

Of course, while the rise to prominence of terrorist networks challenges the long-standing state-centric assumptions of international relations, Jervis offers a useful reminder that state power and its components played pivotal roles in the development of al Qaeda and the execution of the September 11 attacks. Al Qaeda was given refuge and territory by a state government and was funded to a great extent by what amounted to protection money given by the Saudi state. Moreover, a focus on the global dynamics of terrorism should not obscure the fact that al Qaeda targeted prominent symbols of U.S. *state* power such as the Pentagon and the White House, as they had done in their earlier attacks on the USS Cole and the embassy bombings. As Doran points out, dramatic actions against the American state are "propaganda by action" and function as al Qaeda's main recruiting strategy. Finally, while the organization's operations were facilitated by opportunities provided by globalization, states have redoubled their efforts in their response to the network, using an array of traditional instruments of statecraft (diplomatic, financial, and military) to crack down on the group's activities.

It is still unclear whether the geopolitical shifts we have witnessed over the last few months will permanently redefine the contours of the international system. On the one hand, U.S.–Russian relations have arguably improved to a point not reached since World War II. Both countries share a common interest in combating terrorism and mopping up pockets of Islamic fighters in the periphery of the Caucasus and Central Asia. Recent agreements to slash nuclear arsenals by two-thirds and accept Russia as a NATO partner on a number of issues have solidified these new cooperative ties. Moreover, Russia has also emerged as a critical strategic energy partner for the United States, undercutting OPEC's attempts to enact production cuts and providing much needed leverage against the decisions of the oil-producing cartel. Finally, the presence of U.S. troops on former Soviet territory within the Central Asian republics seems likely to continue through the medium-term, as U.S. troops will retain footholds in Tajikistan, Uzbekistan, and Kyrgyzstan, as well as lend counterinsurgency support to the government of Georgia.

---

[2] David Johnston, Don Van Natta, Jr., and Judith Miller, "Qaeda's New Links Increase Threats from Far-Flung Sites," *New York Times*, 16 June 2002.

On the other hand, certain long-standing rivalries and animosities have in recent months dramatically exacerbated the difficulty of the U.S. war on terrorism. The Israeli-Palestinian conflict has escalated to the brink of all-out war, inflaming public opinion throughout Europe and the Arab world and leaving the Oslo Accords and peace process in tatters. Similarly, the bombing of the Indian parliament by Pakistan-based militants initiated a military mobilization on the Indo-Pakistani border and a level of tensions between the subcontinent powers not seen in decades. And the Bush administration repeatedly talks about embarking on a military campaign to topple Sadam Hussein and eradicate the Iraqi threat once and for all.

It also increasingly appears that the American war on terror is likely to solidify entrenched political power in states throughout the world. Governments can now invoke the threat of terrorism as a pretext to combat antistate groups as well as many forms of legitimate political opposition, whether the groups in question really are terrorists (or even religious fundamentalists) or not. European Union (EU) members such as Spain lobbied hard to broaden the body's list of terrorist groups to include organizations and individuals accused of funding terrorism. Russia invoked the threat of terrorism to reinvigorate its operations in Chechnya, while dictatorial leaders like Uzbekistan's President Islam Karimov have exaggerated the threat to political stability posed by Islamic movements in order to justify their increasingly authoritarian practices. Ariel Sharon and his supporters have made a concerted effort to justify all Israeli military actions in the West Bank and Gaza as morally equivalent to the U.S. antiterror campaign, thereby silencing critics of Israel's continued military occupation, settlement building, and use of force. Normatively, fighting terrorism seems to have become an internationally acceptable justification for the violation of human rights, democratic norms, and civil liberties. As such, we can expect that in the near future the global war on terror will favor the domestic political status quo within states—those regimes and ethnic groups in positions of state power—while it will undercut opposition movements and/or antistate secessionist movements.

Finally, on the U.S. domestic front, post-September 11 politics has been characterized by a renewed centralization of power in the federal government. President Bush created an office of homeland security, airline security was federalized, and the increases in defense spending brought the national budget back into deficit. The trend since the Carter administration, continued in Ronald Reagan's "New Federalism," embodied in Bill Clinton's welfare reform proposals, and promised in George W. Bush's presidential campaign to move resources and responsibilities away from the federal government and to the states has definitely been reversed. President Bush's spring 2002 proposal for a new cabinet department of homeland defense takes the trend even further.

With the USA Patriot Act, Congress has given massive authority to the federal executive branch to conduct surveillance and gather needed intelligence by intercepting and monitoring all methods of communication both internationally and within the United States.³ The new legislation also gives to the Immigration and Naturalization Service authority to detain immigrants for long periods of time and sometimes indefinitely when they are suspected of terrorism or have defective visas. Others have been detained by being named as material witnesses. The CIA, established in 1947 with a prohibition against operating within the United States, has now in effect had the prohibition removed. While, as the great civil libertarian Justice Robert H. Jackson wrote, the Bill of Rights was not intended to be a "suicide pact,"[4] the dragnet and detention of thousands, if not carefully done, is a self-imposed danger to our rights and liberties while trying to find terrorists.

DEBATING THE NATURE OF U.S. POWER

Perhaps the greatest debate to emerge from recent events for both academics and policy makers concerns the nature and future orientation of American foreign policy. While our authors agree that the September attacks highlighted the issue of U.S. power and primacy, there are important differences in their approach to the subject and their policy recommendations.

For Betts and Doran, U.S. primacy and power are the major issues that drive al Qaeda, both in its recruiting attempts and its choice of targets and tactics. American primacy has been unquestioned since the cold war and has been achieved on the cheap. Contrary to the military overexpansion and declinism thesis advanced by commentators like Paul Kennedy in the late 1980s, the 1990s did not signal the waning of American power, but rather its unrivaled consolidation.[5] The Gulf War campaign was successful not only in terms of minimizing costs and American casualties, but also in lifting a psychological stigma of U.S. military failure since Vietnam. In retrospect, American military power was unrivaled throughout the 1990s, despite those who envisioned the rise of challenging powers like Japan, China, or a more united European Union.

Along with its military primacy, the United States clearly consolidated its leadership over the international economy. While the Pacific Rim—fashionably viewed in the early 1990s as the powerhouse region of the next century—became mired in economic stagnation and the financial crisis of 1997, the United States enjoyed until 2001 its longest period of post-World War II economic expansion with a booming stock market and fiscal surpluses, making it the envy of every Western industrial democracy. On the international front, the United States exerted its influence through international agencies like the International Monitary Fund (IMF) and World Trade Organization (WTO) to push for increased trade and financial liberalization in the former Eastern bloc and the developing world.

---

[3] The Uniting and Strengthening America by Providing Appropriate Tools to Intercept and Obstruct Terrorism Act of 2001 (USA Patriot Act), P.L. 107-05, 115 Stat. 2721.

[4] *Terminiello v. City of Chicago*, 337 U.S. 934, 69 S.Ct. 1490.

[5] Paul Kennedy, *The Rise and Fall of the Great Powers* (New York: Vintage, 1989).

U.S. power, for Betts, also enabled successive administrations to let moral concerns override purely material-based interests. The humanitarian intervention in Kosovo is one example, as were the earlier interventions in Bosnia and Somalia. However, the greatest favoritism has been extended to Israel, which has received over $100 billion in U.S. aid since its creation. Support for Israel's survival has been unconditional throughout successive administrations beginning with President Harry Truman, although different administrations differed on specific solutions for the Israel-Palestine conflict, especially with respect to support for a Palestinian state. In addition to antagonizing much of the Arab world by supporting Israel, the U.S. government also enraged popular sentiment in the Islamic world by allying with and aiding a number of regimes such as Egypt, Saudi Arabia, and the wealthy Gulf states that are viewed as corrupt, dictatorial, and illegitimate by Islamic fundamentalist groups. Prior to September 11, bin Laden's anti-U.S. speeches were directed primarily against the presence of the American troops in the Middle East, particularly those based in Saudi Arabia. These military forces of the "Great Satan," bin Laden ranted, kept the fundamentalist population from revolting and toppling the apostate and corrupt Arab regimes.

But as Betts warns, even if the United States were now to dramatically alter certain foreign policies—such as withdraw its military forces from Saudi Arabia or halt its support for Israel—it is not clear that such policy shifts would deescalate anti-American terror activity. Rather, the historical record indicates the opposite might happen: policy reversals would signal that the United States is weak and susceptible to intimidation, such as when U.S. forces withdrew from Vietnam, Lebanon, and Somalia. In retrospect, as Doran discusses, it seems reasonable to conclude that both al Qaeda and the Taliban government grossly underestimated the swiftness and effectiveness of the U.S. military response, in part because the United States had previously avoided entanglements in conflicts, especially those likely to yield American casualties. Furthermore, as Doran points out, anti-Americanism will endure as a powerful mobilizing strategy within the Middle East and is unlikely to be abandoned in the future movements even if most of al Qaeda is destroyed.

Other scholars have viewed the scope and nature of this extended period of U.S. primacy as a period of renewed imperial expansion. LaFeber contends that American imperial power is not only projected through conventional means of foreign policy, but is also implicated in the institutions and values of globalization. Thus, the United States is confronted with the classic dilemma of imperial power that must maintain its control while preventing the fragmentation of its power base. The very institutions of openness, liberalization, and mobility that were promoted in the interests of U.S. imperialism have now been turned against the imperial power. Yet, as the events after September 11 have shown, empires do not wither away without a fight, and unlike previous cases of possible imperial overreach—such as Vietnam—the consensus for the "war against terror" is overwhelming in the United States and has not divided American society.

The debate over American primacy or imperialism would not be complete, however, without an understanding of the importance of how power is wielded. As Jervis points out in his conclusion, certain scholars have noted that effective global hegemons have historically bolstered their legitimacy by binding themselves to international institutions and an international collective will.[6] From this perspective, the use of multilateral means to conduct foreign policy is important, because it signals to other major powers a hegemon's willingness to defer to the institutions of the international community.

In the lead-up and aftermath of the 2000 presidential election, George W. Bush emphasized that realist thinking and the pursuit of national interests would dictate the new administration's foreign policy goals and choices. Within a few months of gaining office, the Bush administration expressed its disdain for the Kyoto Treaty on climate control, announced that it would withdraw from the ABM Treaty either with or without Russian consent, and refused to attend the UN Conference on racism in Durban, South Africa. While Europe, Russia, and China expressed concern at Washington's new unilateral tone, administration officials insisted that the United States would no longer meddle in external affairs or involve itself in peripheral peacekeeping operations and interventions. They argued that the previous administration's vigorous mediation of the Israeli-Palestinian conflict in summer 2000 produced disastrous consequences.

Clearly, the events of September 11 forced the Bush administration to change these initial unilateral forays in the interest of forging a coalition against terrorism. For instance, the boastful promise that the United States should not engage in any more "nation-building" has given way to assurances that the United States will never again abandon Afghanistan and the now important Central Asia region. And while a shift towards multilateralism may do little to change perceptions of the U.S. hegemonic power among terrorist groups and their members, U.S. leaders must ensure that they do not delegitimize or destroy the very vehicles that they need to facilitate international cooperation on terror-related issues such as international immigration, law enforcement, money-laundering, and monitoring the proliferation of weapons of mass destruction.

As Jervis points out, such views about exercising primacy through multilateral means may be in vogue among academics, but have yet to be seriously considered in the State Department and Pentagon, despite the debates between these agencies over future military targets. But as we take stock of the challenges of the post-September 11 and post-destruction of the Taliban world, it

[6] G. John Ikenberry, *After Victory: Institutions, Strategic Restraint, and the Rebuilding of Order After Major Wars* (Princeton: Princeton University Press, 2001); and Joseph S. Nye, Jr., *The Paradox of American Power: Why the World's Only Superpower Can't Go It Alone* (New York: Oxford University Press, 2002).

is difficult to imagine how an exclusively unilateral orientation can possibly cope with the structural necessities required to combat the various activities of global transnational terror networks. While American military action might potentially uproot cell activities in areas such as Somalia, the Philippines, Yemen, and Indonesia, it is important to remember that the countries harboring many of the September 11 terrorists included Germany, Belgium, the Czech Republic, Spain, Britain, and also the United States itself. Clearly, if the war on terrorism is to be successful, various U.S. agencies must learn to cooperate and share intelligence with each other and also with their international counterparts.

Already, we have seen signs that the considerable good will and support shown by our Western allies right after September 11 has eroded in response to some of the administration's recent policies. President Bush's axis of evil State of the Union speech in early 2002 with its renewed threat to topple Saddam Hussein's regime not only defocused Americans from the war against al Qaeda terrorism but also became viewed overseas as needlessly inflammatory and provocative. European regimes continue to favor policies of engagement, not confrontation, toward Iraq, Iran, and North Korea. Even Britain, the most publicly supportive of recent U.S. policy, has now stated that it will only back future military action against Iraq if it is supported by the United Nations. Furthermore, the American inability or unwillingness to stop Israel's Sharon government from reoccupying territories and using heavy military force with little care about causing civilian casualties in retaliation for Arab suicide bombings has been used to accuse the United States of employing a more lenient attitude toward the death of Palestinians than the death of Israelis or of Americans. Because of a technological change like the availability of al Jazeera TV in addition to American channels like CNN, Americans see pictures of dead Israelis and their grieving families, while Arabs see pictures of dead Palestinians and their grieving families.

The Future of Fundamentalism

A final issue underscored by the September 11 attacks is that we need a better and more systematic understanding of the causes of religious fundamentalism and the processes by which such groups become violent, seek to direct that violence toward America, and believe that becoming suicide bombers will make them martyrs. Of course, understanding the causes of fundamentalism is not the same thing as "understanding why we are hated," a topic that Jervis effectively deals with in his article. Nor should we accept the statements of bin Laden—uncritically broadcast over al Jazeera, yet curiously accepted at face value by many American academics—as representing the true origins of militant Islamic groups. After all, Islamic fundamentalist movements predate the rise of al Qaeda and are far too ubiquitous throughout the Islamic world to be linked to a single source.

Both Betts and Jervis rightly point out that there is no immediate correlation between poverty and terrorism given the fact that so much of the developing world lives in conditions of socioeconomic malaise. But while there may not be a systematic link between terrorism and poverty, the consensus among scholars of religious fundamentalism is that the links between economic deprivation and the growth of fundamentalist movements are quite strong.[7] The vast majority of fundamentalist group members are unemployed, disenfranchised young men, many of whom have recently moved to urban areas. The basic domestic role of fundamentalist movements is to provide services and functions that the state can no longer afford; in many Arab countries, fundamentalist groups provide alms, education, healthcare, food, and shelter. The growth of fundamentalist religious schools or *madrassahs* in states like Pakistan and Saudi Arabia as alternatives to the crumbling state-education system is a good case in point; while providing basic education, the *madrassahs* also preach hatred of the West and are the sources of many terrorist recruits.

The paradox here is that while many fundamentalist movements sponsor terrorism and maintain active military wings, they also undertake charitable activities that function as implicit critiques of Arab regimes. While anti-Western and anti-Israeli terrorist action is certainly a central factor for gathering popular support, organizations like Hamas, Hezzbollah, Algeria's Islamic Front (FIS), and the Egypt-based Muslim Brotherhood have also gained much of their popular support and political legitimacy by managing the functions of state governance more effectively than the weak state governments that they oppose. As a result, continued intrusion of Western political, economic, and cultural hegemony is only likely to encourage the growth of fundamentalism as an angry and dissenting ideology and vehicle for political opposition.

The problem that U.S. policy makers must confront is that religious fundamentalist movements may be reactions against the West. But they are also separately nourished by certain states and state policies among America's Arab allies. Not surprisingly, many Arab governments have done their best to try to divert social and economic dissatisfactions among their people toward a transnational religious war of Islam against the West. By blaming the events of September 11 on misguided U.S. policies or by advancing outrageous conspiracy theories in state-run media that attributed these acts to the Mossad and CIA, governments in the Islamic world have demonstrated a clear reluctance to confront their own role in the rise of fundamentalism and terror.

Moreover, it is unlikely that the traditional tools of U.S. statecraft can alleviate the problem. For example, continued Israeli-Palestinian violence draws attention from possible terrorist attacks in the United States and only further enflames anti-Israeli and anti-American sentiments throughout the Islamic

---

[7] See John Esposito, ed., *Political Islam: Revolution, Radicalism, or Reform?* (Boulder, CO: Lynne Rienner, 1997); and Mark Juergensmeyer, *The New Cold War? Religious Nationalism Confronts the Secular State* (Berkeley: University of California Press, 1995).

world. Terrorists could not be served better than by having clashes between Israelis and Palestinians broadcast in the international media, thereby splitting the original coalition against terrorism that formed after September 11.[8] Increasing financial and economic liberalization may create new economic opportunities in underdeveloped Muslim countries, but it will also increase those countries' vulnerabilities to severe external shocks as in the cases of Malaysia, Indonesia, and most recently Turkey, thereby potentially triggering an even greater backlash against Western-inspired economic influence. Increasing foreign aid to countries threatened by fundamentalists may marginally keep economies afloat, but it is also likely to heighten the appeals of antigovernment movements that the United States sponsors crony and corrupt governments. Pressing for democratization in countries with little institutional capacity for democratic governance is not likely to be effective, and new parliamentary institutions could be captured by the fundamentalists. Thus the pressing issue for the West is to find new means through which to either coopt or eradicate fundamentalist movements so as to stop them from promoting acts of terror or preaching that fundamentalist Islamic texts justify suicide bombing of innocent civilians, which they do not. This is a task that can no longer be ignored, especially in countries of immense geostrategic importance such as Egypt, Pakistan, and—most of all—Saudi Arabia, the country of citizenship of fifteen September 11 hijackers. But both the secular and religious leaders of those states stay silent so as not to attract attacks on themselves, instead of correcting what the Islamist extremists preach. One of the exceptions among Arab leaders, because he speaks out with correct and nonviolent teachings of Islam, is King Abdullah of Jordan, a brave father's brave son.

Conclusions: What Can the United States Do?

The United States has shown in Afghanistan that its military capacity is more powerful by many orders of magnitude than any other state or terrorist movement. It ranges from high-flying airplanes using smart bombs to small groups of Special Forces on the ground who can mix with the local population while spotting targets for air attacks, and is coupled with a logisitical understructure that can redeploy and resupply American forces across different continents.

When used against a primitive government that provided hospitality to terrorist training camps, American military power can succeed with almost no combat deaths. Such has been the case in Afghanistan with the Taliban regime, although even here the victory was sullied by not being able to capture bin Laden or most of the high al Qaeda and Taliban leadership. One reason is that the American command did not want sizeable U.S. ground troops to engage in the very dangerous task of searching caves and deploying to the east of the al

---

[8] That is why it is of paramount importance that the United States play an active and even-handed role in bringing about a peace settlement and permanent agreement among Israelis and Palestinians.

Qaeda stronghold to keep al Qaeda from escaping to mountains in Pakistan. Nevertheless, this kind of American military power can also be wreaked successfully against terrorist camps in other weak states, such as the almost ungoverned Somalia and Yemen.

But what about terrorist training camps and command headquarters in nations whose governments would not be in our interest to overthrow, some of which are American allies? Apparently the military hardware exists for Special Forces on the ground to light up targets so that smart bombs and missiles could strike them with only minimal risk of killing innocent civilians. But what about terrorist training camps, cells, or command headquarters in nations like Egypt, Pakistan, and Lebanon? What if the United States finds training camps or cells in Iran or Iraq? Would their governments look aside at targeted attacks on al Qaeda camps? Or would they consider it an attack against them and respond? Clearly, while future military action will be an inevitably necessary part of the antiterrorist campaign, the threat of terrorism cannot be fully eradicated by military action alone.

There is no way even with the best intelligence and security to actually stop all terrorist attacks against American targets from succeeding. Richard Betts years ago provided the definitive analysis of why surprise attacks succeed despite various kinds of warning.[9] It was revealed in May 2002 from the administration, the FBI, and the news media that there had been warnings before September 11 about Middle Eastern men enrolled at flight schools; and there were warnings from allies' intelligence agencies that al Qaeda was planning a giant strike. One of the 1993 bombers of the World Trade Center commented then that his group's objective was to topple one of the towers into the other and thus bring them both down. This indicates that American intelligence agencies must set aside their bureaucratic differences and actively share information for the good of the antiterror campaign. With better intelligence and a refocused homeland security, attacks designed to produce huge American casualties could be made much harder to mount and some of them might be aborted.

It is true that we lived with the constant threat of nuclear annihilation—meaning millions of American deaths in a span of hours—by Soviet nuclear missiles for decades, and yet we went about our business without any great concern. But our current situation is different. Except for the thirteen days of the October 1962 Cuban missile crisis, when there was real danger of an actual nuclear exchange, both sides' second-strike capabilities meant that the nuclear weapons would not be used. In those years, mutual deterrence through mutual assured destruction worked.

Since the terrorists have no return address—as a nuclear missile from the Soviet silo would have had—and since terrorist groups are willing not only to risk but even to court death in their attacks to achieve martyrdom, protection

---

[9] Richard K. Betts, "Surprise Despite Warning: Why Sudden Attacks Succeed," *Political Science Quarterly* 95 (Winter 1980–1981).

through deterrence will not work. Nor is it likely that terrorists will adhere to historical norms and conventions among states that have prohibited the use of chemical and biological weapons. The United States needs to engage in a continuous, not an episodic, campaign to strengthen intelligence and to strengthen security of lucrative targets at home while destroying as many terrorist cells as possible both abroad and at home, preferably in close consultation and coordination with international allies.

This campaign must be pursued with a great sense of urgency. It is urgent because using commercial airplanes as missiles did not cause nearly as much destruction—massive as it was—as would terrorist attacks using strategically placed building-buster truck bombs or biological, chemical, or even primitive nuclear weapons.

President George W. Bush, to his credit, has warned the American people that his long-term war on terrorism could produce substantial American military casualties. Unfortunately, that message was blurred by military spokesmen and by the media still unduly playing up a single battle death. Would-be terrorists and their hosts have to learn that even if the United States cannot win a particular campaign "on the cheap"—meaning that it cannot win it without use of substantial ground forces, not just with small groups of Special Forces on the ground and bombs and missiles from safe platforms such as highflying aircraft and naval vessels—it will nonetheless engage in battle, take casualties, and accomplish its objective. There is probably an inverse relationship between the number of military casualties the United States is seen as willing to risk and the number of civilian casualties it will have to absorb. If the United States is seen as only willing to launch campaigns that it can win on the cheap as in Afghanistan, the terrorists will be emboldened to try larger attacks from sites that will be costly and difficult to track down.

September 11 has changed the world for all of us. We should take it for granted that terrorist groups will develop or steal biological, chemical, and nuclear weapons to use against the United States. Sadly there are no shields against such weapons. A greatly strengthened intelligence effort to find and infiltrate these terrorist groups both at home and overseas in order to abort attacks before they take place is about the only card America has to play. President Bush in his commencement address at West Point in June 2002 promised to use "preemptive action" when intelligence finds an attack being readied. The United States is already practicing what is in effect preventive detention of individuals with some kinds of dangerous profiles. The United States should take all constitutional measures likely to reduce the probability of more terrorist attacks, while Americans come to realize that despite what their country does, most likely over the years more people will become victims. But that should not be a reason to give up the fight or not stay the course.

Part II:
The Attacks

The Post September 11 Debate Over Empire, Globalization, and Fragmentation

WALTER LaFEBER

Months before the September 11 attacks, a few observers, working almost entirely within the Washington, DC beltway, argued that the United States was an empire and its people the fortunate Chosen who were to spread an imperialism beneficial to all, apparently whether already stable and functioning parts of the world wanted it or not. Americans, these observers elaborated, were imperial not in the old sense of wanting to hold territory, but in their determination to expand globally American ideas based on capitalism and democracy—two concepts that actually have often been at cross-purposes throughout most of the post-1900 so-called American Century. The new imperialists rightly noted that earlier U.S. imperialism had been linked to American Progressivism and especially to the international, supposedly progressive ideals of Woodrow Wilson and the big-stick diplomacy of Theodore Roosevelt. The twenty-first-century imperialists, however, who defined themselves as Reagan conservatives, concluded that large political payoffs could bless their wing of Republicanism if they could sell the idea of an imperial foreign policy that combined American political and economic principles, unilateralism, a McDonald's-Disney culture, and—the necessary accompaniment—a military that absorbed nearly as much of the gross national product as it did during the height of the cold war, when the GNP was considerably smaller.[1] Such military costs were nevertheless logical, given the ambition.

---

[1] Thomas E. Ricks, "Empire or Not? A Quiet Debate over U.S. Role," *Washington Post*, 21 August 2001; Kevin Baker, "The Fear in Ideas: American Imperialism, Embraced," *New York Times Magazine*, 9 December 2001, 53.

WALTER LaFEBER is a professor of government at Cornell University. He is the author of *America, Russia, and the Cold War* whose just-published 9th edition has a chapter explaining more fully the September 11 aftermath in U.S. foreign relations.

A particular relationship between the old, Progressive imperialists and their early twenty-first-century, self-styled namesakes was notable: both sets of imperialists had to work within a context of rapid globalization. The first age of globalization began in the mid-nineteenth century and expanded until it hit the cataclysm of World War I. The second began with the new technologies of the 1970s and the American triumphalism of the late 1980s and 1990s, then lasted until the September 11 attacks. For both generations of imperialists, the globalization process turned out to be crucial. It gave them the tools and reach to shape and reshape other societies, but it simultaneously destabilized important parts of the globe by widening the gaps between rich and poor, while ironically providing better communications so those gaps became glaringly apparent to the poor. Globalization thus became both a cause and a result of the imperialism.

Evaluation of these themes of globalization and imperialism should briefly note the outcomes of the early, Progressive imperialism. Roosevelt and Wilson's racism and parochial nationalism led to military interventions in Mexico, the Dominican Republic, Haiti, Nicaragua, and Cuba, among other places. These created severe problems, not solutions, in twentieth-century American foreign relations. Leaving such unfortunate results aside, imperialism is still defined as "the policy of extending the rule or authority of an empire or nation over foreign countries." "Imperial," according to *Webster's*, characterizes "the rule or authority of a sovereign state over its dependencies." Applying such definitions to the early twenty-first century seems archaic by a hundred or so years. And especially so since the world of the past quarter-century has become less amenable to a single sovereign state ruling over foreign countries. That is not to say, however, that governments, including American administrations, have not continued to think within the usual box of the 1940s to 1960s world of state-to-state relations, even when such thinking evolved into the belief that properly directed globalization was beneficially reordering the world.

The Present Era of Fragmentation

The globe has instead undergone a fragmentation on a number of levels, which accelerated even as the United States emerged as the sole superpower. The claim that the United States should become a new imperial power is actually a debate over how Americans can (or should) take the lead in retarding the fragmentation and, somehow, create order where division, small self-determining nationalisms, and privatization have produced crises. The debate is ironic in that Americans often espoused the principles and policies that helped generate the chaos of division, self-determination, and privatization. It is doubly ironic in that many analysts who believe nongovernment institutions and trends are the wave of the future, and political officials and observers who hope that multilateralism can ride that wave, are suddenly faced after September 11 with the resurrection of the state, that old agent and protector of interventionism and imperialism.

The September 11 attacks were in one sense a climax of the globe's growing fragmentation, and the U.S.–led response demonstrated how great states attempted to reimpose needed order. Some voices on both sides of the conflict claimed that the response formed part of an attempt to impose an American-led imperial order. Another revealing irony was how the language describing an American empire was used by those who sought to extend its values and also those who used terror to fight it—as if the Americans insisted on using the same language to make a different case, which from the terrorists' perspective appeared to confirm their own claims about the ambitions of U.S. power. Much of the post-1898 American century has been shaped by United States attempts to bring its version of order out of a hundred years of political and economic upheavals, and, especially since the 1950s, political fragmentation. September 11 did mark something new, in part because of the extent of the horror, in part because so many lives were brutally taken on U.S. soil, in part because Americans formed a consensus in back of the president. Such a consensus was not always apparent earlier in the American century when the nation's interests came under attack. The strength of the consensus was surprising, because contrary to the popular Caspar Weinberger/Colin Powell doctrine that the U.S. military should be committed only when the objective and an exit strategy are clearly defined, the Bush administration warned this could be a war lasting many decades, with objectives necessarily changing in a complex, highly unpredictable, global chess game for which the other side made its own rules.

But the attacks in New York City and Washington and the nature of the U.S. response can best be viewed as part of a longer historical process.[2] In 1914, globalization integrated the world according to some criteria (as the percentage of gross domestic product devoted to overseas investments) to a larger degree than in 2000. Only a few imperial powers ordered large parts of that world. If a United Nations had existed in 1500 it could have included more than 300 sovereign units. In 1900 it would have had only thirty to fifty members, but by 2000 the membership was above 190 and rising—an overly simplified but revealing indication of the political fragmentation that occurred during the American century. World War I and the post-1929 economic depression destroyed the momentum of globalization and by the 1930s produced a fragmented world whose major political units attempted to be self-contained, even if in the cases of Germany and Japan this meant undertaking military conquests to achieve an empire. After 1945, U.S. foreign policy, above all, was directed against every effort to fragment and compartmentalize the world along lines bearing any resemblance to the 1930s. Americans are internationally re-

---

[2] A most useful overview, important for its review of the literature as well as its argument, is Ian Clark, *Globalization and Fragmentation; International Relations in the Twentieth Century* (New York: Oxford University Press, 1997), 2. Clark believes that fragmentation "suggests disintegration, autarchy, unilateralism, closure, and isolationism," which occur not only internationally, but "at multiple levels, affecting commitments to internationalism, patterns of regionalism, and even the very cohesion of states themselves."

knowned for their lack of historical knowledge. But their historical memory of the 1930s has shaped the last half-century of their foreign policy. Or more likely, that policy espousing openness and inclusion resulting in open markets and political confederations (as in post-1947 Europe) goes back at least to the 1780s and is so historically rooted that it is part of the political DNA in most Americans who make or seriously study foreign relations.

The superpower rivalry between the United States and the Soviet Union primarily ordered the world for a period after World War II, but quite early that bipolar order began to break down. Tito, deGaulle, Castro, Mao, and above all, the massive decolonization that accelerated after 1956 fractured the so-called two camps. By the 1970s, the political fragmentation was complemented by the new technology of computers, earth satellites, and cables that performed an apparent contradiction by centralizing power in the hands of those who controlled the satellites and cables, while decentralizing power to those who (as in the Iranian Revolution of 1978–1979), discovered how to use new technology to overthrow governments supported by the leading superpower. As Secretary of State George Shultz understood during the 1980s, a fatal weakness of Soviet leadership was its inability to exploit the new technology without modifying the Soviet system to the point where it was modified out of existence. Results included not only a series of independent nations once part of the Soviet empire, but an Afghanistan left fragmented by retreating Soviet troops.

At the same time, another evidence of fragmentation appeared, and again governments were directly challenged, even divided. Nongovernmental organizations (NGOs), as Alexis de Tocqueville noted in the 1830s, are an American strength even (some would say especially) as they can weaken the effectiveness of governmental institutions. A decade after the onset of the cold war, the two superpowers jockeyed back and forth, for example, while the Ford and Rockefeller Foundations rearranged the playing field by conducting their own private foreign policies, not least by sponsoring much of the green revolution that fundamentally changed parts of the globe. By the 1970s, NGOs had grown to the tens of thousands and had become internationalized and adroit in translating their interests into political action.[3] In a pioneering account, Matthew Evangelista has argued that NGOs, especially those involved in arms control, played a critical role in transforming the Soviet Union until it finally fragmented after 1991.[4] In the United States, privatization's influence reached the level of billions of dollars, a level not attainable by many national economies. Thus Ted Turner helped pay for the U.S. debt to the United Nations, and the Bill and Melinda Gates Foundation gave huge grants, often beyond the capacity of indi-

---

[3] An important short historical overview that anticipates his soon-to-be-published monograph is Akira Iriye, "A Century of NGOs," *Diplomatic History* 23 (no. 3, 1999): 421–435; Mark Lytle provides an overview of recent work in "NGOs and the New Transnational Politics," ibid. 25 (no. 1, 2001): 121–128.

[4] Matthew Evangelista, *Unarmed Forces: The Transnational Movement to End the Cold War* (Ithaca, NY: Cornell University Press, 1999).

vidual nations, to combat diseases. These and similar actions, such as George Soros privately financing education and media, especially in eastern Europe, occurred in part because government, including the United States, refused to handle such obligations, even those involving the United Nations. As Tina Rosenberg observed, such NGO activities could be "profoundly subversive" not only in challenging authoritarian governments, but—as with Ford's grants to women's causes and family planning programs—in Third World societies.[5]

Triumphalism and Terrorism

Terrorism built on and accelerated a part of this general fragmentation made possible by the new technologies and post-1950s' political changes. U.S. policy inadvertently helped the terrorists by sending aid to the Afghan resistance to the post-1979 Russian invasion, then leaving Afghanistan after the Soviets retreated in the late 1980s. Out of the resistance movements came leading terrorists who found safety in the chaos of post-1989 Afghanistan, which had successfully defied Moscow's attempts to integrate it into one of the supposed two camps.[6] Throughout the 1980s and 1990s, 871 Americans died worldwide from terrorism, an average of about forty-four each year. As Barton Gellman noted in his important *Washington Post* analyses of pre-2001 terrorism, however, "in actuarial terms, chicken bones were deadlier."

But Gellman and others spelled out how terrorists, led by the al Qaeda network, exploited the political times and new technologies by decentralizing their operations. Not all nongovernmental groups shared Western liberal values or used the new high-tech means for the realization of those values. Instead of using money transfers within the formal international banking system, the network utilized the *hawala* method of quietly transferring money across borders through trusted, informal partners working in such private, small businesses as tea shops, without physically moving the money itself. The Clinton administration rapidly increased antiterrorist funds, especially after 1996, but it could find no government agency in the Treasury Department or out that would try systematically to monitor the *hawala* transactions. As al Qaeda and other terrorist networks decentralized operations and exploited the fragmentation that increasingly characterized the post-1980s world, the United States and other leading governments continued to think within the decreasingly important box of government-to-government relations, whether those relations involved traditional political and strategic questions, or dealing with the different types of diffuse economic networks being established by the terrorists. When Clinton issued the top-secret Presidential Decision Directive 35 in 1995, it gave priority

---

[5] Tina Rosenberg, "Building Their Own Private State Departments," *New York Times*, 12 August 2001.

[6] David M. Shribman, "Campaign May Portend a New Cold War," *Boston Globe*, 23 October 2001, succinctly outlines the process and context.

for intelligence collection to the traditional state enemies of Russia, China, Iraq, and Iran; only in the third tier of priorities did it consider terrorism.[7]

Ironies again appeared. A quality of the American style that Tocqueville and later observers admired—the strength of the nongovernmental organizations and the informal networks they established to create an admirable civil society—was developed with new sophistication by terrorists for considerably less admirable purposes. U.S. officials only slowly realized what was happening. The end of the cold war, for which the first Bush administration happily took credit ("By the grace of God," the President proclaimed in January 1991, "America Won the Cold War"),[8] helped lead not only to the fragmenting of the Soviet Union and a few other states, such as Czechoslovakia, but to the opening of borders and a rapid increase in the free movement of people and goods. Since 1945, Americans had led the fight for this free movement, partly because it would weaken the communist iron curtain, mostly because it fit in with several centuries of American social and economic beliefs. Osama bin Laden understood the double-edged irony of the cold war's end. His al Qaeda network expanded in the early 1990s into as many as twenty countries, and some—Tajikistan and Bosnia—were created by the fragmentation that resulted from the end of the superpower rivalry and the victory of the United States. And bin Laden despised the American triumphalism and the policy, as well as the hubris, that easily flowed from winning the cold war. "The collapse of the Soviet Union," he declared, "made the U.S. more haughty and arrogant and it has started to look at itself as a master of this world and established what it calls the New World Order."[9]

The postwar world and American triumphalism were ready-made for private terrorist networks, which resembled ju-jitsu experts who moved to use the strength of the opponent to defeat that enemy. As al Qaeda broadened its informal, decentralized networks, U.S. officials hoped to use state regimes, especially in Saudi Arabia and Pakistan, to undercut the terrorists. The Saudis not only refused to cooperate, but covertly sent funds to al Qaeda in an attempt to buy protection. Pakistan continually promised to help, but as relations with the United States deteriorated during the 1990s never followed through on its promises. When the Pentagon suggested attacking the *hawala* network, perhaps electronically, others in the Clinton administration doubted it would work; Treasury Secretary Robert Rubin was especially concerned that an electronic attack would be construed as an act of war and open the world's largest banking center, the United States, to a similar kind of new-technology retaliation.[10] Rubin was correct in believing that an integrated, nation-based banking system was

[7] Barton Gellman, "Struggles inside the Government Defined Campaign," *Washington Post*, 20 December 2001.

[8] Text is in the *New York Times*, 29 January 1992.

[9] The bin Laden quote is given and set in context in Peter L. Bergen, *Holy War, Inc.: Inside the Secret World of Osama bin Laden* (New York: The Free Press, 2001), 19–22.

[10] Gellman, "Struggles Inside the Government."

more vulnerable to cyberwar than were the *hawala* networks. More open to question was the extent to which Clinton administration officials could think outside traditional banking categories that were becoming dangerously irrelevant, given the dangers increasingly posed by the decentralized terrorist networks. After all, as the *New York Times* phrased it, Osama bin Laden "fundamentally changed the nature of terrorist financing" by undertaking "a privatization of terror" and "creating a far more diffuse network than any faced in the past." Al Qaeda's evolving, decentralized financial system "transformed the nature of international terrorism."[11]

The course of bin Laden's attacks after 1993 (when terrorists attacked New York City's Trade Center and, according to bin Laden himself, his al Qaeda network was involved with the killing of eighteen U.S. soldiers in Somalia, which forced Clinton to pull the remaining troops out of the East African clan war) until 1998 (when al Qaeda bombed two U.S. embassies in Africa) climaxed with an American response that perfectly caught the fragmentation and privatization of the danger. In retaliation for the embassy attacks, Clinton ordered missiles fired at an area in Afghanistan, where bin Laden was thought to be hiding, and at a plant in Sudan suspected of producing materials for chemical weapons. Sudan was doubly suspect because political chaos in the country had allowed bin Laden to have a safe haven until the Sudanese government finally expelled him in 1996. The missiles missed bin Laden and, as evidence later indicated, the suspected chemical weapons facility had a relationship neither to chemical weapons nor to al Qaeda. Peter Bergen's analysis is revealing: the Clinton administration had earlier attacked Iraq and Serbia, but these targeted governments who were in conflict with the United States; the attacks on the Sudanese plant and the Afghanistan region, however, were "highly unusual" in that "now an *individual* and his followers were the subject of missile attacks directed at two sovereign nations where al Qaeda had some presence."[12]

In the months leading to the September 11 attacks, it seems clear that the Clinton and Bush administrations understood the potential dangers posed by bin Laden and the al Qaeda network, which by now, according to some officials, reached into as many as sixty countries. But they had little sense of how to deal with this brutal and corrupted version of fragmentation and privatization. While the Clinton administration multiplied its resources for fighting terrorism, U.S. officials hoped that the threat could be contained through the assassination of bin Laden; the cooperation of states such as Saudi Arabia and Pakistan, which were familiar with the terrorists's operations; or the destruction of regimes suspected of supporting and supplying the al Qaeda network—above all, Iraq. Clinton, however, could never discover bin Laden's whereabouts long enough to launch an effective military strike; could never convince the Saudis,

---

[11] Kurt Eichenwald, "Terror Money Hard to Block, Officials Find," *New York Times*, 10 December 2001.

[12] Bergen, *Holy War, Inc.*, 119. (Emphasis in original.)

Pakistanis, or any other related state to cooperate in dismantling al Qaeda; and failed utterly to deal with Saddam Hussein's supplying of terrorist networks or his work on weapons of mass destruction.

The reasons for these fatal failures of the 1990s are multiple. Clinton's diplomacy refused to pressure supposed friends such as the Saudis, especially when they were needed for both cheap oil to keep the economy booming and strategic U.S. military bases that institutionalized the power accumulated from the Gulf War. Certainly the failure to continue at least the international inspections of Iraq's plants capable of producing weapons of mass destruction was due to French, Russian, and Chinese resistance, as well as to Saddam Hussein's ability after 1997 to outmaneuver Clinton at every turn. At a more fundamental level, U.S. officials could not recreate a more centralized cold war framework for international relationships (that is, a framework that posited an overwhelming outside threat) in order to achieve dual objectives: force the recalcitrant nations to cooperate against that threat, which in the 1990s appeared to be only a sporadic danger; and convince Americans that privatized terrorism merited the same kind of attention given earlier to the Soviet Union.

This last point needs emphasis, especially since it has received too little emphasis since the September 11 attacks. Tocqueville predicted 170 years ago that Americans would encounter grave difficulties carrying out foreign policies beyond the North American continent, because they paid relatively little attention to diplomacy (little, that is, relative to domestic policy and the drive to make money, which Tocqueville analyzed at length). Nor, he believed, did Americans culturally embody the characteristics needed to wage diplomacy successfully over a period of time—the need for secrecy and consistency, or the understanding (that is the history) of the national interests. The 1990s provided a case study for the accuracy of Tocqueville's thesis. The United States was immersed in the triumphalism that followed the end of the cold war and the Gulf War, consumed after mid-decade with a booming stock market, governed by an administration that put economic success first in its hierarchy of national priorities, and ruled after 1994 by a Republican Congress that unlike the Republican Congresses of 1947–1949 prided itself on ignoring overseas needs and demands while it tried to pass a "Contract for America" that was almost entirely focused on the domestic arena. Thus the years leading up to the September 11 attacks were too much shaped by the parochial priorities of the political elite, media, and public.

A larger question, however, is whether the elite, media, and public, even if they had paid more attention to foreign policy, could have understood what was happening, given the complex and confusing fragmentation that had overtaken much of the globe. Even as Americans celebrated and utilized the growth of NGOs for such purposes as protecting the environment, arms control, human rights, and fighting diseases, and even as many of these Americans preached the values of privatization (and preached even louder when the audience was European or Latin American), they had little interest and less understanding of how terrorist networks were utilizing the approaches of NGOs and privatization, as well as exploiting that third American principle, globalization. The problem posed by Tocqueville—how a highly pluralistic U.S. democracy might somehow formulate and conduct a coherent foreign policy—was solved during the cold war by the threat of communism, possessing nuclear weapons, which forced Americans into a consensus well shaped by Harry Truman and his successors down through Ronald Reagan. Despite Clinton's well-founded reputation for being an exceptionally shrewd politician and communicator, he apparently had little idea of how to deal with this new, post-1989 Tocqueville problem. In any event, he placed his priorities elsewhere and was too often preoccupied with topics associated with tabloids rather than with Tocqueville.

Clinton usually made the right economic choices while too often making the wrong cultural and foreign policy choices. His legacy will not be what many, including the former President himself, think of as the Clinton Doctrine—that is, using U.S. military intervention in such areas as Bosnia and Kosovo to halt further fragmentation, prevent the spread of brutality, and short-circuit possible strategic threats to U.S. interests. The real Clinton doctrine was more closely associated with the astonishing stock market of the 1990s. That doctrine's cornerstones were the North American Free Trade Agreement, the creation of the World Trade Organization, and the President's successful battle for American agreement to China's inclusion in the World Trade Organization (WTO). Clinton was the globalization president during the 1990s, when the processes of globalization and fragmentation went hand-in-hand.[13]

"Globalism Under Siege"

The September 11 attacks with horrible symbolism utilized some of the technologies of globalization to climax a decade of rapid globalization and as a consequence threatened to bring globalization to a standstill, if not throw it into retreat. Within a hundred or so days after the attack, articles appeared in prestigious publications questioning the values, success, and future of the process. The *Wall Street Journal* justifiably headlined a long analysis, "Globalism Under Siege." *Foreign Affairs* labeled several important articles, "Globalization and Its Discontents."[14] At the local levels, antiglobalization protesters who had made headlines with their sometimes violent actions at meetings of international organizations in Seattle, Genoa, and Goteborg, moved into the background after September 11. By mid-December 2001, however, some 80,000 protesters led by labor unions rallied against a European Union summit in Brussels. The antiglobalization leaders in Brussels notably did not oppose the U.S. military campaign in Afghanistan, but argued that a military response was

---

[13] Clark, *Globalization and Fragmentation*, is helpful on the important links and reciprocal relationships between the two processes, esp. 172–196.

[14] John Micklethwait and Adrian Woolridge, "Globalism under Siege," *Wall Street Journal*, 9 November 2001; *Foreign Affairs* 81 (January/February, 2002).

not enough to deal with terrorism's roots. Globalization, they argued, had resulted in ever-widening gaps between rich and poor in key areas of the world, including Saudi Arabia and Egypt, two countries that notably provided the terrorist leadership that carried out the September 11 attacks. To stop the globalization, and the resulting fragmentation, the Brussels protesters asked for government-sponsored massive aid programs to fight poverty and to provide greater protection for domestic industries that could put the impoverished to work.[15]

Other antiglobalization efforts were less constructive. For example, in Pakistan, whose government was the most important U.S. ally in the military campaign against Afghanistan's Taliban government, crowds organized by radical Islamic groups smashed and looted Kentucky Fried Chicken and McDonald's outlets, while burning American flags outside another McDonald's. Rioters also threatened Pizza Huts, Dunkin Donuts stands, a Nike store, and billboards advertising American multinational brands. Henry Kaufman, an economist and former vice chair of Salomon Brothers, concluded that "globalization is going to be at a standstill for awhile, until this high level of uncertainty diminishes." The multinationals tried to deal with these protests by emphasizing how their companies believed in fragmentation, localism, and decentralization. McDonald's was not an American company, the firm insisted, but "a confederation of very local companies" owned and run by local people: "We don't act local; we are local. It's localization, not globalization." One observer who closely studied this apparent fragmentation concluded that the combination of the intense belief that growing profitability rested on globalization, and the consequent threat to local cultures and businesses resulting from the globalizing process, gave multinationals no choice but to emphasize the benefits of decentralization. "McDonald's is like the British empire was," observed Eric Schlosser. "It looks enormous on the map, but it expanded because there were core economic problems at home."[16]

Historians have long observed how empires can be most vulnerable at their outer limits. President John F. Kennedy translated such an observation into a much larger U.S. commitment to Vietnam. Those who want to create or maintain empires, whether formal (as in the British case) or informal (as in the multiple political, economic, military, and cultural levels of the American example) quickly discover the high costs of such commitments. To extend Schlosser's conclusion, not only are McDonald's and other American franchises global, but U.S. troops are also positioned around the globe, including in Saudi Arabia where their presence on soil Islam considers sacred helped drive bin Laden to launch terrorism aimed principally at overthrowing the Saudi ruling families. These franchises and military units are overseas not primarily because of the

---

[15] Philip Shishkin, "Globalization's Foes Reappear in Force at Brussels Project," *Wall Street Journal*, 14 December 2001.

[16] David Barboza, "When Golden Arches Are too Red, White, and Blue," *New York Times*, 14 October 2001; Pamela Constable, "Pakistani Mobs Destroy KFC Outlet and U.S. Flags, *Washington Post*, 13 October 2001.

attractiveness of American culture and military protection, but because of the needs of the United States. The fragmentation of American multinationals and, in a not dissimilar fashion, the post-1980s world, has a price. Those who espouse a new imperial policy in the early twenty-first century understand some of the processes of decentralization and fragmentation, so much so that they demand a much larger U.S. military either to protect or stop (depending on which will more benefit American interests), the process. It is not clear that the new imperialists understand either the complexities of the fragmentation that narrow choices or the price that might be required to bring about the desired order in such a complex empire.

"Hence the worry," as two op-ed writers phrased it in the *Wall Street Journal* two months after September 11, "that the attack on the World Trade Center will prove a turning point [for globalization], just as the assassination of Archduke Ferdinand in Sarajevo in 1914 marked the end of the first age of globalization." Given the editorial page on which they wrote, the authors were necessarily optimistic; more, not less, globalization, they concluded, was the proper solution for dealing with those areas such as Saudi Arabia and other parts of the Islamic world, which had been left out of the process and were now failing to cooperate sufficiently in tracking down terrorists. But even these authors had to admit that "the danger is . . . a process of gradual reversal," because even before September 11 antiglobalization efforts were gathering force. The attacks of that day accelerated those "efforts." For example, "the war against terrorism is . . . demanding tighter controls on immigration and capital." Groups stretching from "European farmers and South Carolina textile workers to African dictators and French culture bureaucrats" were pushing "for more barriers."[17] The authors were twice correct. The post-September 11 antiglobalization efforts had indeed gathered strength and had done so in part because they could point to severe problems within the process that had become apparent before the attacks on New York City and Washington.

One such problem grew from globalization's inability to solve highly dangerous problems of poverty in certain parts of the world out of which the terrorists came. This inability was due less to globalization's excesses than to its limits. It could produce wealth, but it could not necessarily distribute it more equitably or with the necessary intelligence. One analysis concludes that when Tocqueville wrote, the richest country had about three times as much income as the poorest. By 2001, after two long eras of twentieth-century globalization, the richest nation had thirty times the income.[18] During the 1960s and 1970s, U.S. policy makers had mistaken high growth rates in Central America as promises for economic and political stability. Because the growth was so badly distributed, however, it produced a series of revolutions. In the 1980s and 1990s, U.S. policy makers and important members of the business community mistook

---

[17] Micklethwait and Woolridge, "Globalism Under Siege."
[18] Jeff Madrick, "Economic Scene," *New York Times*, 1 November 2001.

globalization for beneficial integration and stabilizing wealth, especially when it was accompanied by the joys of American mass culture. Because the globalization led to an often undesired U.S. presence and a fragmentation caused by local and even national resistance, and because the benefits of globalization were either doubtful or badly distributed, one result was a terrorism that exploited both the globalization and fragmentation.

Americans seemed to understand only one part of the process, globalization; terrorists understood and utilized both parts, globalization and its related fragmentation. U.S. and World Trade Organization officials began in a most preliminary fashion to consider how to fix these fundamental problems in November 2001, when they met in Doha, Qatar to try to establish new guidelines for key parts of the globalization process. The Doha guidelines revealed a notable retreat by the United States and some of its industrialized partners. The Bush administration agreed, for example, to lessen patent protection for brand-name drugs so, at least in emergencies, poorer nations could acquire inexpensive generic versions—especially for AIDS-plagued nations in Africa. Freer trade principles that exploited weaker nations were modified to allow those nations some self-protection. Champions of globalization continued to worry about the post-September 11 onslaught on the process. In the long run, it might provide the rising economic tide to lift all boats. In the short run, however, it did not promise to alleviate the problems of poverty and terrorism that washed over much of the globe. Meanwhile, John Maynard Keynes's dictum about where everyone ends up in the long run still applied.

The Revenge of the State

Keynes's legacy also proved interesting on a related front. Facing a growing recession already in place before September 11, but considerably worsened by the attacks, the George W. Bush administration necessarily ignored its earlier principle that government was best that spent least, and passed a large fiscal stimulus package that in some respects was Keynesian. In other respects, the targeting of wealthier Americans and large corporations for most of the package's benefits, the legislation seemed to recall Andrew Mellon more than Lord Keynes. Worldly Europeans understood what was happening, but expressed puzzlement. For years, they claimed, Americans had preached that the market should decide, subsidies and tariffs be eliminated, and globalization prevail. Then as the U.S. economy headed downhill during the weeks after September 11, the Bush administration threatened to impose antidumping fines to protect the American steel industry. As an anthrax scare settled over the U.S. Post Office and the heavily populated region between New York City and Washington, the administration forgot about its view that drug patents must be protected and instead threatened to bypass Bayer's patent for Cipro so Americans could have cheaper protection against anthrax. Elie Cohen, a leading economist and political adviser in France, where contradictions in U.S. policy never go unnoticed, declared that when "Americans are facing the same problems" Europe and other parts of the world have long faced, the Americans "seem to forget the universal laws of the market."[19]

But this contradiction was only apparent. Americans have seldom been reluctant to fix markets when they deem it in their interest, regardless of their rhetoric. In any event, contradiction was not the most interesting characteristic of the Bush response. The administration's indication about the economic role now to be played by government was only a part of the much larger political, economic, and, especially, military responsibility that was being accepted by Washington both at home and internationally. On a trivial level, President Bush, who while campaigning for the office did not know the names of heads of governments and seemed not to care, conferred with forty-six such figures in the three months after September 11. With some of those leaders, including Vladimir Putin of Russia and Tony Blair of Great Britain, he formed surprisingly close personal and policy ties. On the most important level, the President oversaw the creation of a wartime state apparatus that was as powerful and centralized as any since World War II and gave him executive powers unmatched in perhaps a half-century.

To rephrase, the fragmentation and privatization that helped produce terrorism and an increasingly unstable economic world after September 11 was now to be countered by a new, evolving, considerably more centralized U.S. government that happened to be in the hands primarily of the political party known for urging privatization and decentralization. The world, however, had grown too dangerous for private, marketplace solutions even before the September attacks, and the attacks vividly and literally brought home the dangers.[20] Governmental powers mushroomed until one conservative writer appropriately called it the relegitimation of central institutions.[21] The author was correct in the broad sense, but the institutions had to be relegitimated in part because of Bush and the Republican right's attack on them during the 1990s. Democrat and Republican liberals, although they seldom wanted any longer to identify themselves with the term, had less trouble supporting the revitalization of governmental institutions so they could fight what promised to be a long and costly war against international terrorism. Strong presidential powers were in the tradition of many Democratic chief executives, especially during the frequent wartime years of the twentieth century. Americans not only supported such powers after September 11, but for the first time in more than a generation, a majority told pollsters they trusted the government to do the right thing most of the time.

---

[19] Alan Cowell, "European Converts to Laissez-Faire," *New York Times*, 25 October 2001.

[20] Robert Gilpin, with the assistance of Jean Millis Gilpin, *The Challenge of Global Capitalism: The World Economy in the 21st Century* (Princeton: Princeton University Press, 2000), esp. chaps 10–11, presents the case that the pre-September 11 world of international economics and globalization was in dangerous disarray, indeed, in a race to the bottom, because of the lack of political leadership and involvement.

[21] Michael Kelly, "The Left's Great Divide," *Washington Post*, 7 November 2001.

Bush's centralization of power in the White House after the attacks was breathtaking. He justified it by constantly declaring that this terrorism was an act of war. The country was in a war even though Congress, which according to the Constitution held final authority, had never formally declared war. It was, moreover, a peculiar kind of conflict unlike World Wars I and II or even the Korean war, in which Americans were mobilized and sacrifices demanded. Bush asked not for sacrifice, except from the volunteer military and reserves; instead he pleaded with Americans to spend as much as possible in order to restore a sense of normality and, above all, pump-prime a slowing economy. He centralized power so that Congress and many non–U.S. citizens lost prerogatives, but the rest of the population little noticed or apparently cared—as long as they were told the military campaigns went according to plan, they believed the economy would soon improve, and above all, they felt some confidence that no further major terrorist attacks would occur on American soil.

Bush established a Homeland Security office to oversee continental defense against terrorism. He opposed having Congress grant statutory authority to it, thus its director could refuse congressional requests for him to testify. Attorney General John Ashcroft ruled, without the usual waiting period to hear public comment, that the Justice Department could listen to lawyer-client conversations if Ashcroft believed it necessary, even if the people involved had not been charged and even in the absence of a court order allowing wiretaps. The attorney general ordered the arrest of more than 540 persons charged with only immigration violations. He then held them while refusing to make public why they were being held at such length and declining even to reveal their names. An uproar followed the disclosure by Bush and Ashcroft that military tribunals would be established to try non–U.S. citizens who were suspected of terrorism. The President justified this action on precedents set by Abraham Lincoln and, especially, Franklin D. Roosevelt during World War II. But Bush's order went beyond such previous acts by forcing defendants to testify in secret, allowing evidence to be withheld from defendants, providing for a death sentence if only two-thirds of the judges agreed (instead of the usual required unanimity), and giving those convicted the right of appeal to the Pentagon or the White House instead of to the Supreme Court. Using the military campaigns as cover, Bush also issued an executive order allowing a sitting president to block the release of an earlier president's papers. He thus arbitrarily nullified a law passed by Congress and agreed to by previous chief executives that those papers had to be open (as they were for 200 years) so Americans and their representatives could be properly informed as they made decisions. Cynics noted that Bush's action could prevent disclosure of his father's activities which, for example, included working with Panama's dictator Manuel Noriega and Iraq's Saddam Hussein before the United States decided to go to war against both in 1989–1990. When Bush tried to cut intelligence briefings to congressional intelligence committees, Republican Senator Chuck Hagel of Nebraska said the President "put out a public document telling the world he doesn't trust the Congress."

Bush worked out a compromise, but made the same point again by refusing to send a few treaties that required congressional debate and ratification to Capitol Hill, and instead dealt with some (as the Biological Weapons Convention) so Congress could be circumvented.[22]

Information from the military campaigns in Afghanistan was sketchy as reporters on the scene worked under restrictions that had not been in place during the Vietnam conflict. But this was precisely the point: since that conflict, when factual reporting had undermined the often misleading daily handouts from the White House and Pentagon and fueled an antiwar movement, the military and the White House had determined a certain amount of censorship to be necessary so that the right message would reach Americans. Bush's father had used this censorship successfully in the Panama invasion of 1989 and the Gulf War. Clinton did not get it in place in Somalia during 1993, when the killing and mutilation of American military personnel, graphically shown by new technology earth satellites on American television screens, forced the President to withdraw the remaining troops. The lesson from the past forty years thus seemed clear: the less Americans knew, the more likely they were to support the President's actions overseas. There was also another lesson: the new technology of globalization did not necessarily decentralize knowledge and power, but in certain hands under the right circumstances, could be used to centralize and increase governmental powers.

The White House and the State Department also set up a new office to get its controlled message overseas, especially to Islamic audiences who had been strongly influenced by Osama bin Laden's observations distributed on videos. A former advertising executive, Charlotte Beers, was brought in "to try to make American values as much a brand name as McDonald's hamburgers or Ivory soap," according to one observer. When she briefed foreign journalists in Washington, however, U.S. journalists were excluded. The State Department explained, "We can't give out our propaganda to our own people."[23] Nearly all of these post-September 11 initiatives were excused by the claim that it was a new kind of war, and anyway the President's approval ratings were at historic highs. E. S. Corwin famously noted a half-century ago that in the realm of foreign policy, the Constitution was an "invitation" to a struggle between the President and Congress. After September 11, Congress rapidly lost the struggle.

President Bush's actions were part of the broad campaign to stop the fragmentation of power that had marked the post-1980s era. When he visited China in October 2001, the campaign was explicit. Human rights groups and other NGOs had long criticized and tried to slow the U.S. relationship with China

---

[22] Dana Milbank, "In War, It's Power to the President," *Washington Post*, 20 November 2001, has an overview of the presidential actions; Editorial, "Justice Deformed," *New York Times*, 2 December 2001, critically summarizes the attorney general's actions; while ibid., 18 November 2001, provides a long analysis placing the civil liberty versus security argument in context.

[23] Elizabeth Becker, "In the War on Terrorism, A Battle to Shape Opinion," *New York Times*, 11 November 2001.

because of the communist regime's brutal treatment of dissidents. After September 11, the President made it clear that his administration's desire for China's cooperation against terrorism shaped Washington's approach to the exclusion of nearly all else, including human rights. China's willingness to go along with many of the American initiatives against Osama bin Laden warmed relations between Washington and Beijing that had been under considerable strain before September 11. Leaders of the dissident movements understood Bush's priority, but many, such as Hé Xingtong, whose husband was serving a thirteen-year prison sentence for establishing a short-lived political party, bitterly complained that the President apparently never even mentioned the growing human rights problems to China's leaders.[24] Interests that had especially driven nongovernmental groups had given way to the government-defined and conducted war.

War in Afghanistan targeted the al Qaeda terrorist network and Osama bin Laden. In this sense, it was a different war than Americans had ever fought before. It was a war against an amorphous, decentralized, privatized terrorism instead of a war primarily against formal states. Al Qaeda, however, needed some state support in order to survive, and that need made it easier for the Bush administration to wage the war and explain it to Americans. Thus four months after September 11, and after a series of vigorous military campaigns, the al Qaeda network had been weakened but not destroyed; few of its leaders had been captured; and bin Laden had evaded search teams. But the Taliban regime of Afghanistan that had protected and been handsomely bought off by bin Laden had fallen. The country came under a more traditional and notably decentralized government. It seemed to be only a matter of time until bin Laden, stripped of state support, would be found. The question then became where the U.S. antiterrorist campaign would move next. Again, this question was defined in terms of dealing primarily with states, not only with dispersed, informal terrorist networks. And the state that a growing American and especially Washington consensus seemed to target was Saddam Hussein's Iraq, which had been labeled the K-Mart for international terrorists.

Concluding Themes

If the Bush administration were to decide to overthrow the Iraqi dictator, it would further confirm three broad themes that appeared after September 11. First, a new emphasis on state-to-state relations, especially since a decision to attack Iraq would require the kind of extensive, sensitive, multilateral diplomacy that the Bush administration seemed to relish denigrating before the attacks, was now necessary to bring into a coalition key nations that were most reluctant to wage an all-out military campaign to overthrow Saddam, especially without further evidence of Saddam's involvement with the attacks on New

[24] Philip P. Pan, "Disappointed Dissidents," *Washington Post*, 27 October 2001.

York and Washington. Second, the new importance of nation-building, a task Bush and some of his closest advisers had said before September 11 to be beneath U.S. purposes and beyond American capabilities, now had to be undertaken in Afghanistan and perhaps later elsewhere on a much grander, complex, and dangerous scale. Third, centralized governmental decision making in the United States would necessarily drastically increase both the powers of the President and the importance of state-to-state relations.

The September 11 attacks, therefore, seemed to mark, if not the end, at least a major modification of the post-1980s era of fragmentation. That era had its roots in the cold war, then was notably shaped by the appearance of new, supposedly decentralizing technologies and the end of the Soviet empire. If a new American empire, espoused by some conservative observers in Washington, was to be realized, and a supposedly beneficent American imperialism was to stabilize the world by creating out of the pre-2001 fragmentation an order based on U.S. values, it would be the kind of full-time job that could fully tax Americans' limited attention-span toward foreign policy, not to mention their willingness to sacrifice meaningfully over a long period of time for the sake of the imperium.

During and even before the post-cold-war era of the 1990s, Americans enjoyed democracy on the cheap. Government and political participation were deemphasized. Economic growth, American cultural and technological globalization, and decision-by-marketplace became the conventional answers to the questions of why many Americans grew rich, the stock market went ever upward, and other people loved Nikes and McDonalds. Globalization, however, created a mirror image of fragmentation. Out of that fragmentation came the evil of terrorism, while key governments, following Washington's lead, increasingly defined themselves out of the picture, unless it was to remove barriers to globalization or save such unfortunate parts of the new empire as Mexico and Russia, who could not quite get their roles straight without devaluations and bail-outs. The post-September 11 world will, one hopes, be less shaped by the globalization, unilateralism, and fragmentation that helped produce that world, than it will be by the people who shape governments that are open, cooperative, and knowledgeable about the past that produced the crisis. Nor will that world be shaped by some amorphous transglobal cultural currents that supposedly make all people equally interesting for study in the world's international arena. Simply because of their power, Americans are more equal than others. The question thus becomes not what kind of empire Americans will have, but what kind of democracy. Given the events of the past decade, there is no automatically optimistic answer to that question.

The Soft Underbelly of American Primacy: Tactical Advantages of Terror

RICHARD K. BETTS

In given conditions, action and reaction can be ridiculously out of proportion. . . . One can obtain results monstrously in excess of the effort. . . . Let's consider this auto smash-up. . . . The driver lost control at high speed while swiping at a wasp which had flown in through a window and was buzzing around his face. . . . The weight of a wasp is under half an ounce. Compared with a human being, the wasp's size is minute, its strength negligible. Its sole armament is a tiny syringe holding a drop of irritant, formic acid. . . . Nevertheless, that wasp killed four big men and converted a large, powerful car into a heap of scrap.

—*Eric Frank Russell*[1]

To grasp some implications of the new first priority in U.S. foreign policy, it is necessary to understand the connections among three things: the imbalance of power between terrorist groups and counterterrorist governments; the reasons that groups choose terror tactics; and the operational advantage of attack over defense in the interactions of terrorists and their opponents. On September 11, 2001, Americans were reminded that the overweening power that they had taken for granted over the past dozen years is not the same as omnipotence. What is less obvious but equally important is that the power is itself part of the cause of terrorist enmity and even a source of U.S. vulnerability.

There is no consensus on a definition of "terrorism," mainly because the term is so intensely pejorative.[2] When defined in terms of tactics, consistency

---

[1] William Wolf in Eric Frank Russell, *Wasp* (London: Victor Gollancz, 2000, originally published 1957), 7.

[2] "The word has become a political label rather than an analytical concept." Martha Crenshaw, *Terrorism and International Cooperation* (New York: Institute for East-West Security Studies, 1989), 5.

RICHARD K. BETTS is the Leo A. Shifrin Professor and director of the Institute of War and Peace Studies at Columbia University and was a member of the National Commission on Terrorism. He has written extensively on strategic and tactical issues in national security affairs.

falters, because most people can think of some "good" political cause that has used the tactics and whose purposes excuse them or at least warrant the group's designation as freedom fighters rather than terrorists. Israelis who call the Khobar Towers bombers of 1996 terrorists might reject that characterization for the Irgun, which did the same thing to the King David Hotel in 1946, or some Irish Americans would bridle at equating IRA bombings in Britain with Tamil Tiger bombings in Sri Lanka. Anticommunists labeled the Vietcong terrorists (because they engaged in combat out of uniform and assassinated local officials), but opponents of the Saigon government did not. Nevertheless, a functional definition is more sensible than one conditioned on the identity of the perpetrators. For this article, terrorism refers to the illegitimate, deliberate killing of civilians for purposes of punishment or coercion. This holds in abeyance the questions of whether deliberate killing of civilians can ever be legitimate or killing soldiers can be terrorism.

In any case, for all but the rare nihilistic psychopath, terror is a means, not an end in itself. Terror tactics are usually meant to serve a strategy of coercion.[3] They are a use of force designed to further some substantive aim. This is not always evident in the heat of rage felt by the victims of terror. Normal people find it hard to see instrumental reasoning behind an atrocity, especially when recognizing the political motives behind terrorism might seem to make its illegitimacy less extreme. Stripped of rhetoric, however, a war against terrorism must mean a war against political groups who choose terror as a tactic.

American global primacy is one of the causes of this war. It animates both the terrorists' purposes and their choice of tactics. To groups like al Qaeda, the United States is the enemy because American military power dominates their world, supports corrupt governments in their countries, and backs Israelis against Muslims; American cultural power insults their religion and pollutes their societies; and American economic power makes all these intrusions and desecrations possible. Japan, in contrast, is not high on al Qaeda's list of targets, because Japan's economic power does not make it a political, military, and cultural behemoth that penetrates their societies.

Political and cultural power makes the United States a target for those who blame it for their problems. At the same time, American economic and military power prevents them from resisting or retaliating against the United States on its own terms. To smite the only superpower requires unconventional modes of force and tactics that make the combat cost exchange ratio favorable to the attacker. This offers hope to the weak that they can work their will despite their overall deficit in power.

Primacy on the Cheap

The United States has enjoyed military and political primacy (or hegemony, unipolarity, or whatever term best connotes international dominance) for barely

---

[3] For a survey of types, see Christopher C. Harmon, "Five Strategies of Terrorism," *Small Wars and Insurgencies* 12 (Autumn 2001).

a dozen years. Those who focus on the economic dimension of international relations spoke of American hegemony much earlier, but observers of the strategic landscape never did. For those who focus on national security, the world before 1945 was multipolar, and the world of the cold war was bipolar. After 1945 the United States had exerted hegemony within the First World and for a while over the international economy. The strategic competition against the Second World, however, was seen as a titanic struggle between equal politicomilitary coalitions and a close-run thing until very near the end. Only the collapse of the Soviet pole, which coincided fortuitously with renewed relative strength of the American economy, marked the real arrival of U.S. global dominance.

The novelty of complete primacy may account for the thoughtless, indeed innocently arrogant way in which many Americans took its benefits for granted. Most who gave any thought to foreign policy came implicitly to regard the entire world after 1989 as they had regarded Western Europe and Japan during the past half-century: partners in principle but vassals in practice. The United States would lead the civilized community of nations in the expansion and consolidation of a liberal world order. Overwhelming military dominance was assumed to be secure and important across most of the domestic political spectrum.

Liberal multilateralists conflated U.S. primacy with political globalization, indeed, conflated ideological American nationalism with internationalist altruism.[4] They assumed that U.S. military power should be used to stabilize benighted countries and police international violence, albeit preferably camouflaged under the banner of institutions such as the United Nations, or at least NATO. They rejected the idea that illiberal impulses or movements represented more than a retreating challenge to the West's mission and its capacity to extend its values worldwide.

Conservative unilateralists assumed that unrivaled power relieved the United States of the need to cater to the demands of others. When America acted strategically abroad, others would have to join on its terms or be left out of the action. The United States should choose battles, avoid entanglements in incompetent polities, and let unfortunates stew in their own juice. For both multilateralists and nationalists, the issue was whether the United States would decide to make an effort for world welfare, not whether a strategic challenge could threaten its truly vital interests. (Colloquial depreciation of the adjective notwithstanding, literally vital U.S. interests are those necessary to life.)

[4] Rationalization of national power as altruism resembles the thinking about benign Pax Britannica in the Crowe Memorandum: "... the national policy of the insular and naval State is so directed as to harmonize with the general desires and ideals common to all mankind, and more particularly ... is closely identified with the primary and vital interests of a majority, or as many as possible, of the other nations.... England, more than any other non-insular Power, has a direct and positive interest in the maintenance of the independence of nations, and therefore must be the natural enemy of any country threatening the independence of others, and the natural protector of the weaker communities." Eyre Crowe, "Memorandum on the Present State of British Relations with France and Germany," 1 January 1907, in G. P. Gooch and Harold Temperley, eds., *British Documents on the Origins of the War, 1898–1914*, vol. 3: *The Testing of the Entente, 1904–6* (London: His Majesty's Stationery Office, 1928), 402–403.

For many, primacy was confused with invulnerability. American experts warned regularly of the danger of catastrophic terrorism—and Osama bin Laden explicitly declared war on the United States in his *fatwa* of February 1998. But the warnings did not register seriously in the consciousness of most people. Even some national security experts felt stunned when the attacks occurred on September 11. Before then, the American military wanted nothing to do with the mission of "homeland defense," cited the Posse Comitatus act to suggest that military operations within U.S. borders would be improper, and argued that homeland defense should be the responsibility of civilian agencies or the National Guard. The services preferred to define the active forces' mission as fighting and winning the nation's wars—as if wars were naturally something that happened abroad—and homeland defense involved no more than law enforcement, managing relief operations in natural disasters, or intercepting ballistic missiles outside U.S. airspace. Only in America could the nation's armed forces think of direct defense of national territory as a distraction.

Being Number One seemed cheap. The United States could cut the military burden on the economy by half after the cold war (from 6 percent to 3 percent of GNP) yet still spend almost five times more than the combined military budgets of all potential enemy states. And this did not count the contributions of rich U.S. allies.[5] Of course the margin in dollar terms does not translate into a comparable quantitative margin in manpower or equipment, but that does not mean that a purchasing power parity estimate would reduce the implied gap in combat capability. The overwhelming qualitative superiority of U.S. conventional forces cuts in the other direction. Washington was also able to plan, organize, and fight a major war in 1991 at negligible cost in blood or treasure. Financially, nearly 90 percent of the bills for the war against Iraq were paid by allies. With fewer than 200 American battle deaths, the cost in blood was far lower than almost anyone had imagined it could be. Less than a decade later, Washington waged another war, over Kosovo, that cost no U.S. combat casualties at all.

In the one case where costs in casualties exceeded the apparent interests at stake—Somalia in 1993—Washington quickly stood down from the fight. This became the reference point for vulnerability: the failure of an operation that was small, far from home, and elective. Where material interests required strategic engagement, as in the oil-rich Persian Gulf, U.S. strategy could avoid costs by exploiting its huge advantage in conventional capability. Where conventional dominance proved less exploitable, as in Somalia, material interests did not require strategic engagement. Where the United States could not operate militarily with impunity, it could choose not to operate.

---

[5] At the end of the twentieth century, the combined military budgets of China, Russia, Iraq, Yugoslavia (Serbia), North Korea, Iran, Libya, Cuba, Afghanistan, and Sudan added up to no more than $60 billion. *The Military Balance, 1999–2000* (London: International Institute for Strategic Studies, 1999), 102, 112, 132, 133, 159, 186, 275.

Finally, power made it possible to let moral interests override material interests where some Americans felt an intense moral concern, even if in doing so they claimed, dubiously, that the moral and material stakes coincided. To some extent this happened in Kosovo, although the decision to launch that war apparently flowed from overoptimism about how quickly a little bombing would lead Belgrade to capitulate. Most notably, it happened in the Arab-Israeli conflict. For more than three decades after the 1967 Six Day War, the United States supported Israel diplomatically, economically, and militarily against the Arabs, despite the fact that doing so put it on the side of a tiny country of a few million people with no oil, against more than ten times as many Arabs who controlled over a third of the world's oil reserves.

This policy was not just an effect of primacy, since the U.S.–Israel alignment began in the cold war. The salience of the moral motive was indicated by the fact that U.S. policy proceeded despite the fact that it helped give Moscow a purchase in major Arab capitals such as Cairo, Damascus, and Baghdad. Luckily for the United States, however, the largest amounts of oil remained under the control of the conservative Arab states of the Gulf. In this sense the hegemony of the United States within the anticommunist world helped account for the policy. That margin of power also relieved Washington of the need to make hard choices about disciplining its client. For decades the United States opposed Israeli settlement of the West Bank, terming the settlements illegal; yet in all that time the United States never demanded that Israel refrain from colonizing the West Bank as a condition for receiving U.S. economic and military aid.[6] Washington continued to bankroll Israel at a higher per capita rate than any other country in the world, a level that has been indispensable to Israel, providing aid over the years that now totals well over $100 billion in today's dollars.[7] Although this policy enraged some Arabs and irritated the rest, U.S. power was great enough that such international political costs did not outweigh the domestic political costs of insisting on Israeli compliance with U.S. policy.

Of course, far more than subsidizing Israeli occupation of Palestinian land was involved in the enmity of Islamist terrorists toward the United States. Many of the other explanations, however, presuppose U.S. global primacy. When American power becomes the arbiter of conflicts around the world, it makes itself the target for groups who come out on the short end of those conflicts.

---

[6] Washington certainly did exert pressure on Israel at some times. The administration of Bush the Elder, for example, threatened to withhold loans for housing construction, but this was a marginal portion of total U.S. aid. There was never a threat to cut off the basic annual maintenance payment of several billion dollars to which Israel became accustomed decades ago.

[7] The United States has also given aid to friendly Arab governments—huge amounts to Egypt and some to Jordan. This does not counterbalance the aid to Israel, however, in terms of effects on opinions of strongly anti-Israeli Arabs. Islamists see the regimes in Cairo and Amman as American toadies, complicit in betrayal of the Palestinians.

Primacy and Asymmetric Warfare

The irrational evil of terrorism seems most obvious to the powerful. They are accustomed to getting their way with conventional applications of force and are not as accustomed as the powerless to thinking of terror as the only form of force that might make their enemies do their will. This is why terrorism is the premier form of "asymmetric warfare," the Pentagon buzzword for the type of threats likely to confront the United States in the post-cold war world.[8] Murderous tactics may become instrumentally appealing by default—when one party in a conflict lacks other military options.

Resort to terror is not necessarily limited to those facing far more powerful enemies. It can happen in a conventional war between great powers that becomes a total war, when the process of escalation pits whole societies against each other and shears away civilized restraints. That is something seldom seen, and last seen over a half-century ago. One does not need to accept the tendentious position that allied strategic bombing in World War II constituted terrorism to recognize that the British and Americans did systematically assault the urban population centers of Germany and Japan. They did so in large part because precision bombing of industrial facilities proved ineffective.[9] During the early phase of the cold war, in turn, U.S. nuclear strategy relied on plans to counter Soviet conventional attack on Western Europe with a comprehensive nuclear attack on communist countries that would have killed hundreds of millions. In the 1950s, Strategic Air Command targeteers even went out of their way to plan "bonus" damage by moving aim points for military targets so that blasts would destroy adjacent towns as well.[10] In both World War II and planning for World War III, the rationale was less to kill civilians per se than to wreck the enemy economies—although that was also one of Osama bin Laden's

---

[8] Theoretically, this was anticipated by Samuel P. Huntington in his 1962 analysis of the differences between symmetrical intergovernmental war and asymmetrical antigovernmental war. "Patterns of Violence in World Politics" in Huntington, ed., *Changing Patterns of Military Politics* (New York: Free Press of Glencoe, 1962), 19–21. Some of Huntington's analysis of insurrectionary warfare within states applies as well to transnational terrorism.

[9] The Royal Air Force gave up on precision bombing early and focused deliberately on night bombing of German cities, while the Americans continued to try precision daylight bombing. Firestorms in Hamburg, Darmstadt, and Dresden, and less incendiary attacks on other cities, killed several hundred-thousand German civilians. Over Japan, the United States quickly gave up attempts at precision bombing when weather made it impractical and deliberately resorted to an incendiary campaign that burned most Japanese cities to the ground and killed at least 300,000 civilians (and perhaps more than half a million) well before the nuclear attacks on Hiroshima and Nagasaki, which killed another 200,000. Michael S. Sherry, *The Rise of American Air Power: The Creation of Armageddon* (New Haven: Yale University Press, 1987), 260, 413n43.

[10] The threat of deliberate nuclear escalation remained the bedrock of NATO doctrine throughout the cold war, but after the Kennedy administration, the flexible response doctrine made it conditional and included options for nuclear first-use that did not involve deliberate targeting of population centers. In the Eisenhower administration, however, all-out attack on the Soviet bloc's cities was integral to plans for defense of Western Europe against Soviet armored divisions.

rationales for the attacks on the World Trade Center.[11] In short, the instrumental appeal of strategic attacks on noncombatants may be easier to understand when one considers that states with legitimate purposes have sometimes resorted to such a strategy. Such a double standard, relaxing prohibitions against targeting noncombatants for the side with legitimate purposes (one's own side), occurs most readily when the enemy is at least a peer competitor threatening vital interests. When one's own primacy is taken for granted, it is easier to revert to a single standard that puts all deliberate attacks against civilians beyond the pale.

In contrast to World War II, most wars are limited—or at least limited for the stronger side when power is grossly imbalanced. In such cases, using terror to coerce is likely to seem the only potentially effective use of force for the weaker side, which faces a choice between surrender or savagery. Radical Muslim zealots cannot expel American power with conventional military means, so they substitute clandestine means of delivery against military targets (such as the Khobar Towers barracks in Saudi Arabia) or high-profile political targets (embassies in Kenya and Tanzania). More than once the line has been attributed to terrorists, "If you will let us lease one of your B-52s, we will use that instead of a truck bomb." The hijacking and conversion of U.S. airliners into kamikazes was the most dramatic means of asymmetric attack.

Kamikaze hijacking also reflects an impressive capacity for strategic judo, the turning of the West's strength against itself.[12] The flip-side of a primacy that diffuses its power throughout the world is that advanced elements of that power become more accessible to its enemies. Nineteen men from technologically backward societies did not have to rely on home-grown instruments to devastate the Pentagon and World Trade Center. They used computers and modern financial procedures with facility, and they forcibly appropriated the aviation technology of the West and used it as a weapon. They not only rebelled against the "soft power" of the United States, they trumped it by hijacking the country's hard power.[13] They also exploited the characteristics of U.S. society associ-

---

[11] In a videotape months after the attacks, bin Laden said, "These blessed strikes showed clearly that this arrogant power, America, rests on a powerful but precarious economy, which rapidly crumbled . . . the global economy based on usury, which America uses along with its military might to impose infidelity and humiliation on oppressed people, can easily crumble. . . . Hit the economy, which is the basis of military might. If their economy is finished, they will become too busy to enslave oppressed people. . . . America is in decline; the economic drain is continuing but more strikes are required and the youths must strike the key sectors of the American economy." Videotape excerpts quoted in "Bin Laden's Words: 'America Is in Decline,' the Leader of Al Qaeda Says," *New York Times*, 28 December 2001.

[12] This is similar to the concept of political judo discussed in Samuel L. Popkin, "Pacification: Politics and the Village," *Asian Survey* 10 (August 1970); and Popkin, "Internal Conflicts—South Vietnam" in Kenneth N. Waltz and Steven Spiegel, eds., *Conflict in World Politics* (Cambridge, MA: Winthrop, 1971).

[13] Soft power is "indirect or cooptive" and "can rest on the attraction of one's ideas or on the ability to set the political agenda in a way that shapes the preferences that others express." It "tends to be associated with intangible power resources such as culture, ideology, and institutions." Joseph S. Nye, Jr., "The Changing Nature of World Power," *Political Science Quarterly* 105 (Summer 1990): 181. See also Nye, *Bound to Lead: The Changing Nature of American Power* (New York: Basic Books, 1990).

ated with soft power—the liberalism, openness, and respect for privacy that allowed them to go freely about the business of preparing the attacks without observation by the state security apparatus. When soft power met the clash of civilizations, it proved too soft.

Strategic judo is also apparent in the way in which U.S. retaliation may compromise its own purpose. The counter offensive after September 11 was necessary, if only to demonstrate to marginally motivated terrorists that they could not hope to strike the United States for free. The war in Afghanistan, however, does contribute to polarization in the Muslim world and to mobilization of potential terrorist recruits. U.S. leaders can say that they are not waging a war against Islam until they are blue in the face, but this will not convince Muslims who already distrust the United States. Success in deposing the Taliban may help U.S. policy by encouraging a bandwagon effect that rallies governments and moderates among the Muslim populace, but there will probably be as many who see the U.S. retaliation as confirming al Qaeda's diagnosis of American evil. Victory in Afghanistan and follow-up operations to prevent al Qaeda from relocating bases of operation to other countries will hurt that organization's capacity to act. The number of young zealots willing to emulate the "martyrdom operation" of the nineteen on September 11, however, is not likely to decline.

Advantage of Attack

The academic field of security studies has some reason to be embarrassed after September 11. Having focused primarily on great powers and interstate conflict, literature on terrorism was comparatively sparse; most of the good books were by policy analysts rather than theorists.[14] Indeed, science fiction has etched out the operational logic of terrorism as well as political science. Eric Frank Russell's 1957 novel, from which the epigraph to this article comes, vividly illustrates both the strategic aspirations of terrorists and the offense-dominant character of their tactics. It describes the dispatch of a single agent to one of many planets in the Sirian enemy's empire to stir up fear, confusion, and panic through a series of small covert activities with tremendous ripple effects. Matched with deceptions to make the disruptions appear to be part of a campaign by a big phantom rebel organization, the agent's modest actions divert large numbers of enemy policy and military personnel, cause economic dislocations and social unrest, and soften the planet up for invasion. Wasp agents are infiltrated into numerous planets, multiplying the effects. As the agents' handlers tell him, "The pot is coming slowly but surely to the boil. Their fleets are being widely dispersed, there are vast troop movements from their overcrowded home-system to the outer planets of their empire. They're gradually

---

[14] For example, Bruce Hoffmann, *Inside Terrorism* (New York: Columbia University Press, 1998); Paul R. Pillar, *Terrorism and American Foreign Policy* (Washington, DC: Brookings Institution Press, 2001); Richard A. Falkenrath, Robert D. Newman, and Bradley S. Thayer, *America's Achilles' Heel: Nuclear, Biological, and Chemical Terrorism and Covert Attack* (Cambridge: MIT Press, 1998).

being chivvied into a fix. They can't hold what they've got without spreading all over it. The wider they spread the thinner they get. The thinner they get, the easier it is to bite lumps out of them."[15]

Fortunately al Qaeda and its ilk are not as wildly effective as Russell's wasp. By degree, however, the phenomenon is quite similar. Comparatively limited initiatives prompt tremendous and costly defensive reactions. On September 11 a small number of men killed 3,000 people and destroyed a huge portion of prime commercial real estate, part of the military's national nerve center, and four expensive aircraft. The ripple effects, however, multiplied those costs. A major part of the U.S. economy—air travel—shut down completely for days after September 11. Increased security measures dramatically increased the overall costs of the air travel system thereafter. Normal law enforcement activities of the Federal Bureau of Investigation were radically curtailed as legions of agents were transferred to counterterror tasks. Anxiety about the vulnerability of nuclear power plants, major bridges and tunnels, embassies abroad, and other high-value targets prompted plans for big investments in fortification of a wide array of facilities. A retaliatory war in Afghanistan ran at a cost of a couple billion dollars a month beyond the regular defense budget for months. In one study, the attacks on the World Trade Center and the Pentagon were estimated to cost the U.S. economy 1.8 million jobs.[16]

Or consider the results of a handful of 34-cent letters containing anthrax, probably sent by a single person. Besides killing several people, they contaminated a large portion of the postal system, paralyzed some mail delivery for long periods, provoked plans for huge expenditures on prophylactic irradiation equipment, shut down much of Capitol Hill for weeks, put thousands of people on a sixty-day regimen of strong antibiotics (potentially eroding the medical effectiveness of such antibiotics in future emergencies), and overloaded police and public health inspectors with false alarms. The September 11 attacks and the October anthrax attacks together probably cost the perpetrators less than a million dollars. If the cost of rebuilding and of defensive investments in reaction came to no more than $100 billion, the cost exchange ratio would still be astronomically in favor of the attack over the defense.

Analysts in strategic studies did not fall down on the job completely before September 11. At least two old bodies of work help to illuminate the problem. One is the literature on guerrilla warfare and counterinsurgency, particularly prominent in the 1960s, and the other is the offense-defense theory that bur-

---

[15] Russell, *Wasp*, 64. The ripple effects include aspects of strategic judo. Creating a phony rebel organization leads the enemy security apparatus to turn on its own people. "If some Sirians could be given the full-time job of hunting down and garroting other Sirians, and if other Sirians could be given the full-time job of dodging or shooting down the garroters, then a distant and different life form would be saved a few unpleasant chores. . . . Doubtless the military would provide a personal bodyguard for every big wheel on Jaimec; that alone would pin down a regiment." Ibid., 26, 103.

[16] Study by the Milken Institute discussed in "The Economics: Attacks May Cost 1.8 Million Jobs," *New York Times*, 13 January 2002.

geoned in the 1980s. Both apply well to understanding patterns of engagement between terrorists and counterterrorists. Some of the axioms derived from the empirical cases in the counterinsurgency literature apply directly, and offense-defense theory applies indirectly.

Apart from the victims of guerrillas, few still identify irregular paramilitary warfare with terrorism (because the latter is illegitimate), but the two activities do overlap a great deal in their operational characteristics. Revolutionary or resistance movements in the preconventional phase of operations usually mix small-unit raids on isolated outposts of the government or occupying force with detonations and assassinations in urban areas to instill fear and discredit government power. The tactical logic of guerrilla operations resembles that in terrorist attacks: the weaker rebels use stealth and the cover of civilian society to concentrate their striking power against one among many of the stronger enemy's dispersed assets; they strike quickly and eliminate the target before the defender can move forces from other areas to respond; they melt back into civilian society to avoid detection and reconcentrate against another target. The government or occupier has far superior strength in terms of conventional military power, but cannot counterconcentrate in time because it has to defend all points, while the insurgent attacker can pick its targets at will.[17] The contest between insurgents and counterinsurgents is "tripartite," polarizing political alignments and gaining the support of *attentistes* or those in the middle. In today's principal counterterror campaign, one might say that the yet-unmobilized Muslim elites and masses of the Third World—those who were not already actively committed either to supporting Islamist radicalism or to combating it—are the target group in the middle. As Samuel Huntington noted, "a revolutionary war is a war of attrition."[18] As I believe Stanley Hoffman once said, in re-

---

[17] Mao Tse-Tung's classic tracts are canonical background. For example, "Problems of Strategy in China's Revolutionary War" (especially chap. 5) in *Selected Works of Mao Tse-Tung* (Beijing: Foreign Languages Press, 1967), vol. i, and "Problems of Strategy in Guerrilla War Against Japan," in *Selected Works*, vol. ii (1967). Much of the Western analytical literature grew out of British experience in the Malayan Emergency and France's role in Indochina and Algeria. For example, Franklin Mark Osanka, ed., *Modern Guerrilla Warfare* (New York: Free Press, 1962); Gerard Chaliand, ed., *Guerrilla Strategies: An Historical Anthology from the Long March to Afghanistan* (Berkeley: University of California Press, 1982); Roger Triniquier, *Modern Warfare: A French View of Counterinsurgency*, Daniel Lee, trans. (New York: Praeger, 1964); David Galula, *Counterinsurgency Warfare: Theory and Practice* (New York: Praeger, 1964); Sir Robert Thompson, *Defeating Communist Insurgency* (New York: Praeger, 1966); Richard L. Clutterbuck, *The Long Long War: Counterinsurgency in Malaya and Vietnam* (New York: Praeger, 1966); George Armstrong Kelly, *Lost Soldiers: The French Army and Empire in Crisis, 1947–1962* (Cambridge: MIT Press, 1965), chaps. 5–7, 9–10; W. P. Davison, *Some Observations on Viet Cong Operations in the Villages* (Santa Monica, CA: RAND Corporation, 1968). See also Douglas S. Blaufarb, *The Counter-Insurgency Era: U.S. Doctrine and Performance, 1950 to the Present* (New York: Free Press, 1977); D. Michael Shafer, *Deadly Paradigms: The Failure of U.S. Counterinsurgency Policy* (Princeton: Princeton University Press, 1988); Timothy J. Lomperis, *From People's War to People's Rule: Insurgency, Intervention, and the Lessons of Vietnam* (Chapel Hill: University of North Carolina Press, 1996).

[18] Huntington, "Patterns of Violence in World Politics," 20–27.

bellions the insurgents win as long as they do not lose, and the government loses as long as it does not win. If al Qaeda-like groups can stay in the field indefinitely, they win.

Offense-defense theory applied nuclear deterrence concepts to assessing the stability of conventional military confrontations and focused on what conditions tended to give the attack or the defense the advantage in war.[19] There were many problems in the specification and application of the theory having to do with unsettled conceptualization of the offense-defense balance, problematic standards for measuring it, and inconsistent applications to different levels of warfare and diplomacy.[20] Offense-defense theory, which flourished when driven by the urge to find ways to stabilize the NATO-Warsaw Pact balance in Europe, has had little to say directly about unconventional war or terrorism. It actually applies more clearly, however, to this lower level of strategic competition (as well as to the higher level of nuclear war) than to the middle level of conventional military power. This is because the exchange ratio between opposing conventional forces of roughly similar size is very difficult to estimate, given the complex composition of modern military forces and uncertainty about their qualitative comparisons; but the exchange ratio in both nuclear and guerrilla combat is quite lopsided in favor of the attacker. Counterinsurgency folklore held that the government defenders need something on the order of a ten-to-one advantage over the guerrillas if they were to drive them from the field.

There has been much confusion about exactly how to define the offense-defense balance, but the essential idea is that some combinations of military technology, organization, and doctrine are proportionally more advantageous to the attack or to the defense when the two clash. "Proportionally" means that available instruments and circumstances of engagement give either the attack or the defense more bang for the buck, more efficient power out of the same level of resources. The notion of an offense-defense balance as something conceptually distinct from the balance of power means, however, that it cannot be identified with which side wins a battle or a war. Indeed, the offense-defense balance can favor the defense, while the attacker still wins, because its overall

---

[19] George Quester, *Offense and Defense in the International System*, 2nd ed. (New Brunswick, NJ: Transaction Books, 1988); Robert Jervis, "Cooperation Under the Security Dilemma," *World Politics* 30 (January 1978); Jack L. Snyder, *The Ideology of the Offensive: Military Decision Making and the Disasters of 1914* (Ithaca, NY: Cornell University Press, 1984); Stephen Van Evera, *Causes of War: Power and the Roots of Conflict* (Ithaca, NY: Cornell University Press, 1999), chaps. 6–8; Charles L. Glaser and Chaim Kaufmann, "What Is the Offense-Defense Balance and Can We Measure It?" *International Security* 22 (Spring 1998).

[20] For critiques, see Jack S. Levy, "The Offensive/Defensive Balance of Military Technology," *International Studies Quarterly* 28 (June 1984); Scott D. Sagan, "1914 Revisited," *International Security* 11 (Fall 1986); Jonathan Shimshoni, "Technology, Military Advantage, and World War I: A Case for Military Entrepreneurship," *International Security* 15 (Winter 1990/91); Richard K. Betts, "Must War Find a Way?" *International Security* 24 (Fall 1999); Betts, "Conventional Deterrence: Predictive Uncertainty and Policy Confidence," *World Politics* 37 (January 1985).

margin of superiority in power was too great, despite the defense's more efficient use of power. (I am told that the Finns had a saying in the Winter War of 1939–40: "One Finn is worth ten Russians, but what happens when the eleventh Russian comes?") Thus, to say that the offense-defense balance favors the offensive terrorists today against the defensive counterterrorists does not mean that the terrorists will prevail. It does mean that terrorists can fight far above their weight, that in most instances each competent terrorist will have much greater individual impact than each good counterterrorist, that each dollar invested in a terrorist plot will have a bigger payoff than each dollar expended on counterterrorism, and that only small numbers of competent terrorists need survive and operate to keep the threat to American society uncomfortably high.

In the competition between terrorists on the attack and Americans on the defense, the disadvantage of the defense is evident in the number of high-value potential targets that need protection. The United States has "almost 600,000 bridges, 170,000 water systems, more than 2,800 power plants (104 of them nuclear), 190,000 miles of interstate pipelines for natural gas, 463 skyscrapers . . . nearly 20,000 miles of border, airports, stadiums, train tracks."[21] All these usually represented American strength; after September 11 they also represent vulnerability:

> Suddenly guards were being posted at water reservoirs, outside power plants, and at bridges and tunnels. Maps of oil and gas lines were removed from the Internet. In Boston, a ship carrying liquefied natural gas, an important source of fuel for heating New England homes, was forbidden from entering the harbor because local fire officials feared that if it were targeted by a terrorist the resulting explosion could lay low much of the city's densely populated waterfront. An attack by a knife-wielding lunatic on the driver of a Florida-bound Greyhound bus led to the immediate cessation of that national bus service. . . . Agricultural crop-dusting planes were grounded out of a concern that they could be used to spread chemical or biological agents.[22]

Truly energetic defense measures do not only cost money in personnel and equipment for fortification, inspection, and enforcement; they may require repealing some of the very underpinnings of civilian economic efficiency associated with globalization. "The competitiveness of the U.S. economy and the quality of life of the American people rest on critical infrastructure that has become increasingly more concentrated, more interconnected, and more sophisticated. Almost entirely privately owned and operated, there is very little redundancy in this system."[23] This concentration increases the potential price of vulnerability to single attacks. Tighter inspection of cargoes coming across the

---

[21] Jerry Schwartz, Associated Press dispatch, 6 October 2001, quoted in Brian Reich, "Strength in the Face of Terror: A Comparison of United States and International Efforts to Provide Homeland Security" (unpublished paper, Columbia University, December 2001), 5.

[22] Stephen E. Flynn, "The Unguarded Homeland" in James F. Hoge, Jr. and Gideon Rose, eds., *How Did This Happen? Terrorism and the New War* (New York: PublicAffairs, 2001), 185.

[23] Ibid., 185–186.

Canadian border, for example, wrecks the "just-in-time" parts supply system of Michigan auto manufacturers. Companies that have invested in technology and infrastructure premised on unimpeded movement "may see their expected savings and efficiencies go up in smoke. Outsourcing contracts will have to be revisited and inventories will have to be rebuilt."[24] How many safety measures will suffice in improving airline security without making flying so inconvenient that the air travel industry never recovers as a profit-making enterprise? A few more shoe-bomb incidents, and Thomas Friedman's proposal to start an airline called "Naked Air—where the only thing you wear is a seat belt" becomes almost as plausible as it is ridiculous.[25]

The offense-dominant character of terrorism is implicit in mass detentions of Arab young men after September 11, and proposals for military tribunals that would compromise normal due process and weaken standard criminal justice presumptions in favor of the accused. The traditional liberal axiom that it is better to let a hundred guilty people go free than to convict one innocent reflects confidence in the strength of society's defenses—confidence that whatever additional crimes may be committed by the guilty who go free will not grossly outweigh the injustice done to innocents convicted, that one criminal who slips through the net will not go on to kill hundreds or thousands of innocents. Fear of terrorists plotting mass murder reversed that presumption and makes unjust incarceration of some innocents appear like unintended but expected collateral damage in wartime combat.

Offense-defense theory helps to visualize the problem. It does not help to provide attractive solutions, as its proponents believed it did during the cold war. Then offense-defense theory was popular because it seemed to offer a way to stabilize the East-West military confrontation. Mutual deterrence from the superpowers' confidence in their counteroffensive capability could substitute for defense at the nuclear level, and both sides' confidence in their conventional defenses could dampen either one's incentives to attack at that level. Little of this applies to counterterrorism. Both deterrence and defense are weaker strategies against terrorists than they were against communists.

Deterrence is still relevant for dealing with state terrorism; Saddam Hussein or Kim Jong-Il may hold back from striking the United States for fear of retaliation. Deterrence offers less confidence for preventing state sponsorship of terrorism; it did not stop the Taliban from hosting Osama bin Laden. It offers even less for holding at bay transnational groups like al Qaeda, which may lack a return address against which retaliation can be visited, or whose millenialist aims and religious convictions make them unafraid of retaliation. Defense, in turn, is better than a losing game only because the inadequacy of deterrence leaves no alternative.[26] Large investments in defense will produce appreciable reductions in vulnerability, but will not minimize vulnerability.

---

[24] Ibid., 193–194.

[25] Thomas L. Friedman, "Naked Air," *New York Times*, 26 December 2001.

[26] See Steven Simon and Daniel Benjamin, "America and the New Terrorism," *Survival* 42 (Spring 2000): 59, 66–69, 74.

Deterrence and defense overlap in practice. The U.S. counteroffensive in Afghanistan constitutes retaliation, punishing the Taliban for shielding al Qaeda and sending a warning to other potential state sponsors. It is also active defense, whittling down the ranks of potential perpetrators by killing and capturing members of the Islamist international brigades committed to jihad against the United States. At this writing, the retaliatory function has been performed more effectively than the defensive, as the Taliban regime has been destroyed, but significant numbers of Arab Afghans and al Qaeda members appear to have escaped, perhaps to plot another day.

Given the limited efficacy of deterrence for modern counterterrorism, it remains an open question how much of a strategic success we should judge the impressive victory in Afghanistan to be. Major investments in passive defenses (airline security, border inspections, surveillance and searches for better intelligence, fortification of embassies, and so forth) are necessary, but will reduce vulnerability at a cost substantially greater than the costs that competent terrorist organizations will have to bear to probe and occasionally circumvent them. The cost-exchange ratio for direct defense is probably worse than the legendary 10:1 ratio for successful counterinsurgency, and certainly worse than the more than 3:1 ratio that Robert McNamara's analysts calculated for the advantage of offensive missile investments over antiballistic missile systems—an advantage that many then and since have thought warranted accepting a situation of mutual vulnerability to assured destruction.[27]

The less prepared we are to undertake appropriate programs and the more false starts and confusions that are likely, the worse the cost-exchange ratio will be in the short term. The public health system, law enforcement organizations, and state and local bureaucrats are still feeling their way on what, how, and in which sequence to boost efforts. The U.S. military will also have to overcome the natural and powerful effects of inertia and attachments to old self-conceptions and preferred programs and modes of operation. Impulses to repackage old priorities in the rhetoric of new needs will further dilute effectiveness of countermeasures.

Nevertheless, given low confidence that deterrence can prevent terrorist attacks, major improvements in defenses make sense.[28] This is especially true because the resource base from which the United States can draw is vastly larger than that available to transnational terrorists. Al Qaeda may be rich, but it does not have the treasury of a great power. Primacy has a soft underbelly, but it is

---

[27] Estimates in the 1960s indicated that even combining ABM systems with counterforce strikes and fallout shelters, the United States would have to counter each Soviet dollar spent on ICBMs with three U.S. dollars to protect 70 percent of the industry, assuming highly effective ABMs (.8 kill probability). To protect up to 80 percent of the population, far higher ratios would be necessary. Fred Kaplan, *The Wizards of Armageddon* (New York: Simon and Schuster, 1983), 321–324.

[28] For an appropriate list of recommendations see *Countering the Changing Threat of International Terrorism*, Report of the National Commission on Terrorism, Pursuant to Public Law 277, 105th Congress (Washington, DC, June 2000). This report holds up very well in light of September 11.

far better to have primacy than to face it. Even at an unfavorable cost exchange ratio, a number of defensive measures are a sensible investment, but only because our overwhelming advantage in resources means that we are not constrained to focus solely on the most efficient countermeasures.

At the same time, as long as terrorist groups remain potent and active, a serious war plan must exploit efficient strategies as well. Given the offense-dominant nature of terrorist operations, this means emphasis on counteroffensive operations. When terrorists or their support structures can be found and fixed, preemptive and preventive attacks will accomplish more against them, dollar for dollar, than the investment in passive defenses. Which is the more efficient use of resources: to kill or capture a cell of terrorists who might otherwise choose at any time to strike whichever set of targets on our side is unguarded, or to try to guard all potential targets? Here the dangers are that counteroffensive operations could prove counterproductive. This could easily happen if they degenerate into brutalities and breaches of laws of war that make counterterrorism begin to appear morally equivalent to its target, sapping political support and driving the uncommitted to the other side in the process of polarization that war makes inevitable. Whether counteroffensive operations gain more in eliminating perpetrators than they lose in alienating and mobilizing "swing voters" in the world of Muslim opinion depends on how successful the operations are in neutralizing significant numbers of the organizers of terrorist groups, as opposed to foot soldiers, and in doing so with minimal collateral damage.

Primacy and Policy

September 11 reminded those Americans with a rosy view that not all the world sees U.S. primacy as benign, that primacy does not guarantee security, and that security may now entail some retreats from the economic globalization that some had identified with American leadership. Primacy has two edges—dominance and provocation. Americans can enjoy the dominance but must recognize the risks it evokes. For terrorists who want to bring the United States down, U.S. strategic primacy is a formidable challenge, but one that can be overcome. On balance, Americans have overestimated the benefits of primacy, and terrorists have underestimated them.

For those who see a connection between American interventionism, cultural expansiveness, and support of Israel on one hand, and the rage of groups that turn to terrorism on the other, primacy may seem more trouble than it's worth, and the need to revise policies may seem more pressing. But most Americans have so far preferred the complacent and gluttonous form of primacy to the ascetic, blithely accepting steadily growing dependence on Persian Gulf oil that could be limited by compromises in lifestyle and unconventional energy policies. There have been no groundswells to get rid of SUVs, support the Palestinians, or refrain from promoting Western standards of democracy and human rights in societies where some elements see them as aggression.

There is little evidence that any appreciable number of Americans, elite or mass, see our primacy as provoking terrorism. Rather, most see it as a condition we can choose at will to exploit or not. So U.S. foreign policy has exercised primacy in a muscular way in byways of the post-cold war world when intervention seemed cheap, but not when doing good deeds threatened to be costly. Power has allowed Washington to play simultaneously the roles of mediator and partisan supporter in the Arab-Israeli conflict. For a dozen years nothing, with the near exception of the Kosovo War, suggested that primacy could not get us out of whatever problems it generated.

How far the United States goes to adapt to the second edge of primacy probably depends on whether stunning damage is inflicted by terrorists again, or September 11 gradually fades into history. If al Qaeda and its ilk are crippled, and some years pass without more catastrophic attacks on U.S. home territory, scar tissue will harden on the soft underbelly, and the positive view of primacy will be reinforced. If the war against terrorism falters, however, and the exercise of power fails to prevent more big incidents, the consensus will crack. Then more extreme policy options will get more attention. Retrenchment and retreat will look more appealing to some, who may believe the words of Sheik Salman al-Awdah, a dissident Saudi religious scholar, who said, "If America just let well enough alone, and got out of their obligations overseas . . . no one would bother them."[29]

More likely, however, would be a more violent reaction. There is no reason to assume that terrorist enemies would let America off the hook if it retreated and would not remain as implacable as ever. Facing inability to suppress the threat through normal combat, covert action, and diplomatic pressure, many Americans would consider escalation to more ferocious strategies. In recent decades, the march of liberal legalism has delegitimized tactics and brutalities that once were accepted, but this delegitimation has occurred only in the context of fundamental security and dominance of the Western powers, not in a situation where they felt under supreme threat. In a situation of that sort, it is foolhardy to assume that American strategy would never turn to tactics like those used against Japanese and German civilians, or by the civilized French in the *sale guerre* in Algeria, or by the Russians in Chechnya in hopes of effectively eradicating terrorists despite astronomical damage to the civilian societies within which they lurk.

This possibility would highlight how terrorists have underestimated American primacy. There is much evidence that even in the age of unipolarity, opponents have mistakenly seen the United States as a paper tiger. For some reason—perhaps wishfully selective perception—they tend to see retreats from

---

[29] Quoted in Douglas Jehl, "After Prison, a Saudi Sheik Tempers His Words," *New York Times*, 27 December 2001.

Vietnam, Beirut, and Somalia as typical weakness of American will, instead of considering decisive exercises of power in Panama, Kuwait, Kosovo, and now, Afghanistan.[30] As Osama bin Laden said in 1997, the United States left Somalia "after claiming that they were the largest power on earth. They left after some resistance from powerless, poor, unarmed people whose only weapon is the belief in Allah.... The Americans ran away."[31]

This apparently common view among those with an interest in pinning America's ears back ignores the difference between elective uses of force and desperate ones. The United States retreated where it ran into trouble helping others, not where it was saving itself. Unlike interventions of the 1990s in Africa, the Balkans, or Haiti, counterterrorism is not charity. With vital material interests involved, primacy unleashed may prove fearsomely potent.

Most likely America will see neither absolute victory nor abject failure in the war against terror. Then how long will a campaign of attrition last and stay popular? If the United States wants a strategy to cut the roots of terrorism, rather than just the branches, will American power be used effectively against the roots? Perhaps, but probably not. This depends of course on which of many possible root causes are at issue. Ironically, one problem is that American primacy itself is one of those roots.

A common assertion is that Third World poverty generates terrorism. While this must certainly be a contributing cause in many cases, there is little evidence that it is either a necessary or sufficient condition. Fundamentalist madrassas might not be full to overflowing if young Muslims had ample opportunities to make money, but the fifteen Saudis who hijacked the flights on September 11 were from one of the most affluent of Muslim countries. No U.S. policy could ever hope to make most incubators of terrorism less poor than Saudi Arabia. Iran, the biggest state sponsor of anti-American terrorism, is also better off than most Muslim countries. Poverty is endemic in the Third World, but terrorism is not.

Even if endemic poverty were the cause, the solution would not be obvious. Globalization generates stratification, creating winners and losers, as efficient societies with capitalist cultures move ahead and others fall behind, or as elite enclaves in some societies prosper while the masses stagnate. Moreover, even vastly increased U.S. development assistance would be spread thin if all poor countries are assumed to be incubators of terrorism. And what are the odds that U.S. intervention with economic aid would significantly reduce poverty? Successes in prompting dramatic economic development by outside assistance in the Third World have occurred, but they are the exception more than the rule.

The most virulent anti-American terrorist threats, however, do not emerge randomly in poor societies. They grow out of a few regions and are concen-

---

[30] See data in the study by Barry M. Blechman and Tamara Cofman Wittes, "Defining Moment: The Threat and Use of Force in American Foreign Policy," *Political Science Quarterly* 114 (Spring 1999).

[31] Quoted in Simon and Benjamin, "America and the New Terrorism," 69.

trated overwhelmingly in a few religiously motivated groups. These reflect political causes—ideological, nationalist, or transnational cultural impulses to militant mobilization—more than economic causes. Economic development in an area where the political and religious impulses remain unresolved could serve to improve the resource base for terrorism rather than undercut it.

A strategy of terrorism is most likely to flow from the coincidence of two conditions: intense political grievance and gross imbalance of power. Either one without the other is likely to produce either peace or conventional war. Peace is probable if power is imbalanced but grievance is modest; the weaker party is likely to live with the grievance. In that situation, conventional use of force appears to offer no hope of victory, while the righteous indignation is not great enough to overcome normal inhibitions against murderous tactics. Conventional war is probable if grievance is intense but power is more evenly balanced, since successful use of respectable forms of force appears possible.[32] Under American primacy, candidates for terrorism suffer from grossly inferior power by definition. This should focus attention on the political causes of their grievance.

How are political root causes addressed? At other times in history we have succeeded in fostering congenial revolutions—especially in the end of the cold war, as the collapse of the Second World heralded an End of History of sorts.[33] The problem now, however, is the rebellion of anti-Western zealots against the secularist end of history. Remaking the world in the Western image is what Americans assume to be just, natural, and desirable, indeed only a matter of time. But that presumption is precisely what energizes many terrorists' hatred. Secular Western liberalism is not their salvation, but their scourge. Primacy could, paradoxically, remain both the solution and the problem for a long time.*

---

[32] On why power imbalance is conducive to peace and parity to war, see Geoffrey Blainey, *The Causes of War*, 3rd. ed. (New York: Free Press, 1988), chap. 8.

[33] Francis Fukuyama's thesis was widely misunderstood and caricatured. He noted that the Third World remained mired in history and that some developments could lead to restarting history. For the First World, the defeated Second World, and even some parts of the Third World, however, the triumph of Western liberalism could reasonably be seen by those who believe in its worth (as should Americans) as the final stage of evolution through fundamentally different forms of political and economic organization of societies. See Fukuyama, "The End of History?" *National Interest* no. 16 (Summer 1989); and Fukuyama, *The End of History and the Last Man* (New York: Free Press, 1992).

* The author thanks Robert Jervis for comments on the first draft.

The Pragmatic Fanaticism of al Qaeda: An Anatomy of Extremism in Middle Eastern Politics

MICHAEL DORAN

Al Qaeda's behavior presents us with something of a paradox. On the one hand, the organization stands for the principle that Islamic law is the only proper foundation for social and political life; on the other, it often disregards that law with impunity. For instance, the Islamic rules on warfare forbid attacks on women and children, but Osama bin Laden, in his smoking-gun video, expresses no remorse for having killed many innocents on September 11. On the contrary, he suggests that by doing so he showed the world the true face of Islam.

This supposition raises two central questions: What precisely is the relationship between al Qaeda's zealotry and its pragmatism? And, if not fanaticism, what did cause al Qaeda to misread the balance of power between its forces and the United States? In order to answer these, this article will examine the central doctrines of Islamic extremism, arguing that these ideas virtually compel al Qaeda to behave almost exclusively according to the principle of realpolitik. If the organization is a rational actor, then it is susceptible to the same kinds of analyses that we would apply to any other state or political movement in the Middle East. When viewed in this light, al Qaeda's defeat appears as but one in a series of Middle Eastern military miscalculations that includes, among others, the Egyptian remilitarization of the Sinai in June 1967 and the Iraqi invasion of Kuwait in August 1990. The article will argue that this kind of military disaster occurs with relative frequency in the Middle East as a consequence of the complex balance of power in the region. Fanaticism, therefore, played no role in al Qaeda's miscalculation.

MICHAEL DORAN is assistant professor in Near Eastern Studies at Princeton University. He is the author of *Pan-Arabism Before Nasser*.

September 11 was no isolated example. When it comes to matters related to politics and war, al Qaeda maneuvers around its dogmas with alacrity. Thus in the mid-1990s it "obtained specialized terrorist training" from Iranian government officials working with Hizballah in Lebanon.[1] If viewed through the cold eye of realpolitik, there is nothing surprising about the fact that these two parties found a basis for limited cooperation: Teheran and al Qaeda share the goal in the long term of ending United States hegemony in the Persian Gulf, and in the short term of ousting American troops from Saudi Arabia. However, only inveterate pragmatists on both sides could have turned a blind eye to the religious obstacles that stood in the way of even limited, covert cooperation. The Iranian hardliners are themselves Islamic radicals, but the Sunni-Shiah gulf separates them from al Qaeda, which reviles their Shiah belief as a form of polytheism.

It is important to keep in mind this example of realpolitik, because on the basis of the crushing defeat that al Qaeda has suffered in Afghanistan one might conclude that a single-minded commitment to religion translates into a simple-minded politics. One feels a temptation to interpret the entire trajectory of al Qaeda's career as a consequence of its zealotry. The fanaticism of Osama bin Laden, so the argument would go, won for him the loyalty of suicide bombers, whose willingness to martyr themselves transformed his movement into a force in world politics. At the same time, this fanaticism also compelled bin Laden to launch a war against the greatest power on earth without weighing the consequences of his actions in a fully rational manner. This view assumes that a maniacal anti-Americanism on the part of al Qaeda's rank and file dictates the organization's political strategy. However, it seems reasonable to assume that the pragmatism informing bin Laden's cooperation with Iran in the 1990s is continuing to dictate his strategic thinking in his war on America today.

THE INTELLECTUAL ORIGINS OF AL QAEDA'S REALPOLITIK

When searching for the connection between pragmatism and zealotry, a good place to start is with Ibn Taymiyya, the great Islamic thinker who, though he died in the early fourteenth century, laid the intellectual foundations for Islamic extremism in the twentieth.[2] Ibn Taymiyya was a Janus-faced intellectual, a fire-

---

[1] J. T. Caruso, acting assistant director, Counter Terrorism Division, Federal Bureau of Investigation, "Statement for the Record on al Qaeda International," before the Subcommittee on International Operations and Terrorism, Committee on Foreign Relations, United States Senate, Washington, DC, 18 December 2001, available at http://www.fbi.gov/congress/congress01/caruso121801.htm, 24 April 2002; and Peter L. Bergen, *Holy War, Inc.* (New York: Free Press, 2001), 85.

[2] On the influence of Ibn Taymiyya on modern Islamic extremism, see Johannes J. G. Jansen, *The Dual Nature of Islamic Fundamentalism* (Ithaca, NY: Cornell University Press, 1997); and Emmanuel Sivan, *Radical Islam: Medieval Theology and Modern Politics* (New Haven: Yale University Press, 1985). Osama bin Laden himself quotes Ibn Taymiyya repeatedly in his 1996 "Declaration of War Against the Americans...," which is located at http://www.washingtonpost.com/wp-dyn/nation/specials/attacked/, under the link "Religious Texts," 26 March 2002.

breathing zealot, but he was also a pragmatic man who accepted the political world as he found it.[3] Al Qaeda's understanding of politics owes more to him than to any other source: a brief examination of his ideas against the background of his life helps us to understand why this is so.

At the age of five, Ibn Taymiyya became a refugee. In 1268 he fled his native Iraq for Syria in order to escape from the Mongols, who during the previous decade blew into the Middle East like a storm from Central Asia, destroying the Abbasid Caliphate in the process. They established a center of power in northeastern Iran around Tabriz from which they threatened Syria, Palestine, and Egypt. Consequently, Ibn Taymiyya lived his adult life under the shadow of the Mongol threat, which is the key factor for understanding the two faces of his thought.

In 1300, the reigning Mongol Ilkhan, Ghazan, a direct descendant of Genghis Khan, invaded Syria.[4] Since Ghazan had converted to Islam in 1295, he could project himself as a legitimate Muslim ruler, thereby capitalizing during his Syrian campaign on the strong prohibition in Islam against internecine Muslim fighting. In effect, his conversion sent a message to the Syrians: "Do not resist me; I come not to destroy Islam but to strengthen it." This line did not convince Ibn Taymiyya, who put his genius for Islamic law to work in developing anti-Mongol propaganda. He argued that, although Ghazan sported the appearance of being a Muslim, his policies as a ruler proved that he remained loyal to traditional Mongol law and belief. By having converted to Islam but then having failed to raise up Islamic law in his realm, Ghazan demonstrated that his conversion was a sham. On this basis, Ibn Taymiyya pronounced him an apostate. Because Islam takes a very dim view of apostasy (abandoning the true faith) Ibn Taymiyya had the material at hand to build a strong legal case both for ignoring Ghazan's claims of being a Muslim and for making total war on the partially-Islamized Mongols.

Ibn Taymiyya thus established a boundary between the truly Islamic society and its pseudo-Muslim enemies, who in his view posed a grave threat not just to the Muslims of Syria but to religion itself. The extent of the danger meant that the war against the Mongols was the first priority of the community: prosecuting it required all necessary steps, even if they sometimes contravened the letter of Islamic law. Ibn Taymiyya's pragmatism probably reflected his desire to prevent fighting over matters of religion, so that the Islamic community would be capable of standing united against the external threat. Politics, he might have said, is too serious a business to be left solely in the hands of the men of religion, particularly in a time of war.

---

[3] For a detailed discussion of Ibn Taymiyya's pragmatism, see Michael Cook, *Commanding Right and Forbidding Wrong in Islamic Thought* (Cambridge, UK: Cambridge University Press, 2000), 151–157. For a revealing biographical sketch, see D. P. Little, "Did Ibn Taymiyya Have a Screw Loose?" *Studia Islamica* 41 (1975).

[4] On Ibn Taymiyya's attitude toward Ghazan, see Jansen, *Dual Nature*, 33–39.

Following the procedure that Ibn Taymiyya established, al Qaeda today draws a similar line. The following passage from its manual on guerrilla warfare describes the historical emergence of al Qaeda's primary enemy, the apostate ruler: "After the fall of our orthodox caliphates on March 3, 1924 and after expelling the [European] colonialists, our Islamic nation was afflicted with apostate rulers who took over. . . . These rulers turned out to be more infidel and criminal than the colonialists themselves. Muslims have endured all kinds of harm, oppression, and torture at their hands."[5] This conception is clearly an extension of Ibn Taymiyya's world view to the circumstances of the present day. The role that the Mongols played as the threat to Islamic civilization in the thirteenth and fourteenth centuries is, in the view of al Qaeda and likeminded extremists, currently played by Western civilization.

In this conception, the ruling elite in the Middle East today are latter-day Ghazans, apostate rulers. President George W. Bush is not the enemy closest to home; Pervez Musharraf of Pakistan, Hosni Mubarak of Egypt, and King Fahd of Saudi Arabia are the pseudo-Muslim representatives of an alien civilization. These leaders pretend to follow Islam and to represent their own people when in actuality they stand in thrall to Western culture while serving as the puppets of the Western powers. Since they were born Muslims, profess Islam, and yet do not rule according to Islamic law (as defined by the extremists), they receive at the hands of al Qaeda the same verdict—guilty of apostasy—that Ibn Taymiyya meted out to Ghazan. Toppling them from power is the heart and soul of al Qaeda's politics.

Al Qaeda did not itself apply Ibn Taymiyya's ideas to the modern world. That task fell to Sayyid Qutb, one of the most influential thinkers of the twentieth century.[6] A radical Islamic ideologue, Egyptian authorities executed him in 1966 for, they claimed, conspiring to overthrow the government. Qutb's importance lies in having translated the logic of Ibn Taymiyya's rulings on apostasy into a comprehensive perspective on the problems of Islam in the modern world. Qutb describes modern society as "*jahili*"—a word derived from "*jahiliyya*," the name of the historical period in Arabia before Muhammad began preaching Islam. Related to the Arabic word for "ignorance," "*jahiliyya*" translates roughly as "the Dark Age." In Qutb's use, however, "*jahili*" does not refer, as it traditionally does, to a specific historical stage but rather to a general state of barbarousness and idolatry—a state into which any Muslim society can sink, even after the advent of Islam. In his view, the impact of the West in the modern era did in fact cast Middle Eastern societies adrift, cutting them loose from their Islamic moorings and turning them into realms of idolatry. Idolaters, in the orthodox Islamic tradition, do not benefit from any of the restrictions on violence in the name of religion; they are a legitimate target for holy war.

---

[5] *Al-Qaeda Training Manual*, 7. The manual was discovered in the house of an al Qaeda operative in May 2000, and introduced as evidence at the trial of the East Africa Embassy bombers. It is located at http://www.justice.gov/ag/trainingmanual.htm.

[6] On Sayyid Qutb, see Sivan, *Radical Islam*; and Jansen, *Dual Nature*.

In effect, Qutb exhorts extremists to make war on the ruling elite, which is guilty of allowing idolatry to flourish. His remedy is revolution, but the enemy is not limited to the corrupt elite controlling the Middle East; a global evil threatens to wipe out Islam itself. Failure to bring about the Islamic revolution will, therefore, spell the end of all that is of value in the world.

By describing the present as the new *jahiliyya* and arguing that Islam is in danger of being destroyed by the forces of darkness, Qutb affords extremists like bin Laden easy access to what I will dub "the Hijra model," by which I mean the example set by the Prophet Muhammad of how a Muslim should carry out a revolution.[7] In the face of opposition by unjust rulers, the Prophet founded the Islamic community and defended it against idolatrous enemies. He began by preaching Islam in Mecca, where he achieved notable success when people from a variety of backgrounds broke with their pagan traditions and converted to Islam. This success threatened the reigning oligarchy, which sought to protect its privileged position by persecuting the nascent Islamic community. This step forced Muhammad and his followers to make the *Hijra*, or migration, to Medina, where they established an independent state. With his power base thus secured, Muhammad then conducted a successful war against the Meccan idolaters, the former persecutors of the Muslims, whom he eventually converted to Islam.

This pattern—preaching the true faith, performing *Hijra* to escape oppression, organizing an independent power base, and then conducting war to topple the unbelievers from power—is a blueprint for revolution. It is the model that bin Laden is following; in the context of the new *jahiliyya*, al Qaeda's sanctuary in Afghanistan today is the functional equivalent of the Prophet's community in Medina in 622. Viewing its circumstances today as virtually identical to those of the Prophet when he made war against idolatrous Mecca, al Qaeda sees itself as a tiny colony of true believers who are surrounded on all sides by enemies and on whose shoulders rests the fate of humanity. In some respects, al Qaeda resembles a doomsday cult: it divides the world into absolute categories of good and evil; it has a paranoid siege mentality; it sees in extreme violence a means of cleansing the world; and it believes that all humanity stands on the brink of an unspeakable disaster. "Mankind today," Sayyid Qutb writes in the opening line of his most important book, "stands at the edge of the abyss."[8]

However, the world view of al Qaeda differs from that of a doomsday cult with respect to the role of politics and war. According to al Qaeda, violence will not spark the apocalypse but instead will avert disaster and usher in a new dawn, provided that it destroys the idolatrous rulers, just as the Prophet Muhammad ushered in a new age of light and justice when he defeated idolatrous Mecca and ended the darkness of the *jahiliyya*. According to Qutb, mankind stands at

---

[7] See Michael Cook, *Muhammad* (Oxford, UK: Oxford University Press, 1984), chap. 6.
[8] Sayyid Qutb, *Ma'alim fi al tariq* (np, nd). For an English translation, see Sayyid Qutb, *Signposts on the Road* (Mumbai, India: Bilal Books, 1998).

the abyss because it "is bankrupt in the realm of values that, under their shelter, permit human life to develop in a healthy manner and to progress properly."[9] Al Qaeda's goal is to take control of the state in order to pull humanity back from the abyss by upholding Islamic values throughout society. Its violence, therefore, does not presage a supernatural event: it is part of a wholly conventional war that by keeping alight the flame of Islam will nevertheless have near-cosmic consequences.

If considered together as a comprehensive intellectual system, the thought of Ibn Taymiyya, Sayyid Qutb, and the *Hijra* model of revolution explain the seeming contradiction between al Qaeda's principles and its pragmatism. This intellectual system fosters the creation of an enclave of true believers, who fervently support the principle that Islamic law belongs at the center of social and political life. However, Islamic society faces, in their view, a grave existential threat in the form of Westernization, which has bred several generations of apostate rulers in the Middle East. These rulers are using the power of the state successfully to snuff out true religion. Meeting this existential threat is the first duty of every true Muslim, and the hour is very late. In order to save the world from depravity, it is imperative to topple these rulers from power immediately. In this project, al Qaeda sees itself as *one* military arm of the enclave of true believers. Its overriding priority is to carry out Islamic revolution by whatever means available. Since the salvation of mankind hinges on the political effectiveness of the true Muslims, bin Laden has no intention of going down in a blaze of glory unless this sacrifice would destroy one of the apostate regimes or weaken it considerably. In general terms, however, the needs of the revolution require al Qaeda to preserve itself to fight another day. The gravity of the situation requires al Qaeda to pursue its interests by any means available; conventional morality impinges on its political thought only with regard to its utility in manipulating others. Al Qaeda's long-term goals are set by its fervent devotion to a radical religious ideology, but in its short-term behavior, it is a rational political actor operating according to the dictates of realpolitik.

Anti-Americanism, the Trojan Horse of Extremist Islam

If al Qaeda is, for the purposes of political analysis, a pragmatic revolutionary movement interested in self-preservation, then why did it pick a fight to the death with the greatest power on earth? A look at the background of the two most important men in al Qaeda—Osama bin Laden and Ayman al-Zawahiri—is instructive. These men rose out of local Islamic opposition movements—bin Laden in Saudi Arabia, Zawahiri in Egypt. They took up arms against America when they were forced into exile after failing to reform or topple their governments at home. The trajectory of their careers reflects a general trend in the Middle East: Islamic revolutionaries have been crushed in Syria, Egypt, and

[9] Ibid., 3.

Algeria; in many other countries, such as Saudi Arabia and Jordan, they have been coopted and exiled. Although revolutionary political action has failed, extremists have occupied more cultural space than ever before in the form of voluntary social clubs, welfare organizations, and mosque associations of a variety of different kinds. The war against America must be understood in this context of crushed revolutions in the midst of cultural resurgence.

Since Islamic radicals everywhere see the United States as the neo-Mongol power lurking behind the apostate governments that they seek to topple, attacks on America function as "propaganda by action," as well as direct action itself.[10] These bold acts of defiance have three main purposes: they bolster the morale of extremists around the Islamic world; they call new recruits to the banner of radical Islam; and they discredit the prevailing political order, which benefits from a general feeling that actions of individuals cannot alter the status quo. Operations such as the bombing of the East Africa embassies and the attack on the USS *Cole* sent out a clear message: We radicals have not given up the fight. We will eventually triumph, because America is a paper tiger, as are its stooges currently ruling the Middle East. In an effort to get the message out, al Qaeda celebrated its attacks on video tapes, which it distributed as recruitment material in radical mosques around the Islamic world.

On one level, the terrorist attacks on September 11 are simply the boldest in a series of propaganda actions. On another level, they diverge from this pattern significantly. By striking with such brutality, bin Laden fully intended to spark a conflict in Afghanistan between the United States and al Qaeda.[11] He certainly got his wish, but the war did not proceed as planned. Al Qaeda expected the United States to follow in the footsteps of the Soviet Union, whose Afghan adventure presented the world with the spectacle of a superpower going down slowly in defeat, but not before trampling under its boot tens of thousands of innocent Muslim civilians. Al Qaeda calculated that Washington would also discover Afghanistan to be the burial place of empires. Had the conflict actually proceeded according to al Qaeda's scenario, it would have created severe friction between state and society throughout much of the Middle East. Governments in the region, under pressure from Washington to support its war, would find themselves caught between the demands of their foreign patron and the anti-American sentiments of their own public. The ensuing legitimacy crisis would help to advance the cause of the Islamic revolution, either by actually shaking the regimes to the core or simply weakening them.

Although to some this might at first glance appear to be a somewhat implausible scenario, modern Middle Eastern history does provide a clear prece-

---

[10] Emmanuel Sivan, "The Third Wave of Radical Islam" (lecture delivered at Princeton University, 3 December 2001).

[11] I develop this argument in "Somebody Else's Civil War," *Foreign Affairs* 81 (January/February 2002).

dent for the conflict that al Qaeda envisioned—the Iranian hostage crisis.[12] In 1979, the Ayatollah Khomeini and his radical followers initiated a conflict with Washington and then deftly manipulated it as a means of discrediting their domestic rivals. At the risk of oversimplifying matters, we can divide the revolutionary forces in Iran into two camps, the moderate and the clerical, not at all unlike the division in Iran today between reformers and hardliners. In November 1979, supporters of the clerical camp, calling themselves "students following the Imam's line," stormed the American Embassy in Iran, just as National Security Adviser Zbigniew Brzezinski was meeting in Algiers with the Iranian Prime Minister Mehdi Bazargan, who represented the moderate camp and, therefore, desired cordial relations with Washington. By taking the Americans hostage, the clerical camp toppled the Bazargan government, scoring a blow against the moderate camp and the Americans simultaneously, and also driving them apart from each other.

While the initial blow to the Americans brought significant results, the utility of the conflict with the United States only grew as the crisis between the two countries deepened. By continuing to hold the embassy for many months thereafter, the clerical camp brought the conflict to a fever pitch, creating a wartime atmosphere in Iran—an atmosphere made even more explosive by the failed rescue mission that Washington launched. In this climate, the radicals could tar with the brush of treason any politician or soldier with a history of ties to America. Documents captured from the American Embassy contained many memoranda of conversations with moderate politicians, dating from after the fall of the shah. With the country in the grips of a war psychosis, even innocent exchanges with American officials could be made to appear as convincing proof of participation in a conspiracy against the revolution. The cache of American embassy documents thus functioned as a ready supply of ammunition against the moderates. On top of the contrived charges came the discovery of real conspiracies between the Americans and some moderate forces, particularly in the military. These plots only increased the momentum of the radicals, who eventually succeeded in eliminating their rivals so as to enjoy a free hand in fashioning the institutions of the Islamic Republic.

The clerical camp used the crisis with Washington in order to create an external, "imperialist" threat in the eyes of the Iranian public and simultaneously to capture the moral high ground by posing as the authentic representatives of the nation against its foreign enemy. Using the conflict with America in this way, as a kind of Trojan horse for extremist Islam, is also at the heart of al Qaeda's war on America. Bin Laden's post-September 11 statements reveal his intention to use anti-imperialism as a means of reaching a broader audience than would otherwise be available to him. In early November he described the political situation as follows:

[12] I have based this broad-brush interpretation of the hostage crisis on the detailed narrative and analysis of the revolution provided by Shaul Bakhash, *The Reign of the Ayatollahs* (New York: Basic Books, 1984).

> Amid the huge developments and in the wake of the great strikes that hit the United States in its most important locations in New York and Washington, a huge media clamor has been raised. This clamor is unprecedented. It conveyed the opinions of people on these events. People were divided into two parts. The first part supported these strikes against U.S. tyranny, while the second denounced them. Afterward, when the United States launched the unjust campaign against the Islamic Emirate in Afghanistan, people also split into two parties. The first supported these campaigns, while the second denounced and rejected them. These tremendous incidents, which have split people into two parties, are of great interest to the Muslims. . . .[13]

The two camps that bin Laden promotes here—supporters and opponents of America—are not the same two camps that emerge from his Manichean world view, which separates the enclave of true believers from everyone else. Dividing people according to their attitude toward American power demonstrates an intention to capture for al Qaeda the moral high ground in the struggle against the United States. Like the Iranian radicals in 1979, bin Laden regards the conflict with America as a tool for discrediting the ruling elites aligned with the United States in the Middle East, and thereby creating a revolutionary atmosphere that will, he calculates, benefit his brand of extremism.

Although al Qaeda's use of war with America as a vehicle for polarizing public opinion clearly resembles the Iranian hostage crisis, the two events nonetheless differ significantly in one regard. In contrast to al Qaeda, the Iranian clerical camp operated against rivals inside Iran, where the clerical camp controlled both public space and a coercive apparatus. By contrast, al Qaeda seeks to weaken enemies located far beyond the borders of its sanctuary in Afghanistan. Despite this disadvantage, the tensions between Washington and Riyadh that have risen to the surface since September 11 demonstrate that bin Laden did manage to land a few blows for his cause. Al Qaeda slipped the thin end of a wedge between Washington and Riyadh. A protracted U.S. war in Afghanistan would probably have driven it deep into the structure of the American-Saudi alliance, possibly even tearing the two countries apart.

MIDDLE EASTERN BRINKSMANSHIP

Al Qaeda views the post-September 11 conflict with the Unites States as a variation within an historical process. In the search for metaphors, one is tempted to say that bin Laden considers the struggle in Afghanistan to be a single battle in a long war. This image itself is, however, misleading, because it emphasizes the notion of a bilateral contest. For al Qaeda, the primary struggle is between the apostate rulers in the Middle East and the forces of true Islam, of which al Qaeda is but one representative. The relative strength of each side on the battlefield in Afghanistan, though not unrelated to the primary contest as defined by al Qaeda, is by no means a clear measure of success or failure. If al

---

[13] Text from BBC News Online, 3 November 2001, located at http://www.news.bbc.co.uk.

Qaeda simply lives to regroup and to fight in the next stage of this ongoing process, it has scored a significant victory. On the basis of its world view, even total destruction of the organization does not necessarily constitute failure. If, for instance, al Qaeda's destruction were to result in the weakening of apostate regimes, and at the same time its martyrdom were to inspire a like-minded group to emerge from the enclave of true believers, then the very destruction of al Qaeda would constitute a political success.

This view of the conflict with the West as a process, not a discrete event, does not derive solely from al Qaeda's Islamic world view; some aspects of this perspective are shared by every major Middle East actor seeking to alter the status quo. Yasser Arafat and Saddam Hussein share aspects of this view, as did figures from the past such as Gamal Abdel Nasser and Muhammad Mossadegh. This attitude reflects a coherent approach to the difficult facts of life in the Middle East, where Western influence is permanently present but permanently illegitimate. Western power—political, economic, and military—has been a fixture on the political landscape for two-hundred years, and it shows no signs of being dismantled in the foreseeable future. However, the specific terms of Western engagement with the region are never fixed, often in flux, and therefore always subject to negotiation. At the same time, a number of nationalist ideologies and state interests militate in favor of expelling the West, redrawing borders between states, toppling regimes, and redistributing wealth. Since the Western powers are the ultimate guarantors of international order, the negotiable status of their influence keeps alive the possibility of actually taking steps to revise the status quo along these lines. Given all that such a revision would entail in terms of increased prestige and wealth, leaders have a powerful incentive to challenge the West.

These circumstances give rise to a mode of identity politics that, for lack of a better term, I will dub "anti-Western brinksmanship," by which I mean the tendency of Middle Eastern actors to challenge the interests of a Western power directly, or indirectly, through one of its local allies in order to provoke the threat of Western intervention, if not actual intervention itself. In these crises, Middle Eastern leaders adopt utopian nationalist and religious ideologies tailored to appeal to a number of disaffected groups simultaneously. These ideologies undoubtedly exploit three permanent factors on the political scene: historical grievances against the West; revanchist sentiment toward Israel; and transnational identities, such as Arabism and Islam, which embrace the majority of people throughout the region. Often the response by the West (or Israel) to a provocation allows a Middle Eastern brinksman to achieve results that by his efforts alone would not have been possible. This model accounts for much of the interaction between the Palestinians and the Israelis throughout the history of their conflict, and especially since the beginning of the al Aqsa Intifada. As a political phenomenon, al Qaeda's decision to target the West deserves to be analyzed within this framework rather than as a simple story of religious extremism and virulent anti-Americanism.

One obvious response to this argument is that al Qaeda, unlike, say, Saddam Hussein, is clearly driven by its ideology. While al Qaeda is the ideological organization par excellence, there still exists a gap between its long-term goals set by its religious convictions and its immediate goals set by its understanding of the possible. The structure of the Middle Eastern international system places considerable constraints on successful political action. Consequently, al Qaeda has no choice, if it wishes to be a serious player in the game, but to follow the brinksmanship model, which is one of the few methods available to an anti-status quo power in the region.

Bin Laden virtually announced his use of the model when he invoked the cause of Palestine in his post-September 11 propaganda video tapes. His 1996 "Declaration of War," by contrast, had demonstrated far less interest in Palestine, being primarily concerned with specifically Saudi subjects. Palestine, in the language of Middle Eastern politics, is both a pan-Arab and a pan-Islamic symbol that stands simultaneously for the actual suffering of Palestinians under Israeli occupation and for the suffering of all Arabs and Muslims under the callous domination of the Western world. Bin Laden's late conversion to Palestinian nationalism signaled his intention to project his message to a wider audience in order to trump the West in the arena of identity politics.

If al Qaeda's policies actually reflected the shrewd calculations of a Middle Eastern brinksman rather than the irrational rage of a zealot, then what went wrong? Given the nature of the situation, we will never know for certain; but the brinksmanship model alerts us to the main factors that would have caused al Qaeda to misread the balance of power between itself and the United States.

First of all, bin Laden probably assumed that great power rivalries would place limits on the American ability to dominate Central Asia. He counted in particular on Russia and China constraining the United States; both powers wield influence in the region, and both had for some time expressed deep frustration with the unilateralist streak in President Bush's foreign policy. The Republican administration's insistence on pressing ahead with its missile defense plan had alienated Moscow and Beijing alike; both had threatened to engage in an arms race if Washington refused to respect their interests. For some time prior to September 11, friction between the United States and Russia had developed over the war in Chechnya. Moreover, the general discontent that the Russians had expressed regarding the rise of American power since the fall of the Soviet Union made it appear extremely unlikely that Moscow would have supported a massive and prolonged United States military presence in Central Asia close to the Russian heartland. The same held true for Beijing, where a number of bitter memories were still fresh in everyone's mind, from the bombing of the Chinese embassy in Belgrade, to the conflict over the downed American spy plane, to the ever-present tensions over Taiwan.

If the great power environment appeared propitious, then the regional balance was even more promising for al Qaeda. Middle Eastern brinksmen and Washington approach conflicts very differently. Washington searches for allies, focusing on the stated intentions of governments. The brinksman, by contrast, realizes that the key question with regard to his interests is whether the regional political environment in general will permit Washington to carry out its plans. Formal alliances, therefore, mean very little; the brinksman focuses instead on relations within societies and works to bring about a set of political circumstances that will foil American aims.

Working from this perspective, bin Laden calculated that he could drive a wedge between the Unites States and the local allies that it would need in order to topple him. In this particular case, the decade-long regional struggle for Afghanistan worked in his favor. This geostrategic battle pitted a Russian and Iranian entente, which operated in support of the Northern Alliance against Pakistan, which backed the Taliban. For its part, the United States had traditionally allied itself with Pakistan in this regional contest, although relations between Washington and Islamabad had become strained in recent years. From bin Laden's point of view, this regional balance meant that Washington had only two options: it could align itself with the Northern Alliance or it could work through its traditional ally, Pakistan. Both scenarios appeared highly implausible. If a natural law of international politics is "my enemy's enemy is my friend," then the United States found itself working against nature: Washington's enemy, the Taliban, was the ally of its friend, Pakistan; and Washington's enemy's enemy, the Northern Alliance, was the friend of Washington's enemy, Iran. How could this not have bolstered the confidence of al Qaeda?

Bin Laden did not, however, simply assume that the regional balance of power would take care of everything by itself. He also had at least two cards of his own to play in order to influence the regional environment. First, he assassinated Shah Massoud, the leader of the Northern Alliance. Al Qaeda suicide bombers killed Massoud two days before September 11 by posing as Arab journalists coming from Europe to conduct an interview. By the time of his assassination, the Northern Alliance had in any case been relegated to a sliver of territory in northeastern Afghanistan, and it hardly seemed capable of posing a serious threat to the Taliban and al Qaeda. Nevertheless, bin Laden engineered the decapitation of the Northern Alliance in order to throw it into such disarray that it would be useless to the United States as an instrument of retribution.

Second, bin Laden issued a pan-Islamic appeal over the heads of the Musharraf regime in Pakistan to the people in the street sympathetic to him and hostile to America. Using a tactic perfected by Nasser and Saddam, bin Laden hoped that this appeal would either destabilize Pakistan or, at the very least, scare both Washington and Islamabad with the threat of destabilization. Bin Laden issued his appeal in the full knowledge that any attempt by the United States to ally with the Northern Alliance would inevitably provoke a backlash in Pakistan. In particular, he could count on three elements in Pakistani society that could be expected to react violently to such a provocation: groups in the military and secret services with strong ties to the Taliban and jihadist groups in

Kashmir; Islamic extremist political organizations; and especially, the Pashtun tribesmen along the Afghan border. The last group was of particular importance to bin Laden, because the Taliban represents, in addition to a religious affiliation, Pashtun ethnic dominance of Afghanistan. The fact that the border between Pakistan and Afghanistan dissects the Pashtun ethnic group amplified bin Laden's pan-Islamic ideology considerably; it appealed as a consequence not just to religious sentiment in Pakistan but in addition to Pashtun ethnic nationalism.

The overlap between Sunni Islam and the Pashtun ethnicity also gave bin Laden an advantage in countering any attempt by the United States to cooperate with the Northern Alliance, which in addition to its connections with Pakistan's regional rivals represented all the non-Pashtun and non-Sunni elements in Pakistan—the Uzbeks, Tajiks, and Hazaras. Thus, on September 11, bin Laden probably told himself that strategic, ethnic, and religious factors in Pakistan all militated in favor of Islamabad lobbying Washington with all vehemence to steer clear of the Northern Alliance.

From bin Laden's viewpoint, Washington had only one other option—to pressure Islamabad itself to help destroy the Taliban. For the Americans, this policy would allow them to work with, rather than against, their traditional ally, but it would also require Pakistan to dump a Muslim ally on orders from Washington, whose star had been falling in Pakistan in recent years. Such a radical policy reversal, bin Laden probably calculated, would unmask the Musharraf regime before its own public, revealing it as a puppet of the Americans. Again, bin Laden did not leave matters to chance. In proclamations directed to the Pakistani people, he stated: "The world had been divided into two camps: one under the banner of the cross, as Bush, the head of infidelity said, and another under the banner of Islam. A Muslim is a brother to fellow Muslims. He neither does them an injustice, nor lets them down. The Pakistani Government has fallen under the banner of the cross."[14] Bin Laden was certainly aided in this appeal by the tensions that developed between Pakistan and India over the Kashmir dispute. Even if bin Laden had no direct hand in these events, they were precisely the type of disruption that he envisioned when he provoked America to attack him.

The success of bin Laden's tactics, comparable to the Iranian hostage model, hinged on being able to initiate a controlled conflict with the United States. This, in turn, required being able to deny the United States a firm foothold in the region in order to neutralize American military superiority. Obviously, bin Laden severely miscalculated on many levels at once. The Russians allowed the Americans a free hand. The Musharraf government did manage to reverse its policy, align with the Americans while they cooperated with the Northern Alliance, oust pro-Taliban elements from its military, and rein in militants in Pakistan. Iran turned a blind eye to the American presence. In addition to these

---

[14] Text from BBC News Online, 1 November 2001, located at http://www.news.bbc.co.uk.

misreadings of the regional balance of power, one could add many other miscalculations. To name just one, bin Laden, like most generals, planned for the last war; he failed to perceive the qualitative difference between the Russian army of the 1980s and the high-tech American military of the twenty-first century, which managed to overcome many of the obstacles in Afghanistan that previous outside powers had found insurmountable.

Nonetheless, Nasser in the 1967 Arab-Israeli War and Saddam Hussein in the Gulf War made military miscalculations based on a far less propitious set of circumstances. Like other Middle Eastern brinksmen before him, bin Laden miscalculated the strength of public opinion, and he misread the intentions and capabilities of a superpower. This should not blind us to the fact, however, that he did perceive correctly the general patterns in the relations between the United States and the Islamic world, and he attempted to exploit them with cunning. Moreover, it is too early to judge his errors as complete failures. The consequences of September 11 in Saudi Arabia, Pakistan, and Egypt—to name just three countries—have yet to play themselves out fully. Even if al Qaeda never recovers from the military defeat in Afghanistan, bin Laden may still succeed in his aim of severely weakening the apostate regimes in the Middle East and of inspiring like-minded organizations to emerge from the enclave of true believers. He may even survive to fight another day.

There has been much talk about how September 11 permanently changed the United States and the world. In its relations with the Arab and Islamic peoples, however, Washington can almost certainly count on more of the same. The crash of the tectonic plates of history created the complex balance of power between the Middle East and the West today. This deep historical structure determined the range of choices available to even the most resolute superpower. Before too long, this balance of power will inevitably support the aspirations of another brinksman, who will step to the fore and challenge American hegemony. Bin Laden's miscalculations, even if they do spell total failure for al Qaeda, may well pave the way for somebody else's success.

Part III:
THE AXIS OF EVIL

North Korea's Weapons of Mass Destruction: Badges, Shields, or Swords?

VICTOR D. CHA

On the morning of 30 January 2002, wire reports, television news, and internet chat rooms throughout Asia were abuzz with speculation about phase two of the United States war against terrorism coming to the Korean peninsula. The previous evening, President George W. Bush in his State of the Union address outlined the U.S. mission beyond Afghanistan to include not only the termination of terrorist threats beyond al Qaeda networks, but also the prevention of links between these threats and regimes in an "axis of evil" enumerated as North Korea, Iraq, and Iran, that seek weapons of mass destruction (WMD) to threaten the United States and its allies.[1] Contrary to concerns expressed by many different media circles, the axis of evil speech did not signal imminent military action against the Democratic People's Republic of Korea (DPRK or North Korea). The President calmed any such concerns during his summit meetings with Japanese, Chinese, and especially South Korean leaders shortly after the speech.[2] The axis of evil statement, however, did intimate a harder-line policy toward North Korea at odds with the engagement or "sunshine" policy of ally South Korea. Also, the speech made clear the priority placed by the Bush administration on countering WMD threats as an integral, if not central, component of the post-September 11 American security agenda.

---

[1] Text available at http://www.whitehouse.gov/news/releases/2002/01/20020129-11.html, 28 February 2002.

[2] See "Remarks by President Bush and President Kim Dae-Jung in Press Availability—Seoul, Korea, 20 February 2002," White House Office of the Press Secretary, Washington, DC. (http://www.whitehouse.gov/news/releases/2002/02/20020220-1.html), 24 February 2002.

VICTOR D. CHA is associate professor of government and director of the American Alliances in Asia Project in the Edmund A. Walsh School of Foreign Service, Georgetown University.

These developments point to the renewal in coming months of an acerbic debate that took place at the end of the Clinton administration over the merits of engaging or containing the DPRK. Although the Bush administration's initial review of North Korea policy in June 2001 recommended unconditional engagement with Pyongyang on a broad range of issues including its suspected nuclear weapons program, ballistic missile production and export, and its conventional force posture on the peninsula,[3] this position is far from a conclusive one given the well-known skepticism of North Korean intentions expressed in the Bush's axis of evil speech as well as other statements by administration officials. A confluence of forces, moreover, adds to the likely reemergence of North Korea as a front-burner foreign policy issue after a period of calm and relative stasis in 2000–2001, following the unprecedented thaw created by the summit meeting between the South and North Korean leaders, Kim Dae Jung and Kim Jong Il in June 2000, and by the visit of U.S. Secretary of State Madeleine Albright to Pyongyang in October 2000. The standing nonproliferation agreement between the United States and the DPRK, the 1994 nuclear Agreed Framework, soon reaches critical implementation stages that will test the intentions of both parties and raises debates about American revision or abandonment of the agreement. A presidential election in South Korea in December 2002 has already sparked a contentious debate over the current government's sunshine policy. Japan's normalization talks with North Korea remain stalled since winter 2000 with no sign of resolution. Finally, Kim Jong Il's self-imposed missile testing moratorium, which was contingent on continued progress in U.S.–DPRK dialogue, ends in December 2002.[4]

Engagement with the DPRK, proponents argue, will avert crisis. Carrots in the form of normalized political relations, economic aid and investment, and mutual tension reduction will reduce North Korea's insecurity and offer a path of reform for an end to the proliferation threat and other belligerent DPRK behavior.[5] Skeptics of engagement do not believe that the regime's revisionist

---

[3] For the June 2001 policy review see "Statement by the President," White House Office of the Press Secretary, 13 June 2001 (http://www/whitehouse.gov/news/releases/2001/06/20010611-4.html), 28 February 2002.

[4] See Michael May, ed., *Verifying the Agreed Framework* (Lawrence Livermore National Laboratory, Center for Global Security Research and Center for International Security and Cooperation, Stanford University, April 2001), UCRL-ID-142036 CGSR 2001-001; Donald Gregg, "Collateral Damage in Korea," (http://www.koreasociety.org/TKSQ.html.), *Korea Society Quarterly* (Fall 2001), 25 January 2002; and Hoi-Chang Lee, "Korea at the Crossroads: The Challenges Ahead" (American Enterprise Institute-Heritage Foundation speech delivered at the St. Regis Hotel, Washington, DC, 23 January 2002).

[5] Representative arguments include Leon V. Sigal, *Disarming Strangers: Nuclear Diplomacy with North Korea* (Princeton: Princeton University Press, 1998); Dong-Won Lim, "Inter-Korean Relations Oriented toward Reconciliation and Cooperation," *Korea and World Affairs* 16 (Summer 1992): 213–223; Selig S. Harrison, "The Missiles of North Korea," *World Policy Journal* 17 (Fall 2000): 13–24; Harrison, "Promoting a Soft Landing in Korea," *Foreign Policy* 106 (Spring 1997): 57–76; Bruce Cumings, "Missile Launch Is a Shot over the U.S. Bow," *Los Angeles Times*, 2 September 1998; Soon-Young Hong, "Thawing Korea's Cold War," *Foreign Affairs* 78 (May/June 1999): 8–12; David C. Kang, "We Should Not Fear the North Koreans," *Los Angeles Times*, 13 June 2000; Steven Mufson, "Threat

intentions will change, and therefore the offer of economic and diplomatic carrots only strengthens the hardliners in Pyongyang, exemplifies Western weakness (in DPRK eyes), and ultimately strengthens a regime bent on overturning the status quo on the peninsula. As Douglas Paal has argued, the policy amounts to "conditional appeasement" that does not produce observable change for the better in the DPRK.[6] Rather than rehash the engagement-containment debate, this article tries to address a prior and axiomatic question. The very existence of a vigorous policy debate in Washington, Seoul, and Tokyo indicates not consensus but a fundamental absence of agreement on the nature of the threat that emerges from the DPRK. I take the primary agent of the DPRK "threat" in the post-cold war era—the nuclear weapons program—and seek to explain the context of DPRK weaponization. In short, are these weapons basically built out of insecurity, metaphorically as shields to ensure against acts by the United States and others to crush the regime? Or are they swords built for aggressive and revisionist purposes? Or are these programs essentially badges or symbols of prestige for an otherwise bankrupt regime?[7]

The answers to these questions lie in an investigation of strategic doctrine. It is only by understanding the doctrine in which this weapons capability is em-

---

of 'Rogue' States: Is It Reality or Rhetoric?" *Washington Post*, 29 May 2000; Hazel Smith, "Bad, Mad, Sad, or Rational Actor? Why the 'Securitization' Paradigm Makes for Poor Policy Analysis of North Korea," *International Affairs* 76 (January 2000): 111–132; Michael Gordon, "How Politics Sank Accord on Missiles with North Korea," *New York Times*, 6 March 2001; Chung-in Moon and David I. Steinberg, eds., *Kim Dae-jung Government and Sunshine Policy: Promises and Challenges* (Seoul: Yonsei University Press, 1999); Donald Gregg and James Laney, "Don't Dismantle the Nuclear Framework on Korea," *Washington Post*, 21 September 1998; David I. Steinberg, "A Wrench in the Korean Peace Machinery," *International Herald Tribune*, 1 February 2002; and Michael O'Hanlon, "Choosing the Right Enemies," *New York Times*, 6 February 2002.

[6] Douglas Paal, "Achieving Korean Reunification" in Nicholas Eberstadt and Richard Ellings, eds., *Korea's Future and the Great Powers* (Seattle: University of Washington Press, 2001), 305. Other arguments in this vein include Chuck Downs, "Discerning North Korean Intentions" in Eberstadt and Ellings, *Korea's Future*, 88–105; "Sound the Alarm: Defector says North Korea is Preparing for War," *The Economist*, 26 April 1997; Fred Iklé, "U.S. Folly May Start Another Korean War," *Wall Street Journal*, 12 October 1998; William Taylor, "The Best Strategy is to Do Nothing," *Los Angeles Times*, 2 September 1998; James Risen, "CIA Sees a North Korean Missile Threat," *New York Times*, 3 February 1999; "Sunshine or Moonshine," *Wall Street Journal*, (editorial) 2 March 1999; North Korea Advisory Group, *Report to the Speaker, U.S. House of Representatives*, November 1999, (http://www.house.gov/international_relations/nkag/report.htm), 3 January 2000; Stephen Bradner, "North Korea's Strategy," in Henry Sokolski, ed., *Planning for a Peaceful Korea* (Carlisle, PA: Strategic Studies Institute, 2001), 23–82; Joseph Bermudez and Sharon Richardson, "The North Korean View of the Development and Production of Strategic Weapons Systems," in Sokolski, *Planning*, 83–112; Nicholas Eberstadt, *The End of North Korea* (Washington, DC: AEI Press, 1999); Henry Sokolski and Victor Gilinsky, "Bush is Right to Get Tough with North Korea," *Wall Street Journal*, 11 February 2002; and Margaret Thatcher, "Advice to a Superpower," *New York Times*, 11 February 2002.

[7] I focus primarily on nuclear doctrine rather than the entire portfolio of weapons of mass destruction. Doctrine or strategies for each of these weapons is different and cannot be generalized under a nuclear doctrine. I do include implicitly the ballistic missile program as delivery vehicles for nuclear warheads.

bedded that we can obtain a better sense of how threatening the DPRK may be. For example, if such weapons are developed outside of any semblance of a larger military doctrine, then the likelihood of their random and/or irrational use as weapons of terror is higher and more threatening. But if nuclear and missile weaponization are part of a larger military strategy, then a margin of rationality and predictability obtains with regards to the potential use of such weapons.[8] Better insights into DPRK strategic doctrine, moreover, shed light on two important issues for policy makers: the potential effectiveness of engagement strategies to address the WMD threat; and the likelihood that such capabilities could be rolled back. If the DPRK nuclear program is integral to a defensive/deterrence-based doctrine, then engagement strategies aimed at reducing DPRK insecurity would be warranted: moreover, providing incentives to roll back those capabilities might work. However, if DPRK nuclear weapons are part of a revisionist doctrine, then engagement will fail and rollback will be impossible. The nature of this exercise, given the black box of DPRK intentions, is necessarily a deductive one.[9] I begin with a brief discussion of how others have assessed the DPRK's WMD threat, followed by some elementary theoretical background to explain the importance of strategic doctrine as providing insight into intentions. I then investigate, as a first cut, the regime's overall objectives. The second cut is to understand nuclear and missile weaponization in the context of these objectives. The third analytical cut is to understand any contradictions in the doctrine and the implications for my assessment of the DPRK threat.

WMD Threats and Doctrine

There is no dearth of arguments or scenarios about the ways in which North Korea's WMD capabilities might be threatening. Pyongyang might employ nuclear weapons and ballistic missiles as part of an attempt to overrun the peninsula again; but in the interim, it might utilize strategic deception to lull South Korea and the United States into believing it is interested in a deal on non-

---

[8] This argument does not deny that even a wholly defensive doctrine by a small nuclear power like North Korea can still be threatening in terms of the dangers associated with poor safeguards and accidents often cited about fledgling nuclear programs. On the other hand, given recent revelations regarding the superpowers' nuclear programs during the cold war, there is growing debate about whether such safety arguments are any more applicable to Third World proliferation than they were to the First World. See Waltz's arguments in Kenneth Waltz and Scott Sagan, *The Spread of Nuclear Weapons: A Debate* (New York: Norton, 1996); Peter Feaver, "Optimists, Pessimists, and Theories of Nuclear Proliferation Management," *Security Studies* 4 (Summer 1995); and Ahmed Hashim, "The State, Society, and the Evolution of Warfare in the Middle East," *Washington Quarterly* 18 (Autumn 1995); and Avery Goldstein, *Deterrence and Security in the 21st Century* (Stanford, CA: Stanford University Press, 2000), 276–79.

[9] The propositions I derive here would have to be confirmed by rigorous empirical investigation of DPRK military writings. Nevertheless, I believe this is a useful exercise that provides a testable framework for understanding weaponization choices by the DPRK.

proliferation and tension reduction.[10] Another view, consonant with many reports about DPRK dictator Kim Jong Il before the summit with South Korea in June 2000, argues that the reclusive leader is irrational, unpredictable, and mad enough to use these weapons without probable cause. A third view posits that the threat stems primarily from the DPRK state's collapse or implosion resulting either in the problem of "loose nukes," inadvertent detonation, or accidental use of these weapons.[11] Finally, Kim Jong Il might strike out with these capabilities in a last-gasp act of desperation if the regime faces imminent extinction or perceives an imminent attack.[12]

These are all plausible and real concerns. However, probability estimates for these scenarios generally focus on variables like the regime's viability, the sanity of the leadership, and the strength of U.S.–ROK (South Korea) defense and deterrence capabilities on the peninsula. Assessing the true threat posed by these weapons, however, is a function of two additional factors. First, as Robert Jervis has argued, the offensive or defensive nature of the weapons in question is an important determinant of the security dilemma and, derivatively, the level of threat.[13] Weapons systems that are defense-oriented (fortifications, trenches, short-range fixed artillery sites, recessed force deployments) are less likely to generate insecurities among other states while contributing to the security of arming states. On the other hand, a state's buildup of offensive weapons generates acute security dilemmas and threat perceptions, because potential expansionist intentions behind the buildup cannot be ruled out by the state's competitors. Second, if weapons cannot be clearly distinguished for offensive or defensive purposes,[14] then transparency regarding the threat will hinge on

---

[10] See Eberstadt, *The End of North Korea*; and Chuck Downs, *Over the Line: North Korea's Negotiating Strategy* (Washington, DC: AEI Press, 1999).

[11] On these two views, see Jonathan D. Pollack and Chung Min Lee, *Preparing for Korean Unification: Scenarios and Implications* (Santa Monica, CA: RAND, 1999); Thatcher, "Advice to a Superpower"; Aidan Foster-Carter, "North Korea: All Roads Lead to Collapse" in Marcus Noland, ed., *Economic Integration of the Korean Peninsula* (Washington, DC: Institute for International Economics, 1998); and Edward Olsen, "Coping with the Korean Peace Process: An American View," *Korean Journal of Defense Analysis* 9 (Winter 1997).

[12] On the desperation thesis, see Michael Green, "North Korean Regime Crisis: U.S. Perspectives and Responses," *Korean Journal of Defense Analysis* 9 (Winter 1997); Olsen, "Coping with the Korean Peace Process"; Don Oberdorfer, *The Two Koreas: A Contemporary History* (Reading, MA: Addison-Wesley, 1997), 314; and Victor D. Cha, "Engagement and Preventive Defense on the Korean Peninsula," *International Security* 27 (Summer 2002, forthcoming).

[13] Robert Jervis, "Cooperation Under the Security Dilemma," *World Politics* 30 (January 1978): 167–214; also see John Herz, *Political Realism and Political Idealism* (Chicago: University of Chicago Press, 1951); and Nicholas Wheeler and Ken Booth, "The Security Dilemma" in John Baylis and N. J. Rengger, eds., *Dilemmas of World Politics* (Oxford, UK: Clarendon Press, 1992): 29–60. This is admittedly a pared down version of the argument, largely for the purpose of illustrating to the nonsecurity expert the importance of doctrine in understanding and assessing threats.

[14] For example, tanks are slow and relatively immobile, but they can be used for offensive purposes. Surface-to-air missiles are notionally defensive weapons; but depending on who uses them, they can be seen as offensively intended. Nuclear weapons can be used for offensive (first-strike) or defensive (assured second-strike) purposes.

the doctrine in which the weapons systems are embedded.[15] Whether a given weapon is offensive or defensive greatly depends on the context and circumstances of its use, and often the best indicator of this context is the military doctrine under which the system operates.

Weapons for What Purpose?

Given the importance of strategic doctrine in assessing the WMD threat posed by a state, the next step is to locate a better understanding of a state's pronouncements and writings on the topic. For the declared nuclear powers, this doctrine is usually established, public, and fairly transparent.[16] However, in the case of a proliferating country like North Korea, the task is doubly difficult, because transparency is minimal and the stakes are very high. The government of North Korea does not release any official statements on its nuclear weapons or ballistic missile programs. This stands in stark contrast to another new proliferator, India, which after its nuclear tests released statements explicating the doctrine (however faulty) in which these new capabilities were embedded. Thus, in the opaque case of North Korea, the first step in learning its strategic doctrine might be to understand the government's predominant political objectives. Strategic doctrine and the regime's national objectives are likely to be linked. The *Juche* ideology of "self-reliance" is the most known aspect of North Korea's national strategy.[17] At a minimum, one could posit that a primary political goal of the DPRK regime and its *juche* strategy is state survival and protection of national sovereignty, given the deteriorating domestic and geostrategic conditions since the end of the cold war.

This may appear obvious, but it was a goal taken for granted by the North until the 1990s. From the outset of the regime's creation in 1948, the primary national goal was not merely state survival and protection of sovereignty, but "victorious unification" (*songong t'ongil*) over the rival regime in the South.[18]

---

[15] As Eyre, Suchman, and Alexander note, "[T]echnology is never just technology, . . .every machine has a socially constructed meaning and a socially oriented objective and the incidence and significance of technological developments can never be fully understood or predicted independently of their social context." Cited in Dana Eyre and Mark Suchman, "Status, Norms and the Proliferation of Conventional Weapons" in Peter Katzenstein, ed., *The Culture of National Security* (New York: Columbia University Press, 1996), 86. Also see Robert O'Connell, "Putting Weapons in Perspective," *Armed Forces and Society* 9 (1983).

[16] See Goldstein, *Deterrence and Security.*

[17] Robert Myers, *Korea in the Cross Currents* (New York, M. E. Sharpe, 2000), chap. 9; Eberstadt, *The End of North Korea*; *Juche! The Speeches and Writings of Kim Il Sung*, foreword by Eldridge Cleaver (New York: Grossman Publishers, 1972); and Han S. Park, ed., *North Korea: Ideology, Politics and Economy* (New York: Prentice-Hall, 1996).

[18] For some of the classic works on North Korea during the cold war, see Dae-Sook Suh, *Kim Il Sung: The North Korean Leader* (New York: Columbia University Press, 1988); B. C. Koh, *The Foreign Policy Systems of North and South Korea* (Berkeley: University of California Press, 1984); Robert Scalapino and Chong-Sik Lee, *Communism in Korea* (Berkeley: University of California Press, 1972); and Bruce Cumings, *Korea's Place in the Sun* (New York: Norton, 1997).

Moreover, most economic and military indicators of relative state power substantiated such a goal. Throughout the first three decades of the cold war, the two regimes faced off as relative equals with each buttressed by security guarantees from its great-power patrons. From the early 1960s to 1970s, North Korean gross national product per capita and conventional military capabilities rivaled, if not surpassed, that of its southern counterpart.[19] This relative equality enabled each regime its particular vision of unification, which essentially meant domination of one over the other.

Today, despite rhetoric to the contrary, North Korea no longer sees overthrow of the South and unification of the peninsula as a realistic objective. By the 1990s, an enormous and insurmountable gap emerged between the two countries. Annual 8 percent growth in the ROK (before the 1997 Asian financial crisis) versus successive years of 3–8 percent negative growth in the North between 1991 and 1998 resulted in a nearly twenty-fold gap in the gross domestic product of the two economies and a ratio of South to North per capital income as high as 11:1.[20] Although Pyongyang clings to *juche* and visions of hegemonic unification, even staunch ideologues like Hwang Jang-yop admitted after defecting in 1997 that a communist revolution in the South is no longer a viable DPRK objective.[21] In a similar vein, a low-key but very significant event at the September 1998 session of the Supreme People's Assembly (1st session, 10th term) was abolition of the Unification Committee.[22] Propaganda emanating out of Pyongyang under Kim Jong Il, while still promoting strict adherence to "revolutionary traditions," increasingly admits that "existing theories" may not be sufficient to deal with new problems and developments. Russian observers note that among the core principles that have made up the *juche* ideology, emphasis has shifted over the past year from universal "communization" to "self-dependency" as the ultimate revolutionary goal.[23] The government-run newspaper, *Nodong Sinmun*, in a moment of candor at the end of 2000 admitted how much national goals had changed: "The masses' independent demands grow higher ceaselessly with the times as the revolution develops. . . . Should

---

[19] For economic data, see Bruce Cumings, *The Two Koreas*, Foreign Policy Association, Headline Series No. 269 (May/June 1984): 65–66. The North Korean military grew from 300,000 to over one million troops over the two decades. See Nicholas Eberstadt, "'National Strategy' in North and South Korea," National Bureau of Asian Research, *Analysis* 7 (no. 5, 1996), 10, 12.

[20] For other figures, see Marcus Noland, "Economic Strategies for Unification" in Nicholas Eberstadt and Richard Ellings, eds., *Korea's Future and the Great Powers* (Seattle: University of Washington Press, 2001), 199–202; Pollack and Lee, *Preparing for Korean Unification*.

[21] See Oberdorfer's recounting of conversations between Hwang and Selig Harrison in Don Oberdorfer, *The Two Koreas*, (New York: Addison-Wesley, 1998), 401. Also see Hwang's interview in Myers, *Korea in the Cross Currents*, 140–45.

[22] Inter-Korean matters have been subsumed nominally under the party central committee. See "The DPRK Report," No. 14 (September-October 1998), (Ftp://ftp.nautilus.org/napsnet/RussiaDPRK/DPRK_Report_14.txt), March 2002.

[23] "The DPRK Report," no. 7 (May-June 1997), (Ftp://ftp.nautilus.org/napsnet/RussiaDPRK/DPRK_Report_7.txt), 1 March 2002.

the regime fail to strengthen and develop fast enough to meet the masses' incessantly growing independent demands, the people would turn their back on it and eventually it would collapse."[24] As one expert noted, "[t]hirty years ago a very different verdict on the national strategies of the two Koreas might have been rendered. . . . [T]he North Korean goal of enforcing a Socialist unification upon the South was no mere pipedream."[25] Now, Pyongyang's end game has changed from one of hegemonic unification to basic survival.

SHIELDS?

If one can posit that a critical DPRK national objective is state survival, then insight into the DPRK's strategic doctrine is best broached first by understanding how nuclear proliferation and this survival objective are interlinked. This question is a fundamental one that often gets lost in the debates about the nuclear program, which have fixated on quantities of weapons-grade plutonium accumulated and whether or not the North already has a bomb, rather than on the context of weaponization.[26] If the regime's objective is survival, then one line of argument would posit that the North seeks nuclear weapons as a deterrent. If the DPRK case is typical of new, small and medium-size proliferation in the "second" nuclear age, then the "rules" regarding proliferation and deterrence are substantially different from the first nuclear age.[27] The rationale behind proliferation is not based on achieving assured second-strike capabilities as the backbone of stable deterrence, as was the case between the United States and Soviet Union. Instead, what appears to be the operative doctrine for smaller nuclear powers is existential deterrence: ". . . the mere existence of nuclear forces means that, whatever we say or do, there is a certain irreducible risk that an armed conflict might escalate into a nuclear war. The fear of escalation is thus factored into political calculations: faced with this risk, states are more cautious and more prudent than they otherwise would be."[28] Security for the proliferator is therefore achieved not through assured second-strike capability but by creating "first-strike uncertainty." Deterrence and security derive from hav-

---

[24] Chong-Mi Kim, "The Sagacious Leadership that Keeps Strengthening the People's Regime in Compliance with the Requirements of the Developing Revolution," *Nodong Sinmun*, 27 December 2000 in *Foreign Broadcast Information Service - East Asia* 2001–0117, 27 December 2000.

[25] Eberstadt, "National Strategy," 23; also see Adrian Buzo, *Guerilla Dynasty* (Boulder, CO: Westview, 1999), chap. 8.

[26] For a good critical survey of these debates and speculations, see Sigal, *Disarming Strangers*.

[27] Victor D. Cha, "The Second Nuclear Age: Proliferation Pessimism versus Sober Optimism in South Asia and East Asia," *Journal of Strategic Studies* 24 (December 2001): 79–122.

[28] Marc Trachtenberg, "The Influence of Nuclear Weapons in the Cuban Missile Crisis," *International Security* 10 (Summer 1985): 139; also see McGeorge Bundy, "Existential Deterrence and its Consequences" in Douglas MacLean, ed., *The Security Gamble: Deterrence Dilemmas in the Nuclear Age* (Totowa, NJ: Rowman and Littlefield, 1984), 3–13; and Devin Hagerty, *The Consequences of Nuclear Proliferation: Lessons from South Asia* (Cambridge, MA: MIT Press, 1998), 26.

ing just enough capabilities to raise uncertainty in the mind of the opponent so that it cannot neutralize you with a first strike.[29]

What are some of the parameters by which one could test whether the North's nuclear program is driven by an existential deterrent doctrine? The first are material constraints. Existential deterrent doctrines (as opposed to stable deterrence doctrines) are most likely among proliferating states that are small, limited in resources, and with proximate adversaries. The DPRK's well-documented economic difficulties in the 1990s impose severe resource constraints on closing gaps with rival competitors through modernization and a buildup of conventional forces. As Avery Goldstein argues, the self-help imperatives of anarchy also render reliance on allies for security an unattractive proposition (when abandonment fears are high) or an unfeasible one (when allies do not exist).[30] Nuclear weapons, therefore, offer the most efficient means by which to optimize security needs, abandonment fears, and resource constraints. Nuclear weapons are also more "fungible" than conventional forces in the sense that they remain relevant security assets in most cases regardless of wholesale changes in future adversaries or contingencies.[31] If programs are developed under a veil of secrecy, this often signals existential deterrence, because opacity generates worst-case assessments that tend to err on the side of caution (hence increasing first-strike uncertainty). If the nuclear arsenals are small, inaccurate, and counterforce-oriented, this usually indicates a doctrine not based in nuclear war-fighting or second-strike capabilities.

There is some evidence to suggest DPRK interest in nuclear weapons as part of an existential deterrent doctrine.[32] The geostrategic situation from the

---

[29] The precedent for this form of deterrence had already been set by the second-tier nuclear powers in the first nuclear age. As Goldstein's study shows, existential deterrent doctrines were what drove China, Britain, and France's pursuit of an independent but not second-strike assured nuclear deterrent against their respective superpower adversaries. See Goldstein, *Deterrence and Security*, 44–46. This argument does not deny the vigorous debate on whether existential deterrence is stable, nor does it deny the debates about the safety of small nuclear programs. Illustrative of these arguments, see Waltz and Sagan, *The Spread of Nuclear Weapons*; Peter Feaver, *Guarding the Guardians: Civilian Control of Nuclear Weapons in the United States* (Ithaca, NY: Cornell University Press, 1992); Bruce Blair, *The Logic of Accidental Nuclear War* (Washington, DC: Brookings, 1993); Scott Sagan, *The Limits of Safety: Organizations, Accidents, and Nuclear Weapons* (Princeton: Princeton University Press, 1994); and David Karl, "Proliferation Pessimism and Emerging Nuclear Powers," *International Security* 21 (Winter 1996/97): 87–119. The point is that pursuit of weaponization by small powers like the DPRK may be based in a belief in the efficacy of existential deterrence, regardless of whether this is correct or not.

[30] Goldstein, *Deterrence and Security*, 225; also see Sagan's "security model" in "Why Do States Build Nuclear Weapons?" *International Security* 21 (Winter 1996/97): 54–86; and John Deutsch, "The New Nuclear Threat," *Foreign Affairs* 71 (Fall 1992).

[31] For further discussions on the relative advantages of nuclear over conventional deterrents, see Goldstein, *Deterrence and Security*, 35–40, 54–55.

[32] A peaceful uses of atomic energy agreement between the United States and the Soviet Union in the 1960s enabled North Korea to develop a small nuclear research reactor and a basic understanding of nuclear physics, engineering, and reactor operations. Pyongyang's nuclear industry was capable of supporting a complete nuclear fuel cycle by the 1980s. Subsequent reactors (an operational five megawatt reactor and construction of 50 and 200 megawatt reactors) presaged an annual reprocessed plutonium production capacity that could sustain an excess of ten nuclear weapons. While these activities

early-1990s (when revelations about the nuclear program became front page news) shifted heavily against the North and in favor of its southern rival. Pyongyang's primary cold war patron, the Soviet Union, ceased to exist. Its successor state in Russia normalized relations with Seoul in September 1990 and declared that it would not honor Soviet cold war security guarantees to DPRK defense. Pyongyang's other critical patron, China, sought diplomatic normalization with South Korea in 1992 and also disavowed its "as close as lips to teeth" cold war security relationship with the North. Thus, in a period of three years between 1989 and 1992, the world, as Pyongyang knew it since 1948, changed beyond recognition. Such changes dictated some form of self-help security solution beyond relying on allies. In addition, the insurmountable gap in capabilities with the ROK that emerged at the end of the cold war made regime salvation paramount. Consequently, as one long-time DPRK expert asserts, "The growing political, economic, and military imbalance between the North and South almost forces [the DPRK] to produce nuclear weapons for survival and for security. It is the only alternative to guarantee North Korea's own style of socialism and to insure the continuation of Kim Il Sung's dynasty.[33] The nuclear program was developed with a premium on opacity, and even the most generous estimate would put the arsenal at a handful of primitive weapons. In addition, while much has been made of the DPRK's long-range ballistic missile program in the aftermath of the Taepo-dong test in August 1998, these missiles are notoriously inaccurate with inordinately high circular probability errors. Such missiles as delivery vehicles for nuclear warheads could not practically or effectively be integrated in some doctrine that focused on counterstrike targets, which rely on high accuracy. Inaccurate delivery vehicles could however be evidence of a doctrine that holds countervalue targets (like cities) for deterrence purposes.[34] There is little evidence that the program is integrated into the military structure. Despite the Soviet origins of the nuclear program, the North's military lacks training in nuclear weapons or nuclear war-fighting, which gives the sense that the weapons are for deterrent and not war-fighting purposes. The Korean

---

remain frozen and are subject to dismantlement as a result of the 1994 U.S.–DPRK Agreed Framework, suspicions remain regarding the North's plutonium reprocessing history, alleged covert activities outside Yongbyon, and possible crude nuclear devices. Concerns also abound regarding possible reprocessing activities in 1989 and May-June 1994, which would have provided the DPRK with enough weapons-grade plutonium for several nuclear weapons. See Sigal, *Disarming Strangers*; and Alexandre Mansourov, "The Origins, Evolution, and Current Politics of the North Korean Nuclear Program," *The Nonproliferation Review* 2 (Spring-Summer 1995), internet version, http://cns.miis.edu/pubs/npr/mansou23.htm, 5 May 2000. On the likelihood of the DPRK's nuclear weapons, see Andrew Mack, "Security and the Korean Peninsula in the 1990s" in Mack, ed., *Asian Flashpoint* (Sydney: Allen & Unwin, 1993), 1–20.

[33] Dae-sook Suh, "North Korea: The Present and the Future," *Korean Journal of Defense Analysis* 8 (Summer 1996): 78.

[34] Clearly there are alternative explanations for these traits that do not necessarily mean an existential deterrent doctrine, in particular, resource constraints.

Peoples Army (KPA) is presumably outside of the entire nuclear chain of command.[35]

Most North Korea experts agree that the primary agent in understanding the intentions behind the nuclear program is Kim Il Sung. Initiatives and ideas with regard to the program were Kim's and disseminated sparingly among a small circle of advisers; moreover, these views were never recorded in any of Kim's military writings. In spite of this, there is no denying that the DPRK leader from very early on appreciated the awesome destructiveness and deterrent value of the weapon, particularly as a young guerrilla fighter who witnessed the United States subdue the Japanese with merely two of these weapons.[36] Kim most likely comprehended ex post facto the compellent value of implicit nuclear threats by the United States to end the Korean war in 1953.[37] He consequently sought extended nuclear deterrent guarantees from the Soviet Union, and his interest and activity in pursuing independent capabilities positively correlated over the years with lapses in confidence in the Soviet security guarantee. Kim was clearly affected by the Soviet-South Korea normalization pact, referring to it as a "betrayal of socialism." In perhaps the most direct statement linking the nascent nuclear capabilities with the loss of confidence in Moscow, the DPRK foreign ministry stated in September 1990 that it would take "measures to provide for ourselves some weapons for which we have so far relied on the [Soviet] alliance."[38] The Chinese experience also weighed heavily in Kim's calculations. China in the 1950s was a fledgling regime perceived as besieged and threatened by the United States. However, nuclear capabilities changed China's strategic and political context dramatically and provided it with a measure of security unattainable previously.

Deterrence Operationalized

Hence, an argument could be made for DPRK nuclear weaponization and existential deterrence. There may have been other alternative purposes intended with the weapon, but as Alexandre Mansourov argues, "It appears that Kim Il Sung gave first priority to deterrence when he thought about the possible mission for nuclear weapons in the overall military doctrine of the DPRK."[39] This, as North Korea expert Dae-Sook Suh argues, was for regime survival: "The

---

[35] Mansourov contests this claim by North Korean officials. See "The Origins, Evolution, and Current Politics," 9–10.

[36] Mansourov conversations with Steve Linton cited in ibid., 5–6.

[37] On atomic diplomacy in Korea, see Rosemary Foot, "Nuclear Coercion and the Ending of the Korean Conflict," *International Security* 13 (Winter 1988-89); and Roger Dingman, "Atomic Diplomacy during the Korean War," *International Security* 13 (Winter 1998-89).

[38] Andrew Mack, "The Nuclear Crisis on the Korean Peninsula," *Asian Survey* 33 (April 1993): 342, cited in Herbert Ellison, "Russia, Korea and Northeast Asia" in Eberstadt and Ellings, eds., *Korea's Future and the Great Powers*, 166.

[39] Mansourov, "The Origins, Evolution, and Current Politics," 7.

reason for the North Korean nuclear weapons program is based on its need to survive. It is not to improve its power position vis-à-vis South Korea or to use nuclear blackmail in its international relations. It is not the purpose of the North Korean nuclear weapons program to engage in nuclear arms trade. . . . North Korea thinks it needs such weapons for its survival."[40]

Another longtime North Korea scholar, Bruce Cumings, agrees with this general assessment: "The DPRK probably decided in 1991, if not earlier, to develop a small-state deterrent for a country surrounded by powerful enemies, like Israel: To display enough activity to make possession of a nuclear device plausible to the outside world, but with no announcement of possession. . . . in short, to appear to arm itself with an ultimate trump card and keep everyone guessing whether and when the weapons might become available."[41] Although reliable evidence is lacking, one could surmise the doctrine operationalized as follows: First, defense and deterrence against U.S.–ROK conventional ground invasion accomplished by the forward deployed forces and artillery along the demilitarized zone.[42] Second, existential nuclear deterrent against the United States. The countervalue target of this deterrent would not be South Korea (for tactical as well as nationalist reasons) or the United States (absent long-range delivery capabilities) but Japan.[43] Third, neither-confirm-nor-deny policy with regard to these capabilities. Opacity forces others to "worst-case" the DPRK's capabilities, which then enhances the deterrent value of the threat.

Policy Implication: If Deterrence, then Engagement

The policy implications of an existential deterrent interpretation of DPRK strategic doctrine favor arguments for engagement. The logic of this policy argument would be that a security dilemma operates with regard to DPRK weaponization. Although provocative by violating nonproliferation norms and couched in aggressive rhetoric, this weaponization is largely defensively intended. Moreover, the nuclear program is best ended by the guarantee of regime survival, not by pressure.[44]

Pressing the consistency of the engagement logic further, one might argue that if North Korea's primary interest is survival, why consider giving up the nuclear program? Perhaps Pyongyang just wants the outside world to believe it is interested in a trade while surreptitiously cheating on any agreements concluded. Nuclear and long-range missile capabilities, after all, would be the ultimate equalizer and security guarantor for a weak regime like North Korea. This criticism does not consider the relative unattractiveness of such an option for

---

[40] Suh, "North Korea: The Present and the Future," 74–75.

[41] Cumings, *Korea's Place in the Sun*, 467.

[42] The defensive rationale for forward-deployed forces derives from "use-or-lose" conditions.

[43] For interesting discussions to this effect, see Bermudez and Richardson, "The North Korean View," 83–112; and Mansourov, "The Origins, Evolution and Current Politics," 7–8.

[44] Suh, "North Korea: The Present and the Future," 80.

Pyongyang's overall political objectives. The objective is regime survival. Nuclear weapons and missiles may promise survival through existential deterrence, but they offer nothing else. The objective of survival might be attained but it would be a barren one where the North would remain excluded and alienated from the world community and its benefits. A more desirable outcome for the regime would be what might be called "enriched" survival, a scenario in which the Pyongyang regime endures without nuclear weapons—being able to maintain a credible neither-confirm-nor-deny policy would be optimal—while simultaneously accumulating concessions that improve the overall situation.

Swords?

The existential deterrence argument for North Korea appears logical to many DPRK-watchers and is consonant with much of the small and medium-proliferation cases in the second nuclear age.[45] North Koreans, if asked, would probably offer this rationale for their proliferating as well. However, the deterrence argument is not without its inconsistencies.

North Korean Fears of U.S. Attack

One internal contradiction in particular is devastating. There is no denying that the overriding political objective of Pyongyang in the post-cold war era has been to ensure regime survival; however this has not always been the North's primary concern. For the majority of the regime's existence, survival was not the issue; instead, the primary security contingency that the DPRK feared was defending against unprovoked aggression or preemptive attack by the United States and South Korea.

This has been stated countless times in North Korean propaganda for Western and internal consumption. U.S.–ROK military exercises to maintain combat and defense-readiness (Team Spirit) involving nearly 200,000 men were routinely condemned by Pyongyang as provocative exercises aimed at attacking the North. The Reagan administration's decision in the 1980s to sell advanced F-16 fighter planes to Korea as well as its explication of a "horizontal escalation" doctrine with the Soviet Union reconfirmed North Korean beliefs that the United States was threatening preemptive attack on the North, either directly as a function of the balance on the peninsula or as a response to Soviet actions elsewhere in the world. As Cumings observes, "This scenario truly horrified the North Koreans, and during the remaining Reagan years they shouted themselves hoarse in opposition to U.S. policy."[46] More recently, revelations in the late 1990s regarding revision of the U.S. operational battle plan for Korea (Operation Plan 5027) confirmed the North's view of a salient U.S. threat to

---

[45] Goldstein, *Deterrence and Security*; and Hagerty, *The Consequences of Nuclear Proliferation*.
[46] Cumings, *Korea's Place in the Sun*, 461.

attack. The new plan substantially expanded the target list, timetable, and depth of a U.S. counter-offensive on Pyongyang. Comments by one U.S. official with regard to OP-PLAN 5027 played right into the hands of those in Pyongyang preoccupied with a U.S. attack: "When we're done, [the DPRK] will not be able to mount any military activity of any kind. We will kill them all."[47]

Fears of a preemptive U.S. attack are evident in DPRK conventional military doctrine. Kim Il Sung's Four Military Lines and Three Revolutionary Forces are premised on repelling and rolling back a U.S. attack to Pusan in three days.[48] Nowhere is this fear more evident than in the forward deployment of DPRK forces along the demilitarized zone. These deployments are seen by the West as aggressively-intended; but from a DPRK perspective, they reflect a defensive mentality about fending off a U.S. attack. As General James Clapper (director of Defense Intelligence Agency [1991–94] and former chief of intelligence in Korea and Pacific commands) noted, the North's forward deployments may actually reflect a use-or-lose mentality to compensate for inferiorities in the relative military balance on the peninsula. In other words, the North does not necessarily believe that offense has the advantage but chooses to forward deploy because its main fear is unprovoked U.S. attack. Should the United States undertake an offensive attack (complete with relentless bombing runs as was the case in 1950), anything other than forward deployment would render DPRK forces incapable of mobilizing quickly enough in a counter-offensive or sustaining supply routes with rear-area forces.[49]

The Preemption Contradiction

Most North Korea watchers who agree with the existential deterrent argument and therefore favor engagement would also agree with this assessment of DPRK threat perceptions. Given these traditional DPRK security concerns about a U.S. attack, however, a glaring contradiction obtains. *If the primary military contingency that the regime is preoccupied with is unprovoked U.S. aggression, then nuclear proliferation, rather than deterring, actually increases the likelihood of attack.* As the literature on nuclear deterrence has shown, in security competitions between two states, proliferation by one side dramatically increases the incentives for preemptive attack by the other.[50] Moreover, if a state's prolifera-

---

[47] Richard Halloran, "New Warplan Calls for Invasion of North Korea," Global Beat, 14 November 1998, (http://www.nyu.edu/globalbeat/asia/Halloran111498.html), 12 January 1999; Chong-Hun Yi, "North Korea Beefs Up Demonstrations Denouncing Operation Plan 5027," *Sisa Journal*, 24 December 1998 [in Korean]; and Bruce Bennett, "Conventional Arms Control in Korea: A Lever for Peace?" in Sokolski, *Planning*, 291–328.

[48] Buzo, *Guerilla Dynasty*, chap. 8.

[49] Clapper's analysis as cited in Sigal, *Disarming Strangers*, 21.

[50] Thomas Schelling, *The Strategy of Conflict* (Cambridge, MA: Harvard University Press, 1960), chap. 9; Gordon Chang, *Friends and Enemies: The United States, China and the Soviet Union, 1948–72* (Stanford, CA: Stanford University Press, 1990); and Karl, "Proliferation Pessimists," 96–97.

tion activities are revealed to be small and still incomplete, the window for the adversary is open widest to act preemptively quickly and destroy the program before the capability is acquired. Fledgling nuclear weapons programs in China and Iraq created very strong incentives for the United States and Israel to undertake preemptive strikes against these facilities. In the Iraqi case, such a strike was carried out. In the Chinese case, recently declassified documents show that the United States, despite claims to the contrary, seriously considered a preemptive attack against Chinese nuclear facilities, including intelligence-gathering, contingency planning for air attacks, and discussions with the Soviets.[51]

If the DPRK claims that their nuclear weapons program is embedded in a defensive existential deterrent doctrine, this is effectively an oxymoron. If the motive is defensive, then nuclear proliferation actually makes Pyongyang less secure. Given Pyongyang's long-held fears of a U.S. attack, proliferation raises the likelihood of U.S. preemptive attack.[52]

Nuclear Denial Strategy

The contradiction in the existential deterrent logic requires one to look for alternative strategies in which DPRK nuclear weaponization might be embedded. One possibility that can never be ruled out given past DPRK aggression is nuclear weapons as part of a war-fighting strategy that seeks to deny the United States access to the peninsula. War game scenarios have posited, for example, an all-out DPRK surprise attack on the ROK that attempts to take advantage of an initial indecision by the United States and creates chaos among the South to "liberate" the fatherland.[53] Primary instruments of attack would include heavy artillery barrages destroying U.S.–ROK forward defenses that would hurt and weaken morale among South Korean soldiers. During this frontal barrage, DPRK special operation forces would infiltrate key civilian and military communication and transportation centers from the rear. An integral part of the offensive is to create panic and chaos in Seoul and other major cities, giving rise to refugees and road congestion, which would create maneuverability nightmares for U.S. and ROK forces responding to the attacks. The strategy also banks on a period of political hesitation in the United States with regard

---

[51] William Burr and Jeffrey Richelson, "Whether to 'Strangle the Baby in the Cradle': The United States and the Chinese Nuclear Program, 1960–64," *International Security* 25 (Winter 2000/01): 54–99; Gordon Chang, "JFK, China, and the Bomb," *Journal of American History* 74 (March 1988): 1289–1310; and McGeorge Bundy, *Danger and Survival: Choices about the Bomb in the First Fifty Years* (New York: Vintage, 1990).

[52] This argument in part hinges on the degree of risk acceptance in the North. If the DPRK perceives itself in the domain of losses, it might be more risk-acceptant with regard to proliferating and therefore willing to accept a period of high instability and increased threat of U.S. attack to reach an existential deterrent capability. For this line of inquiry, see Victor D. Cha, "Engaging North Korea Credibly," *Survival* 42 (Summer 2000): 136–55; and Cha, "Engagement and Preventive Defense."

[53] Bermudez and Richardson, "The North Korean View," 6.

to taking casualties in a bloody ground war, and ultimately it aims for defeat of the U.S.–ROK Combined Forces Command (CFC) within seven days.[54]

Nuclear weapons and WMD-armed missiles would play a critical denial role to U.S. reinforcement operations in such a war strategy. In the initial and critical stages of the war, the primary concern for the United States is to have its forces on the peninsula capable of absorbing the DPRK invasion long enough so it can fly in reinforcements for the counter-offensive. For the DPRK, the primary obstacle in the battle plan for invasion is logistics. Given the KPA's inability to sustain ample supply lines from north of the demilitarized zone for any protracted period of time, the strategy requires a quick victory over Seoul from which the advancing KPA forces can then replenish supply lines. In order to avoid a protracted battle over Seoul, the DPRK must disrupt and delay the U.S. ability to flow reinforcements to the peninsula through Okinawa. This could be accomplished through a two-pronged denial strategy of persistent chemical and biological attacks on ports and logistic nodes in South Korea to delay U.S. reinforcements; and/or hold Tokyo or other major population centers in Japan as nuclear hostage to complicate, delay, and ideally deter the U.S. response. The latter could be accomplished either through U.S. indecision or by the Japanese government not granting American access to its bases for Korean defense. It is important to note that the feasibility of the strategy rests not on U.S. and Japanese capitulation but on the allies' indecision for a long enough period of time for KPA forces to overtake Seoul. Once the DPRK holds Seoul, it then exercises considerable leverage. It might choose to prosecute the war further south to take the entire peninsula, which is highly unlikely. Or it might cease hostilities and seek to negotiate from a position of strength given the new status quo post bellum. The introduction of the nuclear component is therefore critical not as part of a defensive existential deterrent doctrine, but an offensive denial strategy.

Ideology and the KPA

Evidence of a nuclear denial strategy is, of course, hard to come by. From a tactical level, if the DPRK were offensively-intended, they would follow the denial strategy secretly while publicly explaining their proliferation as deterrence-based. In addition, if they were truly defensively motivated, then the de-

---

[54] For other details, see Tom Morgan, "Military and Political Alternatives for Reducing Threats" (paper presented at the International Conference on Emerging Threats, Force Structures and the Role of Air Power in Korea, sponsored by RAND and Yonsei University, Seoul, 12 June 1999); and Stephen Bradner, "North Korea's Strategy" in Sokolski, *Planning*. For earlier background on DPRK offensive strategies, see Jong-Chun Baek, "North Korea's Military Capabilities" in Jae Kyu Park, Byung Chul Koh, and Tae-Hwan Kwak, eds., *The Foreign Relations of North Korea* (Boulder, CO: Westview, 1987), 81–105; U.S. Central Intelligence Agency, *Korea: The Economic Race Between the North and South* (Washington, DC: U.S. Government Printing Office, 1978); and Ralph Clough, *Deterrence and Defense in Korea: The Role of US Forces* (Washington, DC: Brookings, 1976).

nial strategy would be irrelevant. In this sense, the absence of explicit evidence of a denial strategy does not necessarily preclude its existence. Hence two alternative avenues of inquiry might be useful. The first is to induce from DPRK propaganda and ideology any evidence of a denial strategy. The second is to observe the extent to which KPA force structure has changed over time. The latter, in particular, might offer clues as to whether DPRK priorities with scarce resources have been focused on defense or offense modernization, which could then offer some insight on the likelihood of a denial strategy.

With regard to ideology and propaganda, as a recent study by General John Tilleli (former head of U.S. forces in Korea) and Major Susan Bryant points out, DPRK rhetoric, even in the face of Kim Dae Jung's sunshine policy and its hapless post-cold war situation, has not formally renounced its intention to reunify the peninsula.[55] Instead, the North has made countless statements about the destruction it would wreak on Seoul if provoked. But perhaps more important as evidence of a denial strategy than this inflammatory rhetoric (which has all but lost its meaning given its persistent use) is the extent to which DPRK ideology is fully accepting of a major bloody conflict as the final outcome of the Korea problem. Kim Il Sung and Kim Jong Il fully accept the tenets of Leninism, which posit violent conflict as a necessary stage for universal communization and wholly reject in the long term any notions of peaceful coexistence with capitalism.[56] The first vice minister of the People's Armed Forces reinforced such a view, stating that "the question is not if there will be another war on the Korean peninsula, but when."[57] Any overt denial strategy would require that the DPRK regime accept without question the untold numbers of casualties that would result on both sides of the demilitarized zone as well as in Japan. Though not confirming evidence, this fundamental assumption of DPRK ideology is not inconsistent with a denial strategy.

With regard to the KPA, anyone who has studied the security balance on the peninsula is familiar with the current profile of the DPRK military: 1.1 million man army, 3,500 tanks, 2,500 armored personnel carriers, 10,600 artillery guns, 2,600 multiple rocket launchers, and 500+ combat aircraft, all forward-deployed near the demilitarized zone. But interesting insights can be drawn from a longitudinal analysis of the evolution and devolution of these forces. From the end of the Korean war until about the mid-1970s, the KPA threat was largely infantry and artillery-based. Heavy fixed artillery was the mainstay of the force (a lesson of the war as artillery dominated) and KPA forces, while larger than during the Korean War, were still only a fraction (400,000) of the

[55] John H. Tilelli and Susan Bryant, *Northeast Asian Regional Security: Keeping the Calm* (Arlington, VA: Association of the United States Army, 2002), 13.
[56] Kim Il-Sung, *For the Independent and Peaceful Reunification of Korea* (New York: Independent Publishers, 1975), 132 as cited in Downs, "Discerning North Korean Intentions," 88–89.
[57] Samuel S. Kim, "Images and Realities of Korean Unity: Whither Inter-Korean Relations?" (paper presented at the "Republic of Korea After 50 Years" conference, Georgetown University, Washington, DC, 2–4 October 1998), 12.

1.1 million benchmark associated with the threat today. Thus in spite of any aggressive intentions explicitly stated by the DPRK for "unification by force" (*songong t'ongil*), their capabilities dictated otherwise.

The KPA significantly improved their offensive capabilities from the 1980s. Not only did ground forces increase greatly (to 700,000 and then to 1.1 million), but the military also underwent significant mechanization (infantry, armor, and artillery forces). These mechanized units were reorganized from separate divisions into corps-level formations, which are more conducive for commanding a sustained offensive deep into the enemy's territory. This offensive modernization and reorganization was complemented by a significant movement of mechanized armored and artillery units southward to the extent that 70 percent of all combat forces are positioned south of Pyongyang, versus 40 percent in 1980. Although energy and food shortages in the 1990s have decreased the overall fighting capability of these forces, the specific capabilities that continue to be augmented do not elicit any sense of a reduced threat. The KPA has added thousands of long-range artillery tubes and substantially added to its special operations forces; the latter can wreak havoc on population centers in the South and the former can sustain in the range of 500,000 rounds of artillery per hour against CFC forces.

The northern side of the demilitarized zone shows no defensive fortifications equivalent to forward edge of battle area zones or concentric defense lines that are clearly observable on the southern side.[58] Although recent North Korean actions in 1999–2000 in response to the ROK's sunshine or engagement policy indicated some degree of political thaw on the peninsula, one cannot wholly rule out hypotheses on an offense-based DPRK war doctrine. As North Korean defector Hwang Jang-Yop stated, "North Korea still believes that it could conquer South Korea—should the Americans ever leave the peninsula. This withdrawal is one of Pyongyang's most important goals in all its international negotiations."[59] In sum, there are logical inconsistencies in the DPRK existential deterrent argument. There is no evidence that explicitly precludes a nuclear denial strategy, especially important given the methodological problems with confirmation through no evidence. The past decade has witnessed a steady and deliberate enhancement of offensive conventional capabilities. These facts render nuclear weaponization as part of an offensive denial strategy as a credible alternative proposition.

Policy Implication: If Denial, then Coercion

If the DPRK practices a denial strategy, then the implications for policy become clear. Engagement will neither reduce tensions on the peninsula nor con-

---

[58] For details, see Ministry of National Defense, *Defense White Paper 1999* (Seoul: Ministry of National Defense, 2000), chap. 3 (http://www.mnd.go.kr/mnden/emainindex.html), 4 January 2001; and Bradner, "North Korea's Strategy."

[59] "Running Against History: Defector Sees Kim's Regime as Increasingly Brittle," *Far Eastern Economic Review*, 15 October 1998, 10–11.

vince the North to give up its proliferation threat. On the contrary, all of Pyongyang's diplomatic contacts and smile diplomacy in 2000–2001 reflect changes in tactics to gain the food and economic aid necessary to keep the regime afloat, but the DPRK's intentions remain fundamentally revisionist. Through strategic deception, Kim Jong Il seeks to lull the West into a false sense of confidence in engagement as the regime secretly continues to improve its WMD capabilities. Any policy other than coercion and/or isolation and robust deterrence will be interpreted as weakness by the North and will buy time for the regime to fulfill its ultimate objective of subverting liberal-democratic South Korea.

Badges?

A third and final set of propositions about DPRK nuclear weaponization has to do with factors not explicitly related to military rationales. This hypothesis derives from the view that small- and medium-scale proliferation cases are the result of internal bureaucratic processes or prestige/status motivations rather than external threats. As Scott Sagan has argued, states acquire nuclear weapons not only to balance against external threats but also for their symbolic power.[60] For many countries in Asia, nuclear weapons and ballistic missiles are today what armies were in the postcolonial era. They serve as marks of modernity and power. Asia is rich with nationalisms growing out of history, colonial legacies, and economic growth. Inherent in this nationalism are aspirations to rise in the international prestige hierarchy and to be treated as a great or major power. Nuclear weapons and ballistic missiles have become an important indicator of this status. In extreme terms, these capabilities almost become like national airlines; countries seek to acquire them because of how they reflect on one's identity and level of development.[61]

Regarding bureaucratic rationales, in some countries the drive for nuclear weapons-related research over the years became the means by which a young, rising, civilian technocratic sector circumvents and displaces the old, corrupt, and inefficient military bureaucracy. This was especially the case in India, where the Atomic Energy Commission, Defense Research and Development Organization, and the Space Program formed a triumvirate of new influential technocratic bureaus that demand respect in Indian society and develop powerful interests in self-perpetuation.[62]

A degree of bureaucratic politics appears relevant in the DPRK case, but this was not central to initial decisions to proliferate.[63] Where nuclear weapons

---

[60] Sagan, "Why do States Build Nuclear Weapons?" 63–65.

[61] Eyre and Suchman, "Status, Norms and the Proliferation of Conventional Weapons"; and Paul Bracken, "Asia's Militaries and the New Nuclear Age," *Current History* 98 (December 1999): 415–421.

[62] George Perkovich, *India's Nuclear Bomb: The Impact of Global Proliferation* (Berkeley: University of California Press, 1999); and Bracken, "Asia's Militaries and the New Nuclear Age," 420.

[63] For critical and comprehensive analysis, see Mansourov, "The Origins, Evolution and Current Politics," 8–15.

may be most relevant to bureaucracies is in their reflection of the military's rise in all sectors of the North Korean state over the past two decades.[64] Since about 1980, the dominance of the party has given way to military-first politics and a garrison state in which virtually all the key positions of power are occupied by the military. This is evident not only in Kim Jong Il's rule from his position in the National Defense Commission (and not the Workers' Party of Korea [KWP]), but also the conspicuous absence of a party congress in over nineteen years.[65] In this sense, internal politics did not drive proliferation in North Korea, but proliferation may be reinforcing internal changes that are in motion.

The international prestige-hierarchy may have been relevant as a driver of proliferation, but not nearly as important as what the program meant for regime self-validation. As Sam Kim argues, nuclear weapons and ballistic missiles were symptomatic of a system trying to fulfill its *kangsong taeguk* (strong and prosperous power) vision, but being blocked in the economic vein and trying to compensate for this in the military.[66] At best, though, these arguments complement but do not supplant the two primary security rationales. If one surveys all the cases of proliferation in the twentieth century (first or second nuclear age), the primary driver of proliferation in the end is security, which takes us back to the deterrence or denial strategies as the primary drivers.[67]

The final observation regards nuclear and missile proliferation and DPRK bargaining leverage. A byproduct of proliferation has been a coercive bargaining strategy adopted by Pyongyang against its adversaries. Pyongyang's *modus operandi* is to undertake or threaten acts of belligerence that violate the peace and disrupt the status quo, usually highlighting some grievance the DPRK holds. This individual action is usually severe enough to raise concerns that if combined with other similar and subsequent actions, it might be the precursor to a larger conflict. At the same time, the individual violent act alone does not warrant all-out retaliation by the United States and ROK. Washington and Seoul are thus manipulated into the awkward position of wanting to punish the initial act but also wanting to avoid an unnecessary and costly escalation of conflict that might follow from such an action. The response that obtains is then to renegotiate a new status quo, coupled with a token verbal denouncement or sanction against the initial act. This has been the most frequent and consistently threatening behavior by the DPRK since the end of the cold war. It is a coercive bargaining strategy, backed by these capabilities, that seeks not to win militarily but to scare the other side into a new negotiation outcome better than the status

---

[64] This school of thought is separate from and inconsistent with the earlier deterrent school, which argued that the military is divorced from the chain of command on nuclear issues.

[65] Samuel S. Kim, "North Korea in 1999," *Asian Survey* 40 (January 2000): 1401–1413.

[66] Ibid., 1408.

[67] Goldstein, *Security and Deterrence*. The exceptions to this rule are countries that "inherit" nuclear weapons (for example, Ukraine), but even in this case as well as other cases of denuclearization (South Africa), the primary rationale for giving up the capability is an amelioration of security threats.

quo ex ante.[68] It is important to note that this bargaining strategy is not a cause of proliferation but a product of it. In other words, Pyongyang's nuclear weaponization may have inadvertently given rise to this pattern of behavior, but weaponization was not sought specifically for this purpose.

THE DPRK AS EVIL OR ENGAGING? A THREE-STEP FRAMEWORK

The debate on the security and foreign policy of the DPRK has taken place in three concentric circles. At the innermost ring were debates and speculation surrounding the regime's survivability at the end of the cold war. This literature was in vogue largely because it dealt with the question that preceded all others about the DPRK in the early 1990s: Could the regime survive for very long?[69] At the next level, particularly after the DPRK's unexpected resilience, were policy-oriented debates about whether to engage or contain North Korea.[70] The third circle of literature focused on negotiating behavior. This body of work emerged out of the West's first substantive interaction or engagement with North Korea in the early 1990s, culminating initially with the 1994 Agreed Framework.[71] Each of these debates was discrete, dealing with a different aspect of North Korea security and foreign policy; at the same time they were interconnected, for one set of works often derived from the success or failures of the previous body of work.

In this article, I have offered a fourth circle of security debate for understanding North Korea. The first circle of debates on DPRK regime survival in the early 1990s was empirically premature and conceptually ill-conceived, neglectful of an understanding and appreciation of the DPRK system's resiliency despite acute hardship. The second and third circles provided illuminating lenses through which to view North Korea. However, as phase one of the antiterrorism war in Afghanistan subsides, questions about implementation of the Agreed Framework surface. Debates about engagement face the United States,

---

[68] For the development of this argument, see Cha, "Engagement and Preventive Defense."

[69] These works speculated on how (not whether) the regime would collapse: by "hard" landing (sudden implosion), by "soft" landing (gradual decline and absorption by South Korea), or by "explosion" (last-gasp spasm of violence). Representative works include Byung-Joon Ahn, "The Man who Would be Kim," *Foreign Affairs* 73 (November/December 1994): 94–108; Choong-Nam Kim, "The Uncertain Future of North Korea: Soft Landing or Crash Landing?" *Korea and World Affairs* 20 (Winter 1996): 623–636; Marcus Noland, "Why North Korea Will Muddle Through," *Foreign Affairs* 76 (July/August 1997): 105–118; Green, "North Korea Regime Crisis"; Eberstadt, *The End of North Korea*; Bruce Cumings, "Feeding the North Korea Myth," *The Nation*, 29 September 1997, 22–24; Robert Scalapino, "North Korea at a Crossroads," *Hoover Essays in Public Policy* No. 73 (Hoover Institution: Stanford University, 1997); and Aidan Foster-Carter, *Korea's Coming Reunification: Another East Asian Superpower?* Economist Intelligence Unit, Special Report no. M212 (London: Economist Intelligence Unit, 1992).

[70] See notes 5 and 6 for literature on this topic.

[71] Scott Snyder, *North Korea Negotiating Behavior* (Washington, DC: U.S. Institute of Peace, 1999); and Chuck Downs, *Over the Line* (Washington, DC: AEI Press, 1999).

South Korean, and Japanese governments, and none of these previous analyses get at the heart of the issue for policy: Upon what assumptions about the DPRK threat should policy be based?

The common perception of North Korean nuclear weaponization is one of unadulterated threat. However, I have argued that understanding the strategic doctrine in which these capabilities are sought offers a true assessment of the nature of the threat. Only then can we define the appropriate policy. Trying to locate inductively the intentions behind one of the blackest of boxes in the world today is nearly impossible, given the paucity of evidence. As an imperfect substitute, this article deduces a three-step model to explain the context and intentions behind DPRK nuclear weaponization. This model provides a framework by which to interpret any new evidence that becomes available.

If evidence emerges about the DPRK that confirms the existential deterrent (shields) hypothesis, then the threat is not nearly as bad as we believe. Security dilemmas can be averted through engagement. Moreover, the potential for denuclearization is real, provided that the North's survival can be guaranteed. If evidence does not support this view, then the next step is to discern whether the evidence validates a prestige-based or badges argument for DPRK weaponization. If so, then the threat is resolvable if status incentives on the part of Pyongyang can be satisfied. This could be accomplished through engagement, particularly in the economic arena such that the DPRK could, as Sam Kim argues, validate its state identity through economic rather than military avenues.[72] The third and most worrying outcome is if evidence surfaces confirming the denial strategy (swords hypothesis). In this case, not only is the threat real (and the regime "evil" in Bush's axis of evil verbiage), but nuclear rollback is highly unlikely, because DPRK intentions are zero-sum and aggressive. Engagement, though well-intentioned, will not work.[73] At best, the policy will build consensus among the United States and its allies that once Pyongyang reveals it true intentions, more coercive measures might be required.*

---

[72] Kim, "North Korea in 1999," 1408.

[73] For elaboration on this viewpoint, see Victor D. Cha, "Korea's Place in the Axis," *Foreign Affairs* 81 (May-June 2002).

* The author thanks Samuel Kim, Jeong-Ho Roh, Scott Snyder, David Steinberg, Henry Sokolski, and the late Joe Lepgold for comments on previous drafts.

U.S. Policy Toward Iraq Since Desert Storm

DANIEL BYMAN

The end of the Persian Gulf War on 28 February 1991 was supposed to have ended the conflict between Iraq and the U.S.–led coalition. Yet Desert Storm was only the beginning. In the years following the Gulf War, the United States and its allies repeatedly used limited force against Iraq, maintained tight sanctions, conducted intrusive inspections of Iraq's weapons of mass destruction (WMD) and missile programs, supported anti-Saddam oppositionists, and otherwise strove to isolate and weaken Baghdad. Ten years after the war ended, a resolution of the conflict seems further away than ever. Since December 1998, the United States and Britain have conducted a sustained, if limited, bombing effort against Iraqi targets.

This massive effort carries a price. Critics claim that the Iraqi people, not the regime, bear the brunt of U.S. efforts to punish Iraq. Contingency operations in the gulf cost roughly $1 billion a year, in addition to the money necessary for overall force posture in the region.[1] The large military presence in the gulf and the need to carry out frequent military strikes have hindered U.S. military preparedness and hurt the morale of U.S. forces.[2] U.S. policy and the associated military presence also anger Islamists and other anti–U.S. radicals, who have at times engaged in terrorist attacks against U.S. soldiers both in and outside the region.

U.S. policy toward Iraq is a regular bone of contention in Washington and abroad. In August 1999, a bipartisan group of members of Congress formally

---

[1] http://www.fas.org/man/dod-101/ops.iraq_orbat.htm [Accessed 3 March 2000].
[2] Paul K. White, *Crises after the Storm: An Appraisal of U.S. Air Operations in Iraq since the Persian Gulf War* (Washington, DC: The Washington Institute for Near East Policy, 1999), 85.

DANIEL BYMAN is the research director of RAND's Center for Middle East Public Policy. His most recent publications include *Confronting Iraq: U.S. Policy and the Use of Force Since the Gulf War* (co-authored with Matthew Waxman) and *Political Violence and Stability in the States of the Northern Persian Gulf* (co-authored with Jerrold Green).

noted in a letter to the president their "dismay over the continued drift in U.S. policy toward Iraq."[3] Dissent is even more pronounced abroad. The gulf states and Turkey in general support a hard line against Iraq, but have at times criticized or opposed key elements of U.S. policy, such as sanctions or military strikes. Among the major powers, only Britain is solidly behind the United States. France, Russia, and China have at times harshly criticized U.S. policy, claiming that it is both ineffective and unfair.

This article seeks to provide a comprehensive evaluation of U.S. policy toward Iraq since the end of Desert Storm. What are U.S. objectives? What constraints inhibit U.S. policy? How effective are the means used to achieve these goals? What obstacles may hinder success in the years to come?

I argue that much of the criticism of U.S. policy toward Iraq is overstated and fails to appreciate many of the accomplishments of the Bush and Clinton administrations and their allies.[4] Most of the criticisms focus on one policy instrument, ignoring how that instrument works in combination with other elements. Thus, sanctions, inspections, or other instruments are denounced as failures even though they contribute in a variety of ways to overall U.S. objectives. Moreover, many assessments miss the range of goals the United States has in the region. Pundits regularly describe U.S. policy as a failure due to Saddam Hussein's survival, even though Iraq since 1991 has not successfully menaced its neighbors—a signal achievement. The United States has accomplished the

---

[3] As quoted in Robin Wright, "U.S. Nearing Key Juncture in Iraq Policy," *Los Angles Times*, 29 August 1999. Other senior lawmakers noted their concern over "signs of a reduced priority in US policy toward Iraq." As quoted in Jonathan S. Landay, "Is Iraq Building Weapons Again?" *Christian Science Monitor*, 30 August 1999.

[4] What works that exist on U.S. policy toward Iraq either fall into the category of punditry or focus only on an aspect of U.S. policy. Tim Trevan provides valuable insights into weapons inspections in *Saddam's Secrets: The Hunt for Iraq's Hidden Weapons* (London: HarperCollins, 1999). On inspections, see also Scott Ritter, *Endgame: Solving the Iraq Problem Once and for All* (New York: Simon and Schuster, 1999). F. Gregory Gause provides an incisive critique of sanctions policy in "Saddam's Unwatched Arsenal," *Foreign Affairs* 78 (May/June 1999): 54–65; see also John Mueller and Karl Mueller, "Sanctions of Mass Destruction," in ibid., 45–53. Works on the Iraqi opposition include Daniel Byman, Kenneth Pollack, and Gideon Rose, "The Rollback Fantasy," *Foreign Affairs* 78 (January/February 1999): 24–41; Daniel Byman, "Proceed with Caution: U.S. Support for the Iraqi Opposition," *The Washington Quarterly* 22 (Summer 1999): 23–37; and David Wurmser, *Tyranny's Ally* (Washington, DC: The AEI Press, 1999). An assessment of the use of force to coerce Saddam can be found in Daniel Byman, Kenneth Pollack, and Matthew Waxman, "Coercing Saddam Hussein: Lessons from the Past," *Survival* 40 (Autumn 1998): 127–152; and Michael Eisenstadt and Kenneth Pollack, "The Crisis with Iraq: Reviving the Military Option," *PolicyWatch* (Washington Institute for Near East Policy), no. 295, 22 January 1998. Probably the best work on Iraqi internal politics since Desert Storm is Amatzia Baram, *Building Toward Crises: Saddam Hussein's Strategy for Survival* (Washington, DC: Washington Institute for Near East Policy, 1998). Regis W. Matlak also provides a superb assessment. "Inside Saddam's Grip," *National Security Studies Quarterly* (Spring 1999), accessed at http://www.georgetown.edu/sfs/programs/nssp/nssq/Matlak.pdf (June 1999). A fine journalistic account is Andrew Cockburn and Patrick Cockburn, *Out of the Ashes: The Resurrection of Saddam Hussein* (New York: HarperCollins, 1999). An assessment of policy alternatives can be found in Patrick Clawson, ed., *Iraq Strategy Review* (Washington, DC: Washington Institute for Near East Policy, 1998).

most important task: keeping Saddam's Iraq contained (or "in the box," in Washington parlance). Because of the U.S. military presence, sanctions, and other measures, Saddam has not been able to attack his neighbors or other U.S. allies. Countering Iraq's WMD programs has met with less success, and the most ambitious objective—removing Saddam from power—appears far off today. The United States has made these limited gains without jeopardizing the stability of regional allies, another impressive accomplishment.

Several instruments have proven particularly effective. The use of force and the broader U.S. regional military presence have contributed to containment's success. Sanctions too have proved effective in containing Iraq, though they have not achieved more ambitious goals. The Iraqi opposition and weapons inspections have made more marginal contributions. For all of these instruments, however, their true contributions must be understood in the context of overall U.S. policy rather than in isolation.

Despite the generally positive U.S. record, considerable room for improvement remains. Perhaps most damning, much of the credit for the limited U.S. successes is due to Saddam's missteps rather than to skilled U.S. diplomacy and planning. Washington also wrongly emphasizes weapons inspections and other elements of the original containment regime despite their declining utility. The United States and its regional allies, which are vital to U.S. policy success, are often at odds over various policy instruments and their application, but U.S. domestic politics reduces policy makers' flexibility. Finally, the United States appears to lack a long-term plan for the region.

The remainder of this article has five parts. The first section describes U.S. goals since Desert Storm and notes how they have changed as the decade progressed. The second part examines constraints that have shaped U.S. goals and the means used to pursue them. Part three assesses the means used to meet these goals, noting what has worked and what has not. With this assessment in mind, section four reconsiders the overall question of whether U.S. policy in the gulf succeeded. Part five concludes by identifying several potential problems that could hinder success in the future.

U.S. OBJECTIVES

To understand whether U.S. policy toward Iraq has failed or succeeded, the most basic step is recognizing U.S. objectives. These include preventing any Iraqi regional aggression; stopping Iraq's nuclear, biological, and chemical and missile programs; and removing Saddam from power. A negative objective—preventing the spread of regional instability—has also guided U.S. actions. The relative priority of these goals shifted as the decade wore on, with concerns about Iraq's WMD programs and an emphasis on changing the regime in Baghdad rising in importance relative to the goals of containing Iraq and preserving regional stability. To meet these objectives, the United States relies on sanctions, weapons inspections, a large military presence, occasional military strikes, and the Iraqi opposition.

Containing Iraqi Aggression

Initial U.S. policy emphasized containing Iraq, preventing any aggression against Kuwait, other gulf states, and U.S. allies more generally.[5] Because Saddam's Iraq remained committed to regional domination despite its defeat in the Gulf War, the United States established a strong military presence in the region to deter, and if necessary defeat, any Iraqi aggression. To demonstrate its commitment, the United States has augmented its forces during crises and at times conducted military strikes. Another key element of containment is keeping Iraq's military forces—both conventional and unconventional—weak. Thus the United States and its allies, working through the United Nations, set limits on Iraqi oil sales and controlled how the money could be spent in order to prevent Iraq from rebuilding its forces.

Preventing a WMD Buildup

Although the conventional military threat Iraq poses remains an important concern, the United States is increasingly focused on Iraq's WMD programs. Before 1990, the world knew little of Baghdad's WMD efforts beyond the fact that Iraq had a proven chemical weapons capability. Moreover, strikes conducted as part of Operation Desert Storm were initially believed to have destroyed much of Iraq's WMD arsenal and capabilities. Information discovered following the Gulf War, however, indicated that Iraq was close to producing a nuclear weapon and had vast chemical weapons stores. After the defection of a key Iraqi regime official in 1995, it became clear that Saddam also had a vast biological weapons program. Military strikes during the war had only destroyed components of these massive programs.

Given Saddam's unrelenting hostility toward the United States and its allies in the region, both in the gulf and Israel, his possession of these weapons, which have the capacity to kill hundreds of thousands if properly delivered, alarmed Washington. Although the focus on WMD weapons began during the months preceding Desert Storm, the United States steadily elevated the WMD problem to near the top of its concerns, with President Bill Clinton declaring in 1998 that their proliferation "constitutes an unusual and extraordinary threat to the national security, foreign policy, and economy of the United States."[6] In various

---

[5] See Zalmay Khalilzad, "The United States and the Persian Gulf: Preventing Regional Hegemony," *Survival* 37 (Summer 1995): 95–120.

[6] As cited in Gerald Steinberg, "U.S. Responses to the Proliferation of Weapons of Mass Destruction in the Middle East," *Middle East Review of International Affairs* 2 (September 1998), electronic version.

crises after 1997, administration spokespeople emphasized Iraq's WMD programs as their justification for confrontation.

Like containment, preventing a WMD buildup requires several different policy instruments. Robust sanctions and import restrictions ensure that Iraq cannot acquire foreign technology and assistance for its WMD programs. Keeping the inspections and monitoring regime strong, however, requires agreement among the major powers at the United Nations, particularly those with strong defense industrial bases. Washington also has used military force to degrade Iraq's WMD capabilities, which in turn requires regional states to provide basing and access for U.S. forces.

Toppling Saddam's Regime

U.S. policy is focused on Saddam himself as well as the broader threat that a powerful Iraq poses to the region. U.S. leaders see Saddam as reckless, vengeful, and bloody—dangerous traits for a leader pursuing WMD weapons whose country is astride much of the world's oil supplies. At the end of the Gulf War, allied leaders assumed that the combination of military defeat and internal unrest would lead to Saddam's fall. To this end, the United States has used a range of instruments to remove Saddam from power. For many years after the Gulf War, Washington tried to foment a coup in Baghdad. The United States also used military strikes to discredit Saddam and to weaken regime protection forces. Policy makers also hoped that sanctions would foster popular and elite unrest, further destabilizing the regime.

In recent years, the most important instrument for removing Saddam has been the Iraqi opposition. According to its rhetoric at least, the Clinton administration is committed to working with the Iraqi opposition to topple the regime, even as it continues to contain Iraq. In November 1998, President Bill Clinton embraced the opposition, promising to work for "a new government" in Baghdad. Caution at home and opposition from major powers and allies in the region have led Washington to avoid the direct involvement of U.S. ground troops or aid to the Iraqi opposition that would require a major U.S. commitment. A policy more reliant on the Iraqi opposition would depend heavily on regional allies, who would be needed to provide bases, training, and support for opposition fighters.

Preserving Regional Stability

The United States has sought to preserve regional stability even as it pursued ambitious objectives regarding Iraq. Most importantly, the United States feared that the U.S. presence and actions necessary to contain Iraq or overthrow Saddam might decrease stability in regional allies. Sanctions are unpopular, as were many military strikes. In response, regional governments have at times criticized U.S. policy, failed to provide necessary support, or otherwise distanced themselves from Washington. Over time, U.S. policy makers have recognized a tension between the use of force and the stability of U.S. allies. Large force increases and the regular use of force against the Iraqi regime have angered many radicals in the region, threatening the stability of U.S. allies and the lives of U.S. personnel. The large and highly visible U.S. regional military presence proved a magnet for critics of gulf regimes, particularly in Saudi Arabia. Terrorist attacks against U.S. servicemen that resulted in the deaths of five Americans in 1995, nineteen in 1996, and seventeen in an attack on a U.S. naval vessel in 2000 highlighted the lethal nature of this threat. In response, Washington often limited the use of force and the scope and visibility of the U.S. presence. For example, the United States has restricted the personal leave of its forces within Saudi Arabia, relocated U.S. forces far from populated areas, and avoided using planes based in Saudi Arabia to conduct direct strikes on Iraq.

The United States has also sought to keep Iraq itself stable. There is little love lost among Iraq's tribal confederations, religious communities, and ethnic groups. Iraqi national identity is weak in comparison to religious or tribal identity, and the collapse of the center could lead to complete disintegration of the state. Moreover, Saddam Hussein has devastated Iraqi civil society, destroying any independent organization and rending ties among citizens. If Saddam falls, as General Anthony Zinni, former commander of the U.S. Central Command, has testified, dozens of opposition groups might compete for power, destabilizing Iraq.[7]

The United States has also tried to prevent radical Shiah from dominating a post-Saddam Iraq. The United States has long worried that a growth in Shiah influence would lead Iraq to tilt toward Iran, support other Shiites abroad, or both. Regional allies are especially concerned about the growth of Shiah influence in Iraq. Saudi Arabia and other gulf states have long feared Iran's revolutionary government, seeing it as seeking to extend its influence over the region, particularly in Shiite-populated areas such as Bahrain, Kuwait, and Saudi Arabia's Eastern Province.

Iran, however, is not likely to dominate a Shiah led Iraq, and there is little reason to think a Shiah regime would be particularly hostile to the United States or its allies. Ethnic divisions between Iraqi Arabs and Persians, and Iran's economic problems, also diminish Iraqi Shiah ardor for Teheran's leadership. Nor have Iraqi Shiites shown a penchant for supporting radicals overseas.

Nevertheless, as a result of these fears, policy makers have hesitated to support efforts that might destabilize Iraq or lead to increased Shiah influence. In general, Washington has avoided policies that might contribute to an Iraqi collapse. It hesitated to support popular resistance to Saddam in the immediate aftermath of Desert Storm. In addition, for most of the 1990s, the United States has preferred a coup as a means of regime change, as this would be more likely to leave a strong government in power than would other methods.

[7] "Commander Opposes White House Strategy to Topple Saddam." *Associated Press*, 28 January 1999.

Constraints On The United States

The United States does not have a free hand to pursue the above objectives. In particular, three concerns have complicated the application of force or otherwise limited U.S. options: a desire to preserve the anti-Iraq international alliance; public and allied concerns over Iraqi suffering; and domestic pressure opposed to any U.S. concessions with regard to Iraq. These three constraints have shaped both U.S. objectives and the means chosen to pursue them.

The United States seeks to preserve the alliance against Iraq forged during the Gulf War. Several core elements of containment and countering Iraqi WMD, particularly sanctions and UN inspections, depended on international support. Without the support of other major powers, sanctions would have little or no impact. UN inspections also require the backing of the Security Council. Furthermore, Washington believes that international support increases the legitimacy of U.S. policy in general, helping sustain the backing of key regional states such as Saudi Arabia and Turkey.

Maintaining an international alliance, however, places severe limits on U.S. freedom of action. With the exception of Britain, allies have tended to be far more skeptical of the need to use force against Iraq. U.S. allies have also been more critical of the humanitarian impact of sanctions, and several states seek renewed commercial ties. Since 1997, China, France, and particularly Russia have also expressed their opposition to a robust inspections regime. Washington has often softened its policy toward Iraq for fear of jeopardizing the anti-Iraq alliance.

The United States and its allies have taken steps to protect Iraqi Shiites and Kurds from the depredations of Saddam's regime, but these steps are limited and evince a weak commitment to humanitarian objectives. Washington backed UN Security Council Resolution 688, which demanded that Iraq respect the human rights of its communities, and has been enforcing a no-fly zone in northern Iraq (and later in southern Iraq) in part to protect Iraq's communities. Despite these diplomatic efforts, Washington has avoided any formal commitment to either the Kurds or to the Shiites and avoided direct military support. In both cases, Washington waited until an outcry in U.S. and international public opinion before acting.

The United States has also sought to limit the impact of economic sanctions in response to criticism along humanitarian lines. After pressure arose on humanitarian grounds over sanctions, Washington backed UN Security Council Resolution 986, which allowed Iraq to sell oil to buy food, medicine, and other humanitarian items.

U.S. ambivalence stems from both ideological and practical concerns. Washington feels little sympathy towards the Kurds, who have few constituents among the U.S. people and who war with each other as much as with Baghdad. Washington is also concerned that any commitments will be difficult to back up should Saddam make a concerted effort to repress these groups.

Domestic concerns are a final constraint. Both the Bush and Clinton administrations successfully forged a solid domestic consensus opposed to Saddam Hussein. The price of this success, however, is severe limits on the U.S. ability to make concessions to Iraq. Any tactical retreats are subject to criticism in Congress and in the media as being soft on Iraq. Political leaders must respond to limited Iraqi provocations to sustain domestic support even when the effectiveness of the response is questionable and the U.S. attacks may alienate vital allies.

Policy Instruments

The United States employs five instruments to meet its objectives, subject to the constraints enumerated above, with varying degrees of emphasis: economic sanctions; weapons inspections; a strong regional military presence; limited military strikes; and support for the Iraqi opposition.

The Limited Benefits of Sanctions

Sanctions on Iraq have served a variety of purposes, helping to contain Iraq and limit its WMD arsenal. Sanctions have threatened at times to loosen Saddam's grip on power, but also have inadvertently strengthened his hand. Sanctions' humanitarian impact and popular hostility to sanctions in the region, however, have hindered U.S. relations with allies and regional stability more broadly.

Sanctions were initially imposed as a pressure tactic following the Iraqi invasion of Kuwait. Once the Gulf War ended, the rationale for maintaining sanctions was ostensibly shifted to Iraq's WMD programs, though the common perception at the time was that sanctions would continue as long as Saddam remained in power. Under UN Security Council Resolution 687, Iraq was to eliminate all its missile systems, WMD, and associated infrastructure in order for sanctions to be lifted.[8] Under restrictions that continue to this day, the United Nations must approve Iraq's purchases, thus reducing Baghdad's ability to obtain arms or technologies related to its WMD programs.[9]

Sanctions have been criticized, often quite severely, on humanitarian grounds. Dennis Halliday, the UN official who coordinated the oil-for-food program in Iraq, has contended that over 500,000 Iraqi children have died as a result of sanctions.[10] Writing in *Foreign Affairs*, F. Gregory Gause acidly argues

---

[8] UN Security Council Resolutions 661, 665, 666, and 678 set the stage for Resolution 687, approving and elaborating on the use of an economic or trade embargo and UN monitoring until Iraqi forces withdrew from Kuwait. Resolution 687 is the basis of postwar sanctions.

[9] Mueller and Mueller, "Sanctions of Mass Destruction," 49.

[10] Gause, "Getting It Backward on Iraq," 58; Mueller and Mueller, "Sanctions of Mass Destruction," 49. Robert A. Pape uses the figure of 567,000 in his critique of sanctions; see "Why Economic Sanctions *Still* Do Not Work," *International Security* 23 (Summer 1998): 76. For an excellent review of sanctions, see Richard Haass, ed., *Economic Sanctions and American Diplomacy* (Washington, DC: Brookings Institution, 1998).

that, "American policymakers need to recognize that the only 'box' into which sanctions put Iraqis is coffins."[11]

Critics of sanctions' humanitarian impact, however, often overlook the oil-for-food program, authorized under UN Security Council Resolution 986, and its countervailing humanitarian impact since it was enacted. Iraq is allowed to sell oil to purchase food, medicine, and other necessities. This arrangement offsets, in theory at least, much of the suffering of innocent Iraqis. Moreover, the oil-for-food arrangement suggests that most of the blame for the suffering under sanctions lies with the Iraqi regime. Under the oil-for-food arrangement, 15 percent of the oil revenue goes to fund humanitarian aid in the northern Kurdish region, which is administered by the UN, while the remainder of the country receives food and medicine distributed by the Baath.[12] Saddam long opposed Resolution 986, even though it decreased popular suffering. Moreover, areas in Iraq under UN control have seen an improvement in health statistics. Finally, the Iraqi regime has smuggled humanitarian goods out of Iraq, preferring black market profits to the well-being of the Iraqi people. The regime has often not purchased humanitarian items, despite the urging of UN officials.[13]

Even if the humanitarian impact of sanctions is overstated (or should be blamed on the Baath regime), the political damage stemming from U.S. support for sanctions has hurt the U.S. position in the Arab and Muslim world. Saddam has successfully attributed the collapse in the Iraqi standard of living to sanctions rather than to his regime's policies. By manipulating the access of the media and humanitarian organizations, the Iraqi regime has created a widespread perception throughout the world that thousands of Iraqi children are dying each month as a result of sanctions, ignoring the countervailing impact of the oil-for-food arrangement and the Baath regime's own responsibility. This perception has generated considerable opposition to sanctions, which are seen in the Arab world, including the people of many gulf allies, as cruel and senseless, a tool that starves innocent Iraqi children while doing little to Saddam. It has also contributed to regional, and to a lesser extent U.S. public, disaffection with U.S. policy.

Given this price, how effective are sanctions in their ostensible purpose—stopping Iraq's WMD programs? Clearly, they have not led Saddam to abandon his WMD programs. Citing UN Special Commission (UNSCOM) reports that Iraq still retains a good-sized WMD program, Gause argues that while sanctions do impede Iraq's WMD programs, they only do so to a limited ex-

---

[11] Gause, "Getting It Backward on Iraq," 56.

[12] Anthony Cordesman and Ahmed Hashim, *Iraq: Sanctions and Beyond* (Boulder, CO: Westview Press, 1997), 148.

[13] "Photos Show Iraq is Smuggling Oil in Violation of UN Sanctions," USIA Information File, 10 December 1999, available at http://www.usia.gov/cgi-bin/washfile/display.pl?p=/products/washfile/geog/nea&f=99121001.nne&t=/products/washfile/newsitem.shtml [Accessed on 13 December 1999].

tent.[14] Yet this criticism uses a false baseline that underestimates the benefits of sanctions. The true baseline should be Iraq's probable WMD status if sanctions had never been imposed. Most experts estimate that if sanctions were lifted Iraq would long ago have produced several nuclear weapons and an even more extensive biological weapons program.[15]

Are sanctions effective in weakening the regime? Saddam's regime controls Iraqi food stockpiles and uses them to bolster the regime's control.[16] Saddam has successfully exploited sanctions, using the money he controls through the black market to shore up support among elites, particularly in the military and the secret police. Like other despotic regimes before him, Saddam has shifted the burden of sanctions from his regime to the Iraqi people in general.[17]

Sanctions have, however, hurt the regime's standing somewhat at home, including with Saddam's core of supporters. The per capita income of Iraqis has plummeted, falling to less than one-fifth of the level Iraq achieved in the 1980s.[18] The Iraqi leader has not increased salaries sufficiently in response to inflation and otherwise let a range of possible supporters suffer. The impoverishment of Iraq has decreased support for the regime in general. Saddam has not been able to shift the entire burden of sanctions on his foes or on the powerless. His power base sees Iraqi prosperity as one measure of Saddam's rule. Thus, Saddam has had to take short-term measures, including accepting the oil-for-food deal, which he otherwise would have refused, in order to keep the economy afloat.[19] Sanctions have had a strong impact on the stability of Saddam's regime, but not enough to topple him.

Sanctions and import restrictions have had a considerable impact on Iraq's conventional readiness, thus augmenting containment. As with other uses of sanctions, they are often effective as a form of "brute force": rendering a target less capable of effective military action or other forms of resistance.[20] Sanctions proved quite devastating in Iraq, in part because of Iraq's dependence on oil, which must be sold on external markets to have value and can be easily monitored, and because it came on the heels of the Gulf War, which had devastated

---

[14] Gause, "Getting it Backward," 57.

[15] Michael Eisenstadt, *Like a Phoenix from the Ashes? The Future of Iraqi Military Power* (Washington, DC: The Washington Institute for Near East Policy, 1993), 39.

[16] Cordesman and Hashim, *Iraq*, 143.

[17] Gause, "Getting it Backward," 57. This problem of shifting the impact of sanctions from elites to the people in general is common. See Robert A Pape, "Why Economic Sanctions Do Not Work," *International Security* 22 (Fall 1997): 93.

[18] Cordesman and Hashim, *Iraq*, 150.

[19] Baram, *Building Toward Crises*, 61–78.

[20] Kimberly Ann Elliott, "The Sanctions Glass: Half Full or Completely Empty?" *International Security* 23 (Summer 1998): 53. The "brute force" vs. coercion distinction was first made by Thomas Schelling, who noted the importance of distinguishing between efforts relying on the threat of force to change behavior (coercion) and those that simply force an adversary to do what the coercer seeks (brute force). See *Arms and Influence* (New Haven: Yale University Press, 1966), 3.

some of Iraq's infrastructure. Iraq's economic strength, the foundation of its military power, suffered dramatically because of sanctions.[21]

This impact is best observed by looking at changes in Iraq's military capacity since the end of Desert Storm. During the 1980s, including after the Iran-Iraq war, Baghdad made massive purchases of a range of weapons systems and was among the world's top arms importers. After the imposition of sanctions, this flood slowed to a trickle. As Iraq depended on imports for logistical and supply assistance, as well as for complete systems, its military readiness and effectiveness has plummeted.[22] Efforts to meet shortfalls through smuggling and by increasing domestic production have largely failed.[23] Iraqi forces have not been able to conduct routine maintenance, let alone modernization. Iraq's military capacity is less than 20 percent of what it was in 1990.[24] Information on the progress of Iraq's WMD programs is limited, but an intuitive argument can be made that a regime under tight international scrutiny, with its dual-use exports being controlled, has made at best limited progress on these programs, particularly when compared to their rapid development in the 1980s.

Sanctions, however, also have had a negative effective on allied stability, particularly with regard to relations with Washington. In part because of the perceived devastating effects of sanctions but also because of a vestige of pan-Arab sentiment and hostility toward the West, many Arab governments are increasingly critical of the U.S.–led containment effort. Among U.S. allies, Egypt has led the effort to end containment. Saudi Arabia, Bahrain, and the United Arab Emirates (UAE) also have questioned sanctions, and when fearing a loss of popular support, they objected to certain U.S. military strikes against Iraq.

This overall finding on the impact of sanctions on Iraq offsets somewhat the generally negative impact of sanctions in general noted by most academic studies.[25] As Elizabeth Rogers has argued, setting up the removal of a regime's leadership as the measurement of success is too demanding a test.[26] Lesser, but still vital objectives have in part been met by sanctions. Moreover, sanctions' impact is best understood by examining their contribution to U.S. objectives in combination with other instruments. Sanctions' ostensible purpose is tied to putting pressure on Iraq because of its WMD programs and is linked to the removal of the Iraqi regime—two goals that have met with limited or no suc-

---

[21] Immediately after sanctions were imposed, Iraqi GNP fell by more than 50 percent and Iraq's currency plummeted. Elizabeth S. Rogers, "Using Economic Sanctions to Control Regional Conflicts," *Security Studies* (Summer 1996): 60.

[22] Cordesman and Hashim, *Iraq*, 225.

[23] Ibid., 227–231.

[24] Anthony Cordesman, "Hearings on the Current Situation in Iraq" Testimony before the U.S. Senate Armed Services Committee, September 1996.

[25] See T. Clifton Morgan and Valerie L. Schwebach, "Fools Suffer Gladly: The Use of Economic Sanctions in International Crises," *International Studies Quarterly* 41 (Spring 1997): 27–50.

[26] Rogers, "Using Economic Sanctions," 61.

cess, respectively. Pressure from sanctions, however, led Saddam to accept weapons inspections in the first place. If weapons inspectors enjoyed any successes (and clearly they did), then sanctions deserve at least some of the credit.[27] Sanctions also serve a brute-force purpose. They augmented containment, hindering Iraq's ability to acquire weapons and technology that can help it build up both its conventional and unconventional forces.

WMD Inspections

On 4 April 1991, the United Nations adopted Resolution 687, which required the destruction of Iraq's WMD programs as a condition for ending sanctions. Iraq was to declare its illegal weapons immediately and to destroy them within a year. The UNSCOM on Iraq was created to catalog Iraq's WMD arsenal and supervise its destruction. In the years that followed, inspections have helped reduce Iraq's WMD arsenal by uncovering and destroying a range of weapons systems, stockpiles, and production equipment. Inspections, however, did little to solve the long-term problem of Iraqi WMD and at times hindered the effective use of force against Iraq.[28]

UNSCOM's task proved to be enormously difficult. Saddam refused to take UNSCOM seriously and neither declared his WMD arsenal nor cooperated in its destruction. He reportedly told his advisers, "The Special Commission is a temporary measure. We will fool them and we will bribe them and the matter will be over in a few months."[29] From the start, Saddam blocked the inspectors' access, lied to them about the extent or even existence of various WMD programs, and otherwise made a mockery of the process.

As the inspections dragged on, Saddam successfully forced concessions to the inspections regime that greatly hindered its effectiveness. In 1997, Iraq declared several sites to be "presidential" sites and thus off limits to inspectors, even though these sites included over 1,000 buildings and storage sites. In a fuzzily-worded Memorandum of Understanding between UN Secretary General Kofi Annan and Iraqi Deputy Prime Minister Tariq Aziz signed on 23 February 1998, the United Nations agreed to respect Iraq's sovereignty and territorial integrity and legitimate concerns related to dignity, making particular reference to presidential sites. By implication, Annan agreed that the inspectors would limit their activities.[30]

In addition to gaining the complicity of officials at the United Nations, Iraq has also gained the tacit and at times overt support of several major powers. France, Russia, and China all became highly critical of both inspections and

[27] Ibid.," 60.
[28] For a review, see Daniel Byman, "'A Farewell to Arms Control," *Foreign Affairs* 79 (January/February 2000).
[29] Cockburn and Cockburn, *Out of the Ashes: The Resurrection of Saddam Hussein*, 96.
[30] See "Interview: Richard Butler," *Talk* (September 1999), electronic version, accessed October 1999.

sanctions. After UNSCOM issued reports citing Iraqi noncompliance, these powers called for the end of sanctions and criticized UNSCOM rather than demand that Iraq respect the Security Council's previous resolutions. In 1997 and much of 1998, the United States did not conduct military strikes to back up UNSCOM, for fear of losing the international consensus behind its actions.[31]

Rather implausibly, Iraq insists that its WMD programs are terminated and demands an end to sanctions as a result. In reality, Iraq's WMD programs may have continued even as inspections went on, and Iraq's efforts probably increased once inspectors' wings were clipped, though information is extremely scarce. A White House report to Congress notes that, "Saddam Hussein has shown no hesitation in developing WMD in the past, and it is prudent to assume that he is still intent on such development."[32] Press reporting indicates that Iraq may also be investigating new types of chemical agents and pursuing components for nuclear weapons.[33]

Despite these formidable challenges, UNSCOM made some progress on identifying and then destroying elements of Iraq's WMD and missile arsenal. UNSCOM (along with the International Atomic Energy Association [IAEA]) has overseen the destruction of dozens of long-range missiles and missile warheads; tens of thousands of chemical munitions and 690 tonnes of chemical weapons agent; a biological weapons production facility; and nuclear weapons production facilities.[34]

Equally important, when the inspectors had relatively free access throughout Iraq, their presence and vigilance made it more difficult for Iraq to continue work on its WMD programs. Although such judgments are difficult counterfactuals, it is plausible that if left to its own devices Iraq could have developed several operable nuclear weapons as well as a more extensive biological and missile program.[35] Thus, as with sanctions, the baseline for success should be comparing what Iraq's WMD programs would have been without inspections rather than simply judging it by the amount of material destroyed or the continued existence of Iraq's programs.

Even when the inspections regime was going full bore, however, its effectiveness was limited. Finding hidden weapons in a vast area is exceptionally difficult, particularly for biological weapons, which require a relatively limited infrastructure and can be easily concealed as legitimate medical or research facilities. The defection of Wafiq al-Samarrai, the former chief of Iraqi military intelligence, led to revelations that Iraq had manufactured and loaded the le-

---

[31] Ibid.

[32] Landay, "Is Iraq Building Weapons Again?"

[33] Richard Z. Chesnoff, "Bad Chemistry," *U.S. News and World Report*, 25 October 1999 (electronic version); Gary Milhollin, "Saddam's Nuclear Shopping Spree," *The New Yorker*, 13 December 1999, 44.

[34] From UNSCOM web-site, http://www.un.org/Depts/unscom/achievement.htm [Accessed 2 March 1999].

[35] Eisenstadt, *Like a Phoenix*, 39.

thal chemical agent VX—a surprise to UNSCOM.[36] Similarly, despite four years of intrusive inspections, the remarkable extent of Iraq's biological weapons program only became clear after the defection in 1995 of Hussein Kamel al-Majid, who headed Iraq's WMD programs. Only after this defection did Iraq admit that it had a large biological weapons program and, even more frightening, that it had weaponized some agents.

Military Presence

The U.S. military presence—as opposed to the actual use of military force—has helped in the containment of Iraq but carries a price in allied stability. After the end of the Gulf War, Washington signed a series of access agreements, sold large quantities of arms to its gulf allies, and arranged for the presence of substantial U.S. forces in the region. Since the end of the Gulf War, the total number of U.S. military personnel present both on the ground and at sea at any one time has fluctuated between 5,000 and 38,000, depending on the regional security environment and on rotation schedules. Troops in the region regularly include about 2,500 soldiers, 8,000 sailors and Marines, and another 1,000 staff from joint headquarters and joint units. In addition, about 200 combatant and direct support aircraft are deployed to the region to conduct Operations Northern Watch and Southern Watch—the no-fly zones over northern and southern Iraq—along with their crews and support staff. Saudi Arabia and Turkey are key states for air bases, but Bahrain, Kuwait, Qatar, and the United Arab Emirates also play an important role.[37]

The most significant augmentation of U.S. forces in response to Iraqi defiance was in October 1994, when intelligence analysts discovered that Iraq was deploying two Republican Guard armored divisions near the Iraq-Kuwait border. Iraq made bellicose statements regarding Kuwait and also threatened to expel UNSCOM inspectors. The United States responded by rapidly deploying troops to the theater (Operation Vigilant Warrior) and threatening large-scale strikes if Iraq did not withdraw. Both the United States and Britain subsequently warned Iraq that they would use force to stop any Iraqi buildup south of the 32nd parallel. In response, Iraq drew back its forces, recognized Kuwait's independent status, and accepted the revised Iraq-Kuwait border. The United Nations Security Council also passed resolution 949, which limited the Iraqi troop presence near the Kuwaiti border—the so-called no-drive zone.

The United States also augmented its regional presence in 1997–1998 in order to make the threat of retaliation plausible after continued Iraqi defiance over weapons inspections. As 1997 drew to a close, Baghdad refused to allow the inspectors access and otherwise hindered the inspection process. In November 1997, the United States deployed the *U.S.S. George Washington*, which

---

[36] Cockburn and Cockburn, *Out of the Ashes*, 111.
[37] http://www.fas.org/man/dod-101/ops.iraq_orbat.htm [Accessed 21 February 1999].

joined the *Nimitz*, sent B-52s to Diego Garcia, and deployed fighters and bombers to Kuwait and Bahrain. Washington also deployed additional troops as negotiations continued, leading to a total presence of 30,000 troops by December 1997.[38]

Tension continued to escalate in the weeks that followed. Iraq again obstructed inspections, leading the United States to deploy the *U.S.S. Independence* in January 1998 to join the other two carriers. In February, the United States deployed a Marine expeditionary force and additional aircraft. The Pentagon announced that the United States was ready to conduct military strikes on Iraq if defiance continued. In response to negotiations by UN Secretary General Kofi Annan, which led to restrictions on the inspectors as well as to an Iraqi agreement to readmit them, Baghdad allowed the inspectors to return. Despite its favorable terms, Baghdad's agreement was only temporary, and Saddam soon refused all cooperation.[39]

The above review suggests that the military presence, like other instruments, had mixed benefits. The military presence contributed to the goal of keeping Iraq contained by diminishing any hope of territorial aggrandizement. High-level defector reporting indicated that Saddam was considering another cross-border attack in 1994 if there was no U.S. response to his buildup.[40] Not only was an Iraqi invasion deterred, but Resolution 949 laid the groundwork for red lines that have since made a surprise attack far less likely. Iraq's subsequent recognition of the Iraq-Kuwait border and of Kuwait's independence both were important U.S. demands, suggesting that Saddam recognized that facts on the ground would not change as long as U.S. forces were in the region.

The impact of the U.S. presence on Iraq's WMD programs, however, was far more limited. Although Saddam did comply briefly with inspections in response to the late 1997 and early 1998 U.S. buildup, this compliance was both half-hearted and short-lived. Saddam also wrung important concessions out of Annan, reducing UNSCOM's ability to conduct intrusive inspections. Thus, while the buildup and the threat of force it conveyed led to token concessions on Iraq's part, it did not contribute substantially to long-term success.

The military presence is costly. These continuing operations and the regular surges required to deploy to the region in response to Iraqi provocations have challenged military rotation and leave schedules. Sustaining the no-fly zones over Iraq has proved draining. The inhospitable welcome often given to West-

---

[38] White, *Crises After the Storm*, 50–51.

[39] Ibid., 51–52.

[40] "Hussein Kamil on Army Strength, Saddam Fedayeen." *Al-Watan al-Arabi*, 24 November 1995, in Foreign Broadcast Information Service-Near East and South Asia, (FBIS-NES-95-227), 27 November, 1995, 33. Saddam may, however, have simply decided to call attention to the region, trying to bully Kuwait to have sanctions removed. The Iraqi dictator may also have been trying to prove to core supporters at home that he could defy the United States. The timing of the provocations suggests the importance of domestic motives: the Iraqi dinar was plummeting, forcing Saddam to increase food prices and otherwise making his regime unpopular. See Baram, *Building Toward Crises*, 79.

ern forces further strains the military. Morale, retention, and overall readiness have fallen as a result.

The U.S. military presence carries a political price as well. In Saudi Arabia in particular, both radical and mainstream dissident groups have focused much of their protest on the large U.S. military presence in the Kingdom. Saudis are particularly upset about the cost of maintaining the U.S. presence and the related arms purchases, arguing that the money could be better spent on services and infrastructure. Much of the business community, many of whom do not strongly oppose the U.S. presence on ideological grounds, criticize U.S. policy in the region because they believe the cost of the U.S. presence has led to a decline in government largesse and is generally bad for business.[41]

Military Strikes

The United States has repeatedly used limited force to achieve its goals. Since the end of the Gulf War, the United States conducted air and cruise missile strikes to compel Iraqi compliance with a range of goals regarding containment and WMD and also tried to use the strikes to foster discontent with the Baath regime. The four major instances are described below.

January 1993 confrontation. In December 1992, Iraq initiated a crisis with coalition forces, making limited incursions in the southern no-fly zone and threatening to shoot down U.S. monitoring aircraft by moving additional surface-to-air missiles to the southern no-fly zone. At roughly the same time, Iraq blocked the inspection of suspected WMD sites. Two-hundred Iraqi troops also made several crossings over the newly-demarcated Iraq-Kuwait border, seizing items that they claimed belonged to Iraq.[42]

To coerce Baghdad to stop these provocations, U.S., British, and French forces conducted air strikes against several military sites. On 13 January, allied warplanes bombed, among other things, command and control facilities and air-defense sites in the southern no-fly zone. Several days later, the United States struck the Zaa'faraniyah nuclear complex outside of Baghdad with forty-five cruise missiles. The following day, allied aircraft again attacked Iraqi military facilities in the no-fly zones.[43]

In the end, Iraq backed down and did not violate no-fly zones or actively challenge UNSCOM inspections for several years. Diplomatic support, however, was uneven. Saudi Arabia allowed strike aircraft to fly from its territory—the last time it authorized such strike missions. Turkey, however, did not sup-

---

[41] Abdullah al-Shayeji, "Gulf Views of U.S. Policy in the Region," *Middle East Policy* 5 (September 1997); Andrew Rathmell, "Terror comes to the Kingdom of Saudi Arabia," *Jane's Intelligence Review* 3 (1 January 1996): 6.

[42] White, *Crises after the Storm*, 20–23.

[43] Ibid., 22–25.

port the attacks, as concurrent attacks on Muslims in the Balkans had made Ankara reluctant to support perceived anti-Muslim operations elsewhere.[44]

Operation Desert Strike (September 1996). In 1996, after months of growing strife, open warfare erupted between the two leading Kurdish factions—the Kurdish Democratic party (KDP) and the Patriotic Union of Kurdistan (PUK)—in northern Iraq, a zone under an ambiguous level of protection by the United States. The PUK, with help from Iran, appeared to gain the upper hand. To avoid defeat, the KDP called on Baghdad to help repel the PUK. On 29 August, Saddam moved into northern Iraq, the area his government had earlier assumed was under U.S. protection, with 30,000-40,000 troops and thousands more police and intelligence personnel, along with several hundred tanks and artillery pieces. Iraqi troops took much of the north, including the Kurdish-held city of Irbil. In addition, Iraqi security forces rounded up hundreds of opposition members and supporters, executing and imprisoning them. Thousands more were evacuated to the United States.[45]

In response to Saddam's attack, the United States launched forty-four cruise missiles at fixed, above-ground targets in southern Iraq, primarily SAM sites, radar installations, and command and control facilities (Operation Desert Strike). In addition to the cruise missile attacks, the United States extended the no-fly zone in the south, which before had ended at the 32nd parallel, to the 33rd parallel. The zone's extension was intended to further limit Iraq's ability to move its forces and to improve the U.S.–led coalition's ability to monitor the regime.[46] By necessity, the U.S. response was limited, as both Saudi Arabia and Turkey refused to allow the United States to attack Iraq with planes based in their territories.[47] Both countries had little sympathy for the Kurds and did not see Saddam's incursion as meriting a large military response. Thus, the cruise missiles were launched from naval assets or from B-52s staging out of Guam.[48]

Saddam responded quickly to the limited U.S. attack. Iraq had concentrated forces near Chamchamal, a Kurdish-held city en route to the PUK's base at Sulaymaniyah. After the strikes, Saddam dispersed the Republican Guard and pulled his forces back to the cease-fire line.

Operation Desert Fox (December 1998). In December 1998, Ekeus's replacement as head of UNSCOM, Richard Butler, reported to the Security Council that Iraq was not complying with its obligations regarding WMD disarmament. This report came after over a year of Iraqi obstruction, backsliding, and outright defiance. In response, the United States and Britain conducted a

---

[44] Ibid., 22–27.
[45] Bruce Reidel, "U.S. Policy Toward Iraq: Balance, Dismember, or Contain?" Testimony before the National Security Subcommittee, U.S. House of Representatives, 26 September 1996.
[46] Ibid.
[47] Cockburn and Cockburn, *Out of the Ashes*, 243.
[48] http://www.fas.org/man/dod-101/ops/desert_strike.htm [Accessed on 18 December 1999].

large-scale, four-day air and cruise missile campaign against Iraqi military targets. The United States and Britain launched roughly 600 aircraft sorties and 400 cruise missile strikes against approximately 100 targets, including Iraqi intelligence and security forces facilities, presidential palaces, air defense systems, WMD sites, and economic targets.

Though far more massive than any previous strike against Iraq since Desert Storm, Desert Fox remained a limited operation. Even though one ultimate aim was to destroy WMD capability, the allied strikes avoided some Iraqi chemical plants, fearing that a strike could unleash poisonous plumes and kill Iraqi civilians. The campaign was ended after only four days to avoid adverse political and diplomatic consequences expected to arise if strikes continued during the Muslim holy month of Ramadan. Nevertheless, France, Russia, China, and Egypt all protested the Desert Fox bombings, and demonstrations were held in much of the Arab world.[49]

Saddam remained defiant of UNSCOM, but his reaction to the strikes indicates that he feared that military strikes might decrease support among his power base. In response to the bombing and overall crisis, Saddam divided Iraq administratively in a manner that would further increase the control of regime loyalists. He also reinforced areas such as Basra that might be prone to unrest and executed several officers who might have been considering a coup. In the following months, he also cracked down on any potential dissent among the Shiites, executing religious leaders.[50]

Tit-for-tat strikes in 1999 and 2000. Following Operation Desert Fox, Saddam repeatedly made limited challenges to the no-fly zone and continued to refuse access to weapons inspectors. In 1999, Iraqi forces made over 400 separate attacks on coalition aircraft, and over 140 violations of the no-fly zones; the figures for 2000 are similar.[51] In response, coalition forces have engaged in limited strikes, primarily against Iraqi air defense sites but also against communications nodes and other targets. As with the response to Operation Desert Fox, Saddam has stepped up efforts to prevent internal unrest.

Taken together, the various military strikes since the end of the Gulf War have helped the United States make marginal progress in keeping Iraq contained. The no-drive zone, enforced by the threat of strikes on any forces that deploy, has made it far harder for Saddam to concentrate his troops, which is necessary for large and sustained attacks across Iraq's borders. The strikes against Iraqi forces have hindered, if only in a limited manner, Iraq's efforts to rebuild its military power, forcing Saddam to rebuild scarce assets. Saddam has also displayed a remarkable sensitivity to military strikes, halting aggression in 1996 despite the pinprick nature of the attacks.

---

[49] Cockburn and Cockburn, *Out of the Ashes*, 284.
[50] See Matlak, *Inside Saddam's Grip*.
[51] http://www.centcom.mil/releases/news_rel [Accessed on 11 December 1999].

Determining the true impact of military strikes is difficult, however, as their greatest impact may have been unseen, enhancing the credibility of U.S. deterrence. Given Saddam's sensitivity to limited strikes, it is reasonable to assume that he fears more massive attacks, which would be likely in response to more serious Iraqi aggression. The repeated strikes on Iraq, however, demonstrate both the limits of U.S. resolve and its depths. On the one hand, the United States has demonstrated that it will attack Iraqi regime assets for relatively minor provocations (interfering with a no-fly zone), suggesting that more considerable Iraqi aggression would result in more severe attacks. On the other hand, the United States appears unwilling to go beyond brief, if rather intense, bombing campaigns such as Desert Fox when seeking to punish or compel Baghdad. This hesitation may undermine many of the credibility benefits gained from the overall willingness to use force.

Destruction of Iraq's WMD programs through air strikes, however, has proved near impossible. Much of Iraq's WMD programs, particularly its biological programs, are difficult to detect even with on-the-ground monitors. Given that UNSCOM inspected and at times oversaw the destruction of the most obvious sites, the additional damage wrought by air strikes was probably limited. Thus, air strikes—including massive efforts such as Desert Fox—may have degraded known sites somewhat, but almost certainly did not represent a major setback for Saddam. Indeed, the WMD destruction effort at times hindered containment. The military posturing and strikes of 1997-1998 increased disgruntlement with containment in general, both in the region and among the major powers. These high profile confrontations and strikes eroded the consensus around inspections and sanctions, thus threatening the core of the anti-WMD efforts.

Military strikes, however, appear to have weakened Saddam at home—though they hardly led to the collapse of his regime. Saddam is intensely sensitive both to internal security and to any perceived loss of face as a leader.[52] The repeated military strikes, which he could do little to counter, undermined his stature among Iraqis. Moreover, when strikes threatened key regime forces, such as the Republican Guard, they directly threatened Saddam's key supporters.

As the years progressed, allies grew less supportive of military strikes on Iraq. Saudi Arabia began curtailing the types of missions that could be flown from its territory, and Turkey at times refused the United States permission to conduct strikes on Iraq. Despite Saddam's defiance over UNSCOM in 1997 and 1998, the United States refrained from attacks until December 1998, in large part because of a lack of allied support. Only Saddam's refusal to offer even a hint of compromise or compliance led to allied support for Desert Fox. The tit-for-tat bombings after Desert Fox, however, represent a reversal of this trend.

---

[52] See Matlak, *Inside Saddam's Grip*; and Baram, *Building Toward Crises*.

Because of their regular and low-level nature, they are off the front pages, thus reducing the pressure on regional allies.

Repeated limits to access suggest a tension, but a manageable one, between the U.S. goals of preserving allied stability and containing Iraq. For lesser U.S. objectives, such as efforts to protect the Kurds or protect the no-fly zones, allies have limited U.S. access and missions to preserve domestic stability. Yet their stability has not been threatened to the point that they refused to cooperate with Washington.

Backing the Iraqi Opposition

A final instrument, one increasingly prominent in recent years, is encouraging the Iraqi opposition to overthrow Saddam. Since the end of the Gulf War, the United States made limited efforts to unite Iraqis opposed to Saddam, helping form the Iraqi National Congress (INC) as an umbrella group and otherwise encouraging anti-Saddam forces. Washington, however, has refrained from providing substantial aid to the Iraqi opposition or direct military support for opposition military activities.

The opposition has met with at best limited success since the end of the Gulf War. Despite widespread hatred of the regime, the INC was not able to forge the opposition into a coherent, anti-Saddam front. The INC and its allies did not provoke significant defections from the regime.[53] Saddam's incursion into northern Iraq in 1996 wiped out the INC's local cadres or forced them into exile. Today, the opposition in the country appears divided by region, religion, and ethnicity and does not act in concert with foes of the regime abroad.

The opposition received far more attention in the United States once it no longer had a presence in Iraq. In 1998, Congress passed the Iraq Liberation Act, which authorized the transfer of $97 million in military equipment to opposition groups as well as other forms of modest aid. In response, the Clinton administration embraced the Iraqi opposition, at least rhetorically. In 1999, Congress supplemented this aid with several million dollars of direct assistance.

The opposition has done little to remove the Baath regime, and its existence may have actually strengthened it. Although the regime has at most limited support even among Iraq's Sunni community, this community fears greater Shiah or Kurdish influence in the country. This fear is particularly strong among Saddam's core supporters, who would pose the greatest threat to his rule if they turned against the regime. Not surprisingly, Saddam has played up fears of Iraq's dismemberment and the shadow of Shiah domination in order to maintain their loyalty.

Efforts on behalf of the opposition also may hurt ties to allies. Saudi Arabia is concerned that any opposition success might increase Shiah influence in Iraq and further destabilize the region. Turkey, for its part, is suspicious of any plan

[53] Cockburn and Cockburn, *Out of the Ashes*, 187–190.

that might augment the military capabilities and increase the political aspirations of the region's Kurds. This skepticism is particularly acute outside the region. European allies oppose a strong commitment to the opposition, and Russia and China are highly sensitive to any U.S. efforts to foster internal unrest. Both states fear the precedent of recognizing insurgents, as they have their own restive minorities who oppose the central government.[54]

The opposition, however, does serve a useful role in the service of containment as long as its activities remain limited. A viable opposition forces the Iraqi regime to use its assets for internal security rather than external aggression. Saddam has also demonstrated a surprising caution when confronting instability, suggesting he is less likely to take risks if an opposition is strong. Washington can thus strike a balance, strengthening opposition forces to some degree without greatly angering U.S. allies. So far, U.S. efforts to back the opposition have not led the gulf states and Turkey to do more than criticize; basing and access remain unaffected.

An Overall Assessment: A Qualified Success

On its own terms, U.S. policy in Iraq is generally successful, though hardly perfect. Most obviously, Iraq has been contained. A robust U.S. regional presence, a rapid surge capacity, and a willingness to use limited force probably have convinced Saddam that regional aggression will not succeed. Moreover, as a result of sanctions and the devastation of the Gulf War, Saddam's Iraq is far weaker than it was in 1990, both in relative and in absolute terms. Baghdad's few friends during Desert Storm, such as Jordan and the Palestinians, have largely abandoned it. Iraq's regional influence, while increased from 1991, remains limited. In Richard Haass's words, Iraq today is "better understood as constituting a dangerous nuisance than an actual strategic threat."[55]

The United States has considerable capabilities to prevent cross-border aggression, and, if anything, the balance has tilted in favor of the United States and its allies since the end of Desert Storm. The United States now has large air forces in the gulf and is prepared to project additional force rapidly to the region. Access agreements have been completed with several gulf states, and prepositioned equipment would help ground troops gain their full strength far more quickly than they did in 1990. Advances in munitions and systems integration enable U.S. air assets to more effectively halt heavy Iraqi forces, which would have to advance through relatively open terrain.[56]

---

[54] Byman, "Proceed with Caution," 26-27. Even Britain has voiced its skepticism over the U.S. embrace of the opposition. See "Fatchett Reply to INC," 16 March letter circulated publicly by "Iraq News," 19 March 1999 (Electronic version).

[55] Richard N. Haass, "U.S. Policy Toward Iraq: Balance, Dismember, or Contain?" Testimony before the National Security Subcommittee, U.S. House of Representatives, 26 September 1996.

[56] See David A. Ochmanek et al., *To Find and Not To Yield: How Advances in Information and Firepower Can Transform Theater Warfare* (Santa Monica, CA: RAND, 1999).

Stopping Iraq's WMD programs has proved far more difficult. Iraq probably has not attained a nuclear weapon; and progress on its biological and chemical programs has probably halted (though data remain scarce)—a clear success when we recognize that without UNSCOM inspections, sanctions, and other measures Iraq would probably have a nuclear weapon and a range of biological weapons. Nevertheless, the broader U.S. goals of discovering the extent of Iraq's programs, destroying them, and preventing Iraq from reconstituting them in the future have not been met. Inspectors never discovered the true scope of Iraq's programs, much less destroyed them. Effective inspections ended in late 1997, and even the pretense of effective arms control has now been abandoned. Saddam is probably trying to continue some programs and certainly will do so in the future if sanctions end.

The long-term prognosis is even bleaker. U.S. actions have not substantially induced a change in Saddam's long-term policies toward acquiring such an arsenal. Given Iraq's long-time rivalry with Iran and current conventional weakness, it is probable that any successor to Saddam would also seek WMD. Although the current level of WMD infrastructure in Iraq may be limited, the country's scientific and engineering base remains robust and has the capability to rapidly restore WMD programs to past levels and beyond should international efforts to prevent this continue to decline.

Maximal U.S. goals were not met. Efforts to change the regime—by inducing Iraqi elites to support a coup or encouraging the Iraqi populace to overthrow Saddam—probably are farther from success than at any time this decade. Saddam Hussein has foiled several coup attempts since the Gulf War, as well as at least two tribal revolts. Iraqi intelligence rolled up the U.S. network in Iraq in 1996.[57] The Iraqi opposition is fragmented. Several Kurdish and Shiah groups maintain some, but very limited, capacity to operate against Saddam; but the regime vigilantly stamps out any sign of unrest.

When trying to overthrow Saddam, whether through a coup or an insurgency, the United States is pitting itself against the Iraqi dictator's strength. In effect, Saddam has "coup-proofed" his regime.[58] Not surprisingly for a man who has made many enemies, Saddam keeps a close watch on any access to his person. Members of his bodyguard are drawn almost exclusively from Saddam's home area. Other key regime protection assets, such as the Special Security Organization and the Special Republican Guard, also recruit largely from Saddam's al-Bu Nasir tribe and other nearby tribes that have good relations with the al-Bu Nasir. A key task of security forces is defending against a military coup.[59]

The United States has largely met its negative objective: preventing regional instability. Instability from Iraq has not spread to Turkey or other U.S.

[57] Baram, *Building Toward Crises*, 27, 48–49; Cockburn and Cockburn, *Out of the Ashes*, 229.

[58] For more on this, see James T. Quinlivan, "Coup-Proofing: Its Practice and Consequences in the Middle East," *International Security* 24 (Fall 1999): 131–165; see also Matlak, *Inside Saddam's Grip*.

[59] Baram, *Building Toward Crises*, 25.

allies. Nor have the U.S. presence and strikes caused massive internal instability or led regional governments to turn against Washington. Although Islamists and other anti-U.S. oppositionists regularly criticize the United States for its military presence in the gulf region, the anti-Iraq campaign is only a limited source of their anger, and various strikes on Iraq have only marginally increased their resentment.[60]

Potential Future Problems

The successes that the United States and its allies have attained should not obscure potential weaknesses in regional policy. Four weaknesses are particularly acute: a reliance on Saddam Hussein's missteps; an overemphasis on keeping the forms of containment intact even when their utility has declined; a neglect of U.S. allies for the sake of domestic politics; and a lack of a long-term solution to the Iraq problem. These weaknesses could derail containment or otherwise gravely harm U.S. policy in the region.

Dependence on Saddam. The maintenance of sanctions and of allied support for military strikes depends in part on Saddam's mistakes. His utter refusal to make even token concessions regarding inspections, for example, has made it difficult for Russian and French apologists to press his cause. Similarly, his blistering rhetorical attacks alienated potential sympathizers among his neighbors, leading them to support U.S. military basing and strikes. A pretense of cooperation and repentance, while perhaps harming Saddam at home, would make it more difficult for the United States to maintain sanctions or attack Iraq. Thus, if Saddam becomes more temperate, sustaining containment will become more difficult.

Overcommitment to the forms of containment. The United States has also committed itself to several policies that no longer serve their original purposes yet are draining, both politically and operationally. For example, inspections are overvalued. Given the concessions made by Ekeus and particularly Annan regarding where the inspectors could go and how much notice was required, the inspectors cannot be expected to make major new discoveries or otherwise hinder Iraq's programs. The renewal of inspections under current conditions might actually hasten the end of sanctions and thus assist Iraq's WMD programs.

The United States nevertheless clings to the pretense of inspections, because retreat might be seen at home as well as in Iraq as backing down to Saddam. Washington, however, has weathered far more painful defeats, such as Saddam's invasion of the north in 1996, without suffering a fatal blow to its

---

[60] Daniel Byman and Jerrold Green, *Political Violence in the States of the Northern Persian Gulf* (Santa Monica, CA: RAND, 1999).

regional position. The United States has put its credibility on the line unnecessarily, making the continuation of inspections an end in and of itself. Changing course, however, requires the political courage to withstand criticism at home about being soft on Iraq, regardless of its validity.

Neglecting regional allies. The United States runs the risk of letting domestic pressures hinder vital relations with regional allies. Maintaining the no-fly zones requires constant basing and support from regional allies. Although policy makers have gone to great lengths to minimize resentment, particularly from Saudi Arabia, regional allies may also turn against U.S. policy if American backing of the Iraqi opposition is not handled carefully.

Focusing on the short-term. The long-term resolution of the Iraq problem will not come even if the United States meets its most ambitious objective with Saddam's death. Rather, stability (and perhaps better governance) will only come to the region when Iraq is integrated into a regional structure that provides security. Baghdad's desire for WMD, mistreatment of national minorities, and irredentist ambitions are likely to live beyond Saddam Hussein. Although a long-term solution remains far off today, the United States needs a blueprint for the region that goes beyond the removal of a particular leader. Only then, can its current short-term strategy serve long-term objectives.

Although U.S. policy toward Iraq is far from perfect, most critical assessments are a clear case of moving the goalposts. Based on initial U.S. goals, the Bush and Clinton administrations have scored an impressive success: Iraq has not invaded its neighbors and remains militarily weak. Although containment is a frustrating policy, the persistent problems Saddam's Iraq poses should not drive us to despair. The post-Gulf War containment of Iraq demonstrates that the threat posed by aggressive regional powers can be managed, if the United States and its allies can continue demanding and at times unpopular policies to limit adversaries' powers and restrict their freedom of action.*

---

* The author would like to thank Nora Bensahel, Jeremy Shapiro, and Matthew Waxman for their comments on previous versions of this article.

CIA's Strategic Intelligence in Iraq

RICHARD L. RUSSELL

The CIA was the only agency to dissent: on the eve of the ground war, it was still telling the President that we were grossly exaggerating the damage inflicted on the Iraqis. If we'd waited to convince the CIA, we'd still be in Saudi Arabia.
 —H. Norman Schwarzkopf, IT DOESN'T TAKE A HERO

War is the realm of uncertainty; three quarters of the factors on which action in war is based are wrapped in a fog of greater or lesser uncertainty.
 —Carl von Clausewitz, ON WAR

The role of strategic intelligence in the foreign policy decision-making process at the highest echelons of government remains a neglected field of study. Much of the scholarly literature on intelligence is written from the perspective of intelligence officers, while significantly less is written from the perspective of policy makers. As Robert Gates observes, "A search of presidential memoirs and those of principal assistants over the past 30 years or so turns up remarkably little discussion or perspective on the role played by directors of central intelligence [DCIs] or intelligence information in presidential decision making on foreign affairs," while "in intelligence memoir literature, although one can read a great deal about covert operations and technical achievements, one finds little on the role of intelligence in presidential decision making."[1]

The study of intelligence from the policy maker's perspective would potentially yield a more robust understanding of the strengths and weaknesses of strategic intelligence and focus attention on areas where intelligence collection

---

[1] Robert M. Gates, "An Opportunity Unfulfilled: The Use and Perceptions of Intelligence at the White House," *Washington Quarterly* 12 (Winter 1989): 35.

RICHARD L. RUSSELL is professor at the Near East–South Asia Center for Strategic Studies, the National Defense University. He previously served for seventeen years as a political-military analyst at the Central Intelligence Agency, where he specialized on security issues in the Middle East and Europe. Russell is working on a book on power politics, weapons proliferation, and war in the Middle East and South Asia.

and analysis need improvement. The need for improving strategic intelligence performance was painfully made clear to Americans by the tragic events of September 11, 2001, in which their intelligence community failed to detect the Osama bin Laden-orchestrated conspiracy that killed several thousand civilians on American soil.

In the United States, the principal intelligence entity responsible for providing strategic intelligence to the president is the Central Intelligence Agency (CIA). Despite media-inflated public perceptions, strategic intelligence generally plays only a modest role in the day-to-day affairs of statecraft. Michael Herman correctly points out, "Those in CIA who produce the President's Daily Brief [PDB] and the National Intelligence Daily [NID] do not expect them to lead regularly to immediate action, any more than newspapers expect to change the world with every issue. Of all the contents of daily and weekly high-level intelligence summaries only a minute proportion feed directly into decisions."[2] Herman notes that "the role of most intelligence is not driving decisions in any short term, specific way, but contributing to decision-takers' general enlightenment; intelligence producers are in the business of educating their masters."[3]

Strategic Intelligence and the Senior Bush Administration

The impact of strategic intelligence on the American policy-making process reached an apex with President George Herbert Walker Bush. During his administration, the United States had its first commander-in-chief who had previously served as a DCI. Few, if any, presidents had had Bush's grasp of the power—and limitations—of intelligence before occupying the Oval Office. The president who probably comes closest to Bush with prior intelligence experience was Dwight Eisenhower who, as commander of Allied forces in Europe during World War II, had relied heavily on intelligence, particularly intercepted German communications, to inform strategy. As Christopher Andrew observes, Bush's "experience as DCI was to give him a clearer grasp than perhaps any previous president of what it was reasonable to expect from an intelligence estimate."[4] Ironically, Bush had accepted his appointment as DCI by President Gerald Ford with significant reservations. From his post in Beijing as chief of the U.S. Liaison Office, Bush in November 1975 telegraphed President Ford and Secretary of State Henry Kissinger his acceptance of the nomination as DCI out of a sense of duty. Bush remarked in the cable: "I do not have politics out of my system entirely and I see this as the total end of any political future."[5]

---

[2] Michael Herman, *Intelligence Power in Peace and War* (Cambridge, UK: Cambridge University Press, 1999), 143.

[3] Ibid., 144.

[4] Christopher Andrew, *For the President's Eyes Only: Secret Intelligence and the American Presidency from Washington to Bush* (New York: HarperPerennial, 1995), 504.

[5] "Telegram from George Bush to the President through Secretary Kissinger," 2 November 1975, George Bush Personal Papers, Subject File—China, Pre-CIA, Classified [1975–1977], George Bush Presidential Library.

Bush proved to be less than prophetic on this score, but, as president, he personally paid close attention to intelligence and sought to integrate it into the policy-making process. Bush held a daily national security briefing at which CIA briefed him on the latest world developments. In attendance at these briefings were the President, his national security adviser Brent Scowcroft or his deputy Robert Gates—himself a former high-level CIA official and later to be DCI—his chief of staff, and once or twice per week DCI William Webster. The CIA briefer would present the PDB, a printed book, with a rundown of important intelligence reports and analyses. Bush read the PDB in the presence of the CIA briefer and Scowcroft or Gates in order to task the briefer to provide more information or have his National Security Council (NSC) staff lieutenants field policy-related questions as they emerged in the course of discussion of the intelligence briefings.[6]

The Bush administration is a particularly lucrative case for the study of the role of strategic intelligence in statecraft for several additional reasons. Most notably, the United States under Bush's leadership waged a major war in the Persian Gulf. CIA influenced the decision-making process to a degree well beyond that exercised in peacetime, because of insatiable policy-maker appetite for intelligence on Iraq and the region given the high risks to American national interests. In addition, many of the key policy makers who received a daily flood of intelligence during the war have published accounts of their time in office, which give outsiders invaluable insight into the policy-making process and can be mined for evidence of the impact of strategic intelligence on decision making. Finally, many military accounts of the war by scholars, journalists, and military officers are windows through which to view how policy makers and military commanders used intelligence during the Gulf crisis.

This article serves several purposes. First, it attempts to help fill a major gap in intelligence literature on the role of strategic intelligence in informing statecraft. Strategic intelligence in this article refers to the use of information—whether clandestinely or publicly acquired—that is synthesized into analysis and read by the senior-most policy makers charged with setting the objectives of grand strategy and ensuring that military force is exercised for purposes of achieving national interests.[7] Strategic intelligence is a tool to help ensure that civilian authorities control military means for achieving political objectives, as Clausewitz sagely wrote of war. Second, the article traces the uses and limitations of strategic intelligence in major dimensions of the Gulf War to include the warning and waging of war. The article concludes with an assessment or balance sheet of the strengths and weaknesses of strategic intelligence during the Gulf crisis. It draws insights from this case study to inform the future evolu-

---

[6] George Bush and Brent Scowcroft, *A World Transformed* (New York: Vintage Books, 1999), 30.

[7] For treatments of strategic intelligence, see Adda B. Bozeman, *Strategic Intelligence and Statecraft* (Washington, DC: Brassey's Inc., 1992); and Sherman Kent, *Strategic Intelligence for American World Policy* (Princeton: Princeton University Press, 1951).

tion of American intelligence and its support of statecraft, particularly in situations where policy makers face dilemmas posed by the use of armed force.

WARNING OF INVASION

American intelligence effectively tracked the physical build-up of Iraqi forces across the border from Kuwait in mid-July 1990. Details of the President's Daily Brief in the run-up to Iraq's invasion of Kuwait have not been publicly disclosed. Nevertheless, information from the National Intelligence Daily, CIA's current intelligence publication that received a wider dissemination among policy officials than the more tightly controlled PDB, has made its way into the public domain. The NID warned on 24 July that "Iraq now has ample forces and supplies available for military operations inside Kuwait" and during that day doubts grew as to whether Saddam Hussein was bluffing.[8] DCI Webster traveled to the White House on 24 July and briefed Bush on satellite imagery showing the movement of two Republican Guard divisions from garrisons in central Iraq to positions near the Kuwait border.[9] The NID on 25 July published an article "Iraq–Kuwait: Is Iraq Bluffing?" which stated that unless Kuwait meets Iraq's oil production demands—the ostensible Iraqi reason for military posturing along the border—Baghdad will step up pressure on Kuwait. The NID article, however, lacked specific intelligence on Saddam's intentions.[10] Working-level analysts at CIA—primarily in the Directorate of Intelligence's Office of Imagery Analysis (OIA) and Near East and South Asia Analysis (NESA)—were the authors of analyses published in the NID.

One high-level intelligence official on the National Intelligence Council (NIC), charged with advising the DCI, was more forward leaning than the analytic judgments published in the NID. The National Intelligence Officer (NIO) for Warning Charles Allen on 25 July issued a "warning of war" memorandum in which he stressed that Iraq had nearly achieved the capability to launch a corps-sized operation of sufficient mass to occupy much of Kuwait. The memo judged that the chances of a military operation of some sort at better than 60 percent.[11] Allen on 26 July visited NSC's senior director for the Middle East Richard Haass and briefed him with satellite imagery that showed the magnitude of Iraq's military build-up near Kuwait.[12] Allen on 1 August personally informed Haass that an Iraqi attack against Kuwait was imminent. Haass, in

---

[8] Lawrence Freedman and Efraim Karsh, *The Gulf Conflict, 1990–1991: Diplomacy and War in the New World Order* (Princeton: Princeton University Press, 1993), 50.

[9] U.S. News & World Report, *Triumph without Victory: The History of the Persian Gulf War* (New York: Times Books, 1993), 21.

[10] Ibid., 31–32.

[11] Charles E. Allen, "Warning and Iraq's Invasion of Kuwait: A Retrospective Look," *Defense Intelligence Journal* 7 (no. 2, 1998): 40.

[12] Michael R. Gordon and Bernard E. Trainor, *The Generals' War: The Inside Story of the Conflict in the Gulf* (New York: Little, Brown and Company, 1995), 16.

turn, informed Scowcroft, but the White House refrained from moving to a crisis mode.[13] Other analytic voices coming from the NIC may have significantly softened the alarm of Allen's warnings in the ears of key Bush administration policy makers. The NIO for the Near East and South Asia—more directly responsible for analysis of Iraq than Allen as the NIO for Warning—wrote in a 31 July memorandum that Iraqi military action, such as seizing the Rumaila oil field straddled on the border or Kuwait islands, was likely unless Kuwait made oil concessions. The NIO for the Near East and South Asia judged, however, that a major attack to seize most or all of Kuwait was unlikely.[14]

While strategic intelligence performed well in detecting and tracking the buildup of Iraqi military hardware along the border with Kuwait, there was a dearth of human source reporting on Saddam's intentions. Such reporting was needed to give a weight of evidence to competing analytic judgments between the NIOs and the working-level CIA analysts. Although a critical mass of intelligence led CIA to conclude by the afternoon of 1 August that an Iraqi invasion was imminent, the magnitude of Iraqi invasion plans was not anticipated by working-level analysts.[15] Deputy Director for Central Intelligence Richard Kerr briefed the mainstream analytic assessment to a Deputies Committee meeting of key policy makers chaired by Undersecretary of State Robert Kimmit late in the day on 1 August. Kimmit and other participants recall that Kerr emphasized the limited land grab Iraqi option, not a massive invasion of Kuwait.[16] Other accounts stressed that Kerr emphatically told the Deputies Committee meeting that the "Iraqis were ready to move."[17]

And move they did. Iraqi forces began their invasion of Kuwait at 0100 on the morning of 2 August. The invasion was led by two Republican Guard armored divisions, the Hammurabi and the Medina, and eventually included about 140,000 troops and 1,800 tanks. The armored divisions moved rapidly to Kuwait City, while Iraqi Special Force commandos attacked the city in advance of the armored divisions. Commandos loaded on helicopters seized key positions throughout Kuwait, including Bubyian and Warba Islands in the northern Gulf. On 3 August, a Republican Guard mechanized division secured Kuwait's border with Saudi Arabia. The 16,000-man Kuwait Army was overwhelmed. Iraqi forces fully occupied Kuwait in about twelve hours.[18]

Despite CIA's intelligence warning in the week before the invasion, Iraq's behavior had defied the Agency's earlier assessments of the regime. CIA judged in a 1989 National Intelligence estimate, "Iraq: Foreign Policy of a Major Regional Power," published under NIC auspices, that Baghdad after its bloody eight-year war with Iran needed time to rest, recuperate, and rebuild both its

---

[13] Ibid., 5–6.
[14] Ibid., 25.
[15] Freedman and Karsh, *Gulf Conflict*, 73.
[16] Gordon and Trainor, *Generals' War*, 28.
[17] U.S. News & World Report, *Triumph Without Victory*, 33.
[18] Freedman and Karsh, *Gulf Conflict*, 67.

conventional and unconventional military power before undertaking another major war.[19] As Michael Gordon and Bernard Trainor point out, CIA and intelligence community analysts suffered from "mirror imaging" in which they projected their own American values to the Iraqis. They assumed that because the United States had needed time to rest and rebuild after its major wars, the Iraqis would have to do the same.[20]

Iraq's situation was fundamentally different than that of the United States, however. Saddam had a large standing military and no doubt feared that demobilization would let loose unemployed and weapons-trained young men into the streets who would pose a risk to his regime. Saddam, moreover, preferred to launch a war against a minor power rather than suffer humiliation from the burden of debt that he acquired to the Gulf states during his war with Iran. Paul Wolfowitz, undersecretary of defense for policy during the Gulf War, also faulted the intelligence community for not warning the policy community about the changing character of Saddam's public statements in early 1990. He has suggested, "Somebody should have catalogued his increasingly belligerent rhetoric, compared and contrasted his statements to prior formulations, and laid out one or more plausible explanations for the change."[21]

In defense of CIA analysis though, its assessment on the eve of Iraq's invasion that Saddam would likely launch a military campaign to seize a limited piece of Kuwaiti territory was forward leaning at the time. Many of the most astute observers of Middle East politics, including Arab heads of state intimately familiar with Saddam Hussein such as King Hussein of Jordan and President Hosni Mubarak of Egypt, were predicting that Iraq was militarily posturing to politically pressure the Kuwaitis over oil production levels. King Hussein even assured President Bush in a 31 July phone conversation that the crisis between Iraq and Kuwait would be resolved without fighting. The king told Bush, "On the Iraqi side, they send their best regards and highest esteem to you, sir."[22]

A major shortcoming in warning of the Gulf war was the lack of human intelligence to help decipher Saddam's political intentions. As Norman Schwarzkopf observed after the war, "our human intelligence was poor."[23] Civilian policy makers shared his assessment of human intelligence during the war. As Secretary of State James Baker characterized the situation, "U.S. intelligence

---

[19] Gordon and Trainor, *Generals' War*, 9.

[20] Ibid., 11.

[21] Jack Davis, "Paul Wolfowitz on Intelligence–Policy Relations," *Studies in Intelligence* 39 (no. 1, 1995): 7.

[22] Memorandum of Telephone Conversation, "Telephone Conversation with King Hussein," 31 July 1990, OA/ID CF01043, Richard N. Haass Files, Working Files-Iraq, National Security Council, George Bush Presidential Library.

[23] H. Norman Schwarzkopf and Peter Petre, *It Doesn't Take a Hero* (New York: Bantam Books, 1992), 319.

assets on the ground were virtually nonexistent."[24] He judged that "there wasn't much intelligence on what was going on inside Iraq."[25]

JUDGING THE DANGER OF WIDER WAR

Notwithstanding CIA human intelligence shortcomings in warning of war, CIA's analysis was effective in gauging the magnitude of Iraq's invasion and potential repercussions on the international political landscape. At the first meeting of the NSC convened on 2 August to discuss the crisis, the tone of participants was that of accepting Iraq's invasion as a *fait accompli*.[26] CIA analysis delivered in the following NSC meeting on 3 August appears to have influenced the discussion of participants to a more assertive American policy stance. DCI Webster told the President and NSC officials that Saddam was consolidating his hold on Kuwait, and intelligence showed that he would not pull out despite Saddam's public pledges to do so in a couple of days. Webster warned that Saddam would control the second- and third-largest proven oil reserves with the fourth-largest army in the world, Kuwaiti financial assets, access to the Gulf, and the ability to devote money to a military buildup. Webster also noted that there was no apparent internal rival to Saddam's rule, and his ambition was to increase his power.[27] The NSC participants also discussed CIA analysis that argued that "the invasion posed a threat to the current world order and that the long-run impact on the world economy could be devastating. Saddam was bent on turning Iraq into an Arab superpower—a balance to the United States, the Soviet Union, and Japan."[28] As General Colin Powell, then chairman of the Joint Chiefs of Staff, recalled, Webster "gave us a bleak status report," which prompted Scowcroft to declare that "We've got to make a response and accommodating Saddam is not an option."[29]

Strategic intelligence painted a dismal picture of the threat to Saudi Arabia posed by the Iraqi military behemoth in Kuwait. Saudi forces were no match for the Iraqis, and CIA estimated that Iraqi forces could reach Riyadh—located about 275 miles south of Kuwait—in three days.[30] In the 5 August NSC meeting,

---

[24] James A. Baker III with Thomas M. DeFrank, *The Politics of Diplomacy: Revolution, War and Peace, 1989-1992* (New York: G. P. Putnam's Sons, 1995), 7.

[25] Ibid., 267–268.

[26] Bush and Scowcroft, *World Transformed*, 317.

[27] Ibid., 322–323. The oil-related estimates in Webster's brief probably originated in an analytic paper on world oil reserves prepared by economists in CIA's Office of Resource, Technology, and Trade. See U.S. News & World Report, *Triumph Without Victory*, 65. For a first-hand account of the NSC meeting, see Memorandum for Brent Scowcroft, "Minutes from NSC Meeting, 3 August 1990, on Persian Gulf," OA/ID CF01518, Richard N. Haass Files, Working Files-Iraq, National Security Council, George Bush Presidential Library.

[28] Bob Woodward, *The Commanders* (New York: Simon & Schuster, 1991), 237.

[29] Colin L. Powell with Joseph E. Persico, *My American Journey* (New York: Random House, 1995), 463–464.

[30] Freedman and Karsh, *Gulf Conflict*, 88.

Webster reported that CIA was uncertain about Saddam's intentions and that it would be difficult to provide warning of an attack on Saudi Arabia. Webster remarked, moreover, that Iraqi forces were massing on the Kuwait-Saudi border, and reinforcements were on the way giving Iraq more forces in the area than were needed solely for occupying Kuwait.[31] The minutes of the 5 August NSC meeting indicate that CIA analysts were more concerned about the potential for Iraqi offensive operations into Saudi Arabia than their Defense Intelligence Agency (DIA) counterparts.[32] By Schwarzkopf's account, it was not until mid-September that intelligence showed that Iraqi forces were moving to a defensive posture in Kuwait as Republican Guard divisions pulled back from the Saudi border and were replaced by tens of thousands of infantry digging trenches and building barricades, preparing for a long siege.[33]

The debate over whether Saddam ever had designs on Saudi Arabia continues today. The Gulf War Air Power Survey (GWAPS) concluded in retrospect that it was unlikely that Iraq had intended to invade Saudi Arabia immediately after seizing Kuwait, because Iraqi forces assumed a defensive posture to hold Kuwait rather than to prepare for further land advances.[34] Nevertheless, over the medium to longer runs, had Iraq been allowed to consolidate control over Kuwait and had the United States not intervened on the ground to defend Saudi Arabia, the Kingdom would have been an attractive target of opportunity for Saddam's forces. Saudi forces standing alone would have collapsed in the face of a massive Iraqi air and ground campaign much as the Kuwaiti military had.

Assessing Measures Short of War

In the aftermath of the Iraqi invasion, many in the United States, particularly those in the halls of Congress, were looking for American policy options short of waging war against Iraq. Many viewed economic sanctions as the best policy option to avoid the direct engagement of American troops in war overseas.

CIA analysis of international sanctions against Iraq became entangled in the policy debates taking place between the White House and Capitol Hill.[35] Webster in early August approved the dissemination of CIA's weekly reports on the effectiveness of international sanctions against Iraq to the President, De-

---

[31] Bush and Scowcroft, *World Transformed*, 334.

[32] Memorandum for William F. Sittman from Richard N. Haass, "Minutes of NSC Meeting on Iraqi Invasion of Kuwait, 5 August 1990," 18 August 1990, OA/ID CF00873, Richard N. Haass Files, Working Files-Iraq, National Security Council, George Bush Presidential Library.

[33] Schwarzkopf and Petre, *It Doesn't Take a Hero*, 346.

[34] Thomas A. Keaney and Eliot A. Cohen, *Revolution in Warfare? Air Power in the Persian Gulf* (Annapolis, MD: Naval Institute Press, 1995), 4. This book is an unclassified summary of the multivolume Gulf War Air Power Study led by Cohen and commissioned by Secretary of the Air Force Donald Rice in 1991.

[35] For an analysis of CIA's unique bureaucratic position, situated between the executive and legislative branches of government, see Robert M. Gates, "The CIA and Foreign Policy," *Foreign Affairs* 66 (Winter 1987/88): 215–230.

partments of State and Defense, as well as the Senate Select Committee on Intelligence and the House Permanent Select Committee on Intelligence. In general, CIA analysts judged that in the short to medium terms, sanctions seemed unlikely to force Saddam out of Kuwait.[36] Webster passed along this analytic judgment when he testified to Congress in December 1990 and said that economic sanctions had little prospect for forcing Saddam to withdraw his forces from Kuwait. Webster later reiterated this assessment in a 10 January letter to Congressman Les Aspin. He wrote that "Our judgment remains that, even if the sanctions continue to be enforced for another six to twelve months, economic hardship alone is unlikely to compel Saddam Hussein to retreat from Kuwait or cause regime-threatening popular discontent in Iraq. . . . He [Saddam] probably continues to believe that Iraq can endure sanctions longer than the international coalition will hold and hopes that avoiding war will buy him time to negotiate a settlement more favorable to him."[37] To a Congress eager to seek economic sanctions as a way of escaping the hard issues raised by the prospect of sending American forces to the region, CIA's bleak analytic assessment of their efficacy was not welcome news. To his credit, Webster refused to submit to the congressional browbeating intended to force him to change the Agency's assessment.

The congressional and public discourse over the wisdom of sanctions was moot, because President Bush had already determined that war probably would be necessary. After an 11 October White House meeting, Bush and his top advisers had concluded that military action, not economic sanctions, would almost certainly be needed to evict Iraq's military from Kuwait. The President also had accepted the view of Chairman Colin Powell that airpower alone was unlikely to achieve the task.[38] Historical hindsight and the eleven-year experience with the United Nations' failure to use international sanctions to compel Saddam to alter course—particularly in regard to fully disclosing the scope of his weapons of mass destruction programs—shows that CIA's judgment that sanctions would not significantly change Saddam's political behavior was accurate.

Gauging Conventional and Unconventional Military Capabilities

Intelligence estimates of Iraqi conventional military power stressed the mass of Iraqi ground forces coupled with their battlefield experience fighting the eight-year war with Iran. U.S. intelligence assessed that beyond the Republican Guard divisions and eight to ten regular army divisions, the quality of Iraqi divisions significantly decreased.[39] American intelligence was effective in identi-

---

[36] U.S. News & World Report, *Triumph Without Victory*, 150.
[37] Letter, William H. Webster to Les Aspin, 10 January 1991, OA/ID CF 01361, Virginia Lampley Files, National Security Council, George Bush Presidential Library.
[38] Gordon and Trainor, *Generals' War*, 139.
[39] Freedman and Karsh, *Gulf Conflict*, 288.

fying the locations of these less capable regular Iraqi army units along the Kuwaiti border as well as those of the more capable Republican Guard units, which backed-up frontline forces in a strategic reserve in northern Kuwait and southern Iraq. CIA in late 1990 assessed that Iraq would defend in place, try to force the coalition into a war of attrition on the ground, and attempt to create a stalemate that would undermine American political resolve.[40] From Saddam's perspective, the strategy had proved its worth in Iraq's war against Iran. He probably judged that the United States, with its purported fear of casualties, would be even more vulnerable to the strategy than Iran had been.

The Agency correctly anticipated the impact of Iraq's Air Force on the course of battle. CIA in October 1990 assessed that "The Iraqi Air Force would not be effective because it would either be neutralized quickly by Coalition air action or it would be withheld from action in hardened shelters. Within a few days, Iraqi air defenses would be limited to AAA [anti-aircraft artillery] and hand-held and surviving light SAMs [surface-to-air missiles]."[41] The course of battle clearly showed CIA analysis to be on the mark, although it had not anticipated that many Iraqi pilots would flee with their aircrafts to Iran rather than face coalition pilots in air-to-air combat.

CIA analysis paid close attention to Iraq's unconventional weapons capabilities that Baghdad worked assiduously to hide from the world. CIA had tracked the development of Iraqi chemical weapons in the course of Baghdad's war with Teheran. CIA estimated before the war that Saddam's chemical stockpile was more than a thousand tons and included artillery rounds, bombs, and caches possibly moved into Kuwait. In fall 1990, CIA assessed that Iraq would use those stocks in the event of war with the coalition.[42] These estimates had an impact on American policy makers. As Powell recalls, "We knew from CIA estimates that the Iraqis had at least a thousand tons of chemical agents. We knew that Saddam had used both mustard and nerve gases in his war against Iran. We knew that he had used gases on Iraq's rebellious Kurdish minority in 1988, killing or injuring four thousand Kurds."[43] CIA's grasp of Iraq's biological warfare program, however, was sketchy at best. In October 1990, American intelligence warned that Iraq's biological weapons capability was sufficiently sophisticated to cause coalition casualties within four hours after the weapons were used."[44]

American intelligence had closely watched the growth of Iraq's ballistic missile capabilities, some of which were demonstrated in the missile exchanges between Baghdad and Teheran during the "war of the cities" in their eight-year struggle. Shortly before the war with the coalition, intelligence estimated that

---

[40] Keaney and Cohen, *Revolution in Warfare?* 108.
[41] Ibid., 108.
[42] Rick Atkinson, *Crusade: The Untold Story of the Persian Gulf War* (Boston: Houghton Mifflin, 1993), 86.
[43] Powell, *My American Journey*, 468.
[44] Atkinson, *Crusade*, 88.

Iraq's inventory of Scud missiles was about 300–700, but it was uncertain as to how many were Soviet-supplied Scud-Bs and how many were longer-range Iraqi modified variants.[45] American intelligence also had identified twenty-eight concrete launch pads for the Scuds in western Iraq, while it estimated that Iraq had thirty-six mobile launchers, both Soviet-supplied and Iraqi manufactured.[46]

Intelligence estimates on Iraq's nuclear weapons program were less confident than on its ballistic missile programs and grew more conservative and alarmist as the eve of the coalition ground war approached. Before Iraq's invasion of Kuwait, intelligence judged that Iraq would not acquire nuclear weapons for five to ten years. In July 1990, Israel shared with Secretary of Defense Richard Cheney evidence that Iraqi work on high-speed centrifuges needed to enrich uranium for nuclear weapons was progressing fast, which in turn instigated a new American intelligence estimate. A special estimate prepared for President Bush in fall 1990 concluded that it would take Iraq six months to a year and probably longer to acquire a nuclear weapon.[47]

Postwar revelations made largely by United Nations weapons inspections teams gave a truer picture of the scope of Iraq's weapons of mass destruction programs. Despite the air campaign against Iraq's chemical weapons facilities, UN inspectors discovered about 150,000 chemical munitions that survived the war.[48] American intelligence, moreover, failed to detect prior to the war that Iraq had more than seventy chemical warheads for its Scud missiles.[49] UN inspectors helped to lift the shroud of secrecy surrounding the massive Iraqi nuclear weapons program. In January 1992, Iraq admitted having a uranium enrichment program to produce nuclear weapons. Baghdad had bought the components for as many as 10,000 centrifuges for the large-scale production of fissile material. Had Iraq's efforts not been interrupted by the war, Baghdad could have produced enough uranium for four bombs per year.[50] The GWAPS assessed that Iraq's nuclear weapons program was fiscally unconstrained, closer to fielding a nuclear weapon, and less vulnerable to destruction by precision bombing than U.S. intelligence realized before the war. The target list on 16 January contained two nuclear-related targets, but after the war, UN inspectors uncovered more than twenty sites involved in the nuclear weapons program, sixteen of which were described as "main facilities."[51]

Controversy in War

In the midst of the air campaign against Iraq, major analytic disputes erupted between CIA civilian analysts and their uniformed counterparts in the Penta-

---

[45] Gordon and Trainor, *Generals' War*, 230.
[46] Ibid., 230.
[47] Freedman and Karsh, *Gulf Conflict*, 220.
[48] Keaney and Cohen, *Revolution in Warfare?* 71.
[49] Gordon and Trainor, *Generals' War*, 183.
[50] Freedman and Karsh, *Gulf Conflict*, 321.
[51] Keaney and Cohen, *Revolution in Warfare?* 67.

gon and in Schwarzkopf's Central Command (CENTCOM) staff. The initial conflict occurred over the battle damage assessment (BDA) of CENTCOM's efforts to destroy Iraqi ballistic missiles and their mobile launchers. The political pressure on Schwarzkopf to stop Iraqi missile attacks against Israel and Saudi Arabia was intense and caused him to divert substantial military resources against the problem and away from his primary concern to prepare the theater for a ground campaign to evict Iraqi troops from Kuwait. The second controversy between CIA and CENTCOM emerged over the BDA of Iraqi ground forces, which for Schwarzkopf was a barometer for determining the kick-off of the ground campaign.

A major rift in analysis emerged during the war between CIA and CENTCOM intelligence analysts over the BDA of Iraqi Scuds and mobile launchers. During the air war in January 1991, Schwarzkopf told a television interviewer that thirty fixed Scud sites had been destroyed and that his forces may have destroyed as many as sixteen of about twenty suspected mobile launchers. Behind the scenes though, CIA heatedly contested Schwarzkopf's BDA of the Iraqi missiles and launchers. CIA analysts argued that there was no confirmation that any mobile launcher had been destroyed.[52]

The military continued to dispute CIA's analysis of the issue well after the war. Coalition aircrews reported destroying about eighty mobile launchers, while special operations forces claimed about twenty more, according to the GWAPS. Most of these reports stemmed from attacks against decoys or vehicles and equipment such as tanker trucks, which from a distance resembled Scud mobile launchers.[53] The GWAPS concluded after painstaking research that "there is no indisputable proof that Scud mobile launchers—as opposed to high-fidelity decoys, trucks, or other objects with Scud-like signatures—were destroyed by fixed-wing aircraft."[54] That judgment vindicates CIA's wartime analysis—largely conducted by its Office of Imagery Analysis—and belies the critical appraisals of CIA analysis made by Schwarzkopf and other senior commanders.

The controversy over the BDA of Iraqi ground forces had its origins in Schwarzkopf's determination that the transition from the air campaign to a ground war would occur at the point at which Iraqi ground forces had suffered a 50 percent attrition. By his own admission, the figure was solely a benchmark and not a "hard and fast rule" for gauging how much Iraqi combat power had been eroded by the air campaign. Schwarzkopf in his autobiography acknowledged that the 50 percent attrition of Iraqi order of battle was an arbitrary figure: "Pulling a number out of the air, I said I'd need fifty percent of the Iraqi occupying forces destroyed before launching whatever ground offensive we might eventually plan."[55]

---

[52] Atkinson, *Crusade*, 144–145.
[53] Keaney and Cohen, *Revolution in Warfare?* 73.
[54] Ibid., 78.
[55] Schwarzkopf and Petre, *It Doesn't Take a Hero*, 319.

Nevertheless, Schwarzkopf reinforced the importance of this 50 percent figure in deliberations with his civilian policy masters, who were eager to achieve that mark and to kick off the ground war. As with many things though, the devil of this BDA benchmark was in the details. As the GWAPS points out, no one really knew what would constitute a measurable 50 percent attrition of Iraqi combat effectiveness. CENTCOM staffers merely applied the indicators to measurable military equipment such as tanks, armored personnel carriers, and artillery in the Kuwaiti theater of operations.[56]

CENTCOM was assessing in February 1991 that the air campaign was close to achieving the 50 percent attrition benchmark, but CIA analysts were substantially more conservative in their BDA of Iraqi ground forces. CENTCOM, for example, estimated in mid-February that it had destroyed about 1,700 Iraqi tanks or nearly 40 percent of Iraqi armor in the theater. CIA analysts, however, by examining satellite photography for blown tank turrets and shattered hulls could only confirm about one-third destroyed.[57]

CIA brought the discrepancy in BDA to the President's attention. In a PDB memorandum, it reported that CIA was unable to confirm all of CENTCOM's reported damage to Iraqi forces. CIA informally sent the PDB memorandum to Schwarzkopf who went into a rage, because he was about to make the decision to launch the ground attack. He viewed CIA as cynically hedging its bets and providing itself with an alibi in the event that the Iraqis inflicted heavy casualties on U.S. forces.[58]

President Bush asked Scowcroft to investigate the BDA dispute. On 21 February, Webster along with his NIO for conventional forces, retired Army General David Armstrong, met with Powell, Secretary of Defense Richard Cheney, and a CENTCOM representative. Armstrong argued that aside from the dispute over the numbers of tanks destroyed, CIA was not interested in usurping Schwarzkopf's command prerogatives. Armstrong reiterated that regardless of the tank tally, Iraq's army was "highly degraded."[59] Despite CIA's argument, Scowcroft realized that rejecting CENTCOM's BDA would signal a devastating loss of confidence in the military. He saw no political alternative but to side with CENTCOM in the dispute. Subsequently, Powell announced that CIA was not to conduct and report BDA, which set the precedent for the loss of that responsibility long after the Gulf War.[60]

Notwithstanding policy-maker difference to CENTCOM's BDA, postwar analysis showed CIA analysis to be superior. The House Armed Services Committee concluded that Schwarzkopf's BDA on Iraqi tanks was exaggerated by perhaps as much as 134 percent. For example, postwar analysis confirmed that 166 tanks from three Republican Guard divisions were destroyed, while CENT-

---

[56] Keaney and Cohen, *Revolution in Warfare?* 40–41.
[57] Atkinson, *Crusade*, 345.
[58] Ibid., 266.
[59] Ibid., 346.
[60] Ibid., 347.

COM had estimated during the war that 388 had been destroyed.[61] As had been the case in the BDA of ballistic missiles, CENTCOM's overestimation of the BDA of Iraqi ground forces was in large measure due to an overreliance on pilot reports to estimate destroyed Iraqi equipment. Pilots fly high, fast, and in hostile territory under enemy fire and have only fleeting moments to see bomb impacts. They have too small an opportunity to assess damage fairly. In contrast, satellite imagery taken after the battlefield dust has had a chance to settle is a more consistently accurate means of gauging BDA.

Drawing a Balance Sheet and Future Lessons

Before addressing the specifics of strategic intelligence performance during the Gulf War, a broad characterization of the quality of the intelligence picture at the disposal of Iraqi and American policy makers and military commanders is in order. The Iraqis, for their part, lacked an accurate strategic intelligence picture of the theater. They were blind as to the coalition force deployments that made possible the operational concept for nearly enveloping Iraqi forces in the Kuwaiti theater in the ground campaign. In marked contrast, the American intelligence community provided its consumers one of the broadest and clearest pictures of an adversary that any American president and high command has ever had in the nation's history. The United States, by Schwarzkopf's own admission during the war, had managed to identify Iraqi units "practically down to the battalion level."[62] The House Armed Services Committee concluded that American intelligence had an excellent handle on the units, locations, and equipment of Iraqi forces.[63]

That performance is hard to reconcile with the disparaging postwar assessments of CIA's performance made by Schwarzkopf and other CENTCOM commanders. One wonders what General George Patton would have given to have had a comparable picture of opposing German forces in Europe during World War II. These criticisms, moreover, neglect the fact that CIA is not designed to be a "combat support agency." CIA's charter has been to provide strategic-level intelligence primarily to civilian policy makers and not tactical intelligence to battlefield commanders. While military commanders are prone to fault CIA for perceived shortcomings, they appear reticent to fault their own military service intelligence shops and DIA whose charters are to provide tactical combat support to field commanders. Accordingly, DIA and military intelligence manpower for conducting tactical military analysis dwarfs that of CIA.

---

[61] U.S. House of Representatives, Committee on Armed Services, Subcommittee on Oversight and Investigations, "Intelligence Successes and Failures in Operations Desert Shield/Storm," August 1993, 4 and 31. Hereafter cited as House Report. CIA published an unclassified study "Operation Desert Storm: A Snapshot of the Battlefield" in September 1993, which graphically depicts the highlights of battle in the Kuwait theater of operations.

[62] Powell, *My American Journey*, 474.

[63] House Report, 4.

The House Armed Services Committee noted that at the height of the Gulf War, about one-third of DIA's several thousand employees were assisting the war effort, a number that exceeds CIA's total analytic workforce.[64]

These observations aside, what does a balance sheet of American strategic intelligence during the Gulf War look like? On the plus side, CIA's analysis gave warning of war days before Iraq's invasion of Kuwait. CIA analysis gauged fairly well the threat posed to Saudi Arabia by a potential follow-on Iraqi attack, an assessment that probably had a major influence on the Bush administration's decision to counter and reverse Iraq's military land grab. CIA accurately assessed the dim prospects for international economic sanctions compelling Saddam to withdraw his forces from Kuwait. The international sanctions that have been on Iraq since the Gulf War have yet to compel Saddam to comply with UN demands, and it is doubtful that sanctions would have forced him to vacate Kuwait without war.

In hindsight, CIA analysts—in many cases imagery analysts—scored high marks for making accurate BDA of ballistic missile capabilities and the attrition of Iraqi ground forces even though their analysis is much maligned in the common wisdom of the lessons of the war perpetuated by military commanders. A small group of CIA imagery analysts stood alone in informing civilian policy makers that, contrary to Schwarzkopf's extravagant claims, CENTCOM had not destroyed a single Scud missile or launcher during the war. CIA's BDA, which caused substantial controversy toward the eve of the ground war, was proved with postwar analysis to be much closer to ground truth than CENTCOM's inflated BDA of Iraqi forces.

Strategic intelligence in the Gulf War has a fair number of entries in the debit side of the balance sheet. The greatest weakness of CIA's performance was its lack of human assets inside the Iraqi regime able to report on Saddam's plans and intentions. As Christopher Andrew points out, "Though a limited number of agents had been recruited in Iraqi diplomatic and trade missions abroad, none seems to have had access to Saddam's thinking or to his inner circle."[65]

The lack of human intelligence contributed to an inadequate assessment of the magnitude of Iraq's ballistic missile and weapons of mass destruction capabilities. The House Armed Services Committee judged that the intelligence community had a good estimate of Iraqi chemical weapons, while it was hard to assess the performance on the biological warfare program because the UN had extracted very little information from the Iraqis on that issue. A debate also continues as to how many ballistic missiles and mobile launchers Iraq could have preserved during the war. Strategic intelligence performed badly against Iraq's nuclear weapons program. The House Armed Services Committee report assessed that American intelligence was unaware of more than 50 percent of all major nuclear weapons installations in Iraq.[66] To fill in the intelligence

---

[64] House Report, 7.
[65] Andrew, *For the President's Eyes Only*, 533.
[66] House Report, 30.

gaps created by poor human intelligence, moreover, CIA analysts resorted to mirror imaging, which led analysts to judge that Iraq would only go for a limited land grab against Kuwait instead of an all-out occupation.

The poor human intelligence performance is not a lone incident in CIA's history. CIA has traditionally performed poorly in human operations against the United States's most ardent adversaries. In evaluating the performance of human intelligence one should point out the distinction that many intelligence professionals and scholars make between secrets and mysteries. Secrets are facts that can be stolen by human intelligence collectors. Mysteries, on the other hand, are projections of the future that are less vulnerable to human collection and tend to be the bailiwick of analysis.[67] As Gates reflects on CIA's human intelligence operations for gaining access to the intentions of our adversaries during the cold war, "We were duped by double agents in Cuba and East Germany. We were penetrated with devastating effect at least once—Aldrich Ames—by the Soviets, and suffered other counterintelligence and security failures. We never recruited a spy who gave us unique political information from inside the Kremlin, and we too often failed to penetrate the inner circle of Soviet surrogate leaders."[68] CIA has done a better job of human operations against lesser nation-state threats and at stealing technical secrets, but has failed too often in the human intelligence game against the intentions of the most formidable risks to American security. With the benefits of time, hindsight, and independent review, the lack of robust human intelligence sources is likely to be found as one of the prime root causes of the intelligence failure witnessed on 11 September 2001 in New York and Washington.

In the post-cold war age, American security has a narrower margin for error because of technological advances that allow nation-states as well as nonstate actors to project force farther and weapons of mass destruction that allow them to strike with more devastating effects. In this environment, the United States needs to rectify the substantial shortcomings in human intelligence collection operations if it is to successfully deal with issues of war and peace in the future. CIA must reform and make qualitative improvements in its human intelligence operations to increase the odds that American policy makers and military commanders will have access to the thoughts and intentions of their adversaries. Even if the intentions of U.S. adversaries prove elusive and remain hidden, a critical task for human intelligence is to illuminate the policy pressures at play on foreign leaders and to help analysts narrow the range of ambiguity for American policy makers. Substantially improved human intelligence capabilities will help ensure that in the event of a future war with Iraq or any other adversary armed with ballistic missiles and weapons of mass destruction (WMD) the United States has

---

[67] The author is indebted to Robert Gates for reminding him of this important distinction. For a discussion of the role of secrets and mysteries in intelligence estimates, see Joseph S. Nye, Jr., "Peering into the Future," *Foreign Affairs* 73 (July/August 1994): 82–93.

[68] Robert M. Gates, *From the Shades: The Ultimate Insider's Story of Five Presidents and How They Won the Cold War* (New York: Simon and Schuster, 1997), 560.

the strategic intelligence needed to target WMD assets before these weapons are used against American troops and citizens.

A Gulf War legacy that must be redressed is the removal of a civilian check of military BDA in wartime. The civil-military intelligence controversies that emerged during the Gulf War were reminiscent of arguments during the Vietnam War, in which civilian CIA analysts were more objective than the politically and operationally tainted analyses coming from DIA and military intelligence services. Since the Gulf War, CIA has been relieved of any responsibility for BDA, and its once impressive imagery analytic capabilities have been stripped from the Agency and moved to the National Imagery and Mapping Agency, a designated combat support agency controlled by the Pentagon. To ensure that accurate and objective strategic intelligence reaches senior civilian policy makers, CIA needs to resume its exercise of independent imagery analysis and again be charged with critical reviews of military intelligence analyses in peace and war to avoid future policy debacles like those suffered—although increasingly forgotten—during the Vietnam conflict. The absence of an independent civilian analytic check on military intelligence threatens American civilian control of the military instrument for political purpose.*

---

* The author would like to express his appreciation to the George Bush Presidential Library Foundation and the George Bush School of Government and Public Service's Center for Presidential Studies for an O'Donnell Grant to support research for this article at the George Bush Presidential Library. The author particularly appreciated the special interest that then director of the Center for Presidential Studies, George Edwards, III, showed in this project. A word of thanks is due to Archivist John Laster for his gracious help in the Bush Library and to Roger Harrison and Bruce Pease for their comments on earlier drafts. A special word of thanks is due to Robert Gates for taking the time to read and thoughtfully comment on an earlier version of this article. The author also is indebted to Michael Warner, with whom he delivered a joint lecture on the Gulf War to students at CIA's Sherman Kent School for Intelligence Analysis. That joint lecture germinated the interest that drove the research and writing of this article. The views expressed in this article are those of the author and do not reflect the official policy or position of the National Defense University, the Department of Defense, or the U.S. government.

Contradictions in Iranian and Indonesian Politics

DANIEL BRUMBERG

The election of Mohammad Khatami in May 1997 surprised Westerners and Iranians alike. Khatami's assertion that Islam would be strengthened by getting the state out of the business of imposing religion defied the most sacred premises of the Islamic Revolution. That Iran's new president, himself a cleric, argued for the rule of the people while affirming the right of Khomeini's heir, Ayatollah Seyed Ali Khamanei, to serve as the "Supreme Leader," suggested the sudden emergence of a profound ideological divide at the very pinnacle of the state.

Yet such anomalies were hardly new, nor unique to Iran. In Teheran, as much as in Rabat, Amman, or Jakarta, politics pivots around the institutionalization and strategic manipulation of symbolic contradictions. That this dynamic has received so little attention reflects an abiding conviction, particularly among students of Islamic politics, that authority systems must ultimately be based on one dominant form of legitimacy or domination.[1] Thus John Esposito and John Voll argue that by reinterpreting "core concepts ... central to the political positions of virtually all Muslims," Islamists have forged notions of "Islamic democracy" that are as coherent and legal-rational as any secular vision of democracy.[2] Similarly, scholars who hold that Islam's quest to link politics

---

[1] This conviction is central to Weber's own concept of domination. As Reinhard Bendix has noted, while "in Weber's view every historical relation between rulers and ruled contains heterogeneous elements" (or bases of authority), "the predominance of one or another of these elements in the organization and rule ... is related to certain more or less enduring historical configurations." See Reinhard Bendix, *Max Weber: An Intellectual Portrait* (Berkeley: University of California Press, 1977), 297.

[2] John Esposito and John Voll, *Islam and Democracy* (Oxford: Oxford University Press, 1996), 23. While the authors acknowledge that the "Western experience continues to have great influence on the Islamic debates," they believe that the "older modernist approach to Islamic democracy" is now giving way to "coherent theories and structures of Islamic democracy that are not simply reformulations of Western perceptions in some Muslim idiom."

DANIEL BRUMBERG is associate professor of government at Georgetown University and author

to religious norms precludes democracy nevertheless argue that efforts to blend democracy and Islam will either provoke a backlash from conservatives determined to protect Islam from Western encroachment;[3] or by forcing a choice between tradition and modernity, will inadvertently legitimate secular ideologies.[4] Viewed through this linear prism, one can only predict that the struggle for political reform in Iran will either fail, or as one Iranian scholar suggests, "open the gates of the secular city."[5]

This article challenges such conventional wisdom by investigating the dissonant institutionalization of symbolic contradictions in Islamic polities. This dynamic invites forms of political change that have often been misunderstood or unanticipated precisely because they are messy and indeterminate. To grasp this nonlinear dynamic requires a paradigm shift in how we think about authority structures, the states that support them, and the various forms of political change and ideological innovation that such states promote or hinder. I begin by sketching a theory of dissonant politics. Taking a cue from new institutionalist analysis, I highlight the tendency of dissonant states to bequeath multiple legacies or paths.[6] These competing paths create institutional and symbolic space through which elites redefine contending visions of political community. This dynamic hardly makes democracy or pluralism inevitable; the manipulation of institutional and ideological legacies often facilitates the survival strategies that autocrats use to undermine pressures for a substantive transition to competitive democracy. Yet, this same dynamic can also create space for interelite accommodations that can slowly transform politics in ways often unaccounted for in the conventional transitions literature.

To explore these changes I trace the genesis and evolution of institutional and symbolic legacies in Iran and Indonesia, and then consider how recent struggles to redefine these legacies have facilitated the efforts of regime and opposition elites to discredit, challenge, or renegotiate the rules of the game. In Iran, the struggle of the Islamic left to reinterpret Khomeini's legacy in a more pluralistic light helped set the stage for a reform movement. But because this movement has clashed with a rival institutional-ideological path that was controlled by the Supreme Leader and his allies in powerful state institutions,

---

of *Reinventing Khomeini: The Struggle for Reform in Iran*. He has published widely on issues of political and socioeconomic reform in the Middle East.

[3] See Nadav Safran, *Egypt in Search of Political Community: An Analysis of the Intellectual and Political Evolution of Egypt 1804–1952* (Cambridge: Harvard University Press, 1961).

[4] Albert Hourani held that by equating Islam with those ideas and institutions that secured the public interest (*maslaha*), the reformists inadvertently invited a "*de facto* separation of the sphere of civilization from that of religion" that opened "another door to secular nationalism." Albert Hourani, *Arabic Thought in the Liberal Age, 1798–1939* (Cambridge: Cambridge University Press, 1962), 344.

[5] Ahmad Sadri, "Reintroducing the Wheel," *The Iranian*, September 1996, (www.iranian.com/Sep96/Opinion/Democracy).

[6] See Kathleen Thelen and Seven Steinmo, "Historical Institutionalism in Comparative Politics" in Kathleen Thelen, Steven Steinmo, and Frank Longstreth, eds., *Structuring Politics : Historical Institutionalism in Comparative Analysis* (Cambridge: Cambridge University Press, 1996), 1–33.

efforts to liberalize the political system have been stymied. In contrast to this example of bipolar dissonant conflict, Indonesia provides an example of multipolar competition between and within competing Islamic and secular groups. I focus particularly on the competition between two of the most important Islamic groups, one of whose leaders—Abdurrahman Wahid—played a key role in forging a contentious experiment in confessional power sharing virtually unprecedented in the Islamic world. My conclusion contrasts politics in dissonant states with their conceptual opposite: harmonic states. By narrowing the space for regime-opposition accommodations and by glorifying the notion of the state as the sole voice of the community, harmonic states invite a fight to death between hegemonic and counter-hegemonic forces. While Algeria offers the most dramatic example of this destructive zero-sum logic, it may not be the last one to pay the high costs that ensue from a legacy of harmonic authoritarianism.

Dissonant Institutionalization: A Theoretical Sketch

This article is informed by Theda Skocpol's assumption that "various sorts of states . . . give rise to various conceptions of the meaning and method of 'politics' itself, conceptions that influence all groups and classes in national societies."[7] I push this famous observation one step further by conceptualizing how particular types of states facilitate particular types of political and ideological change. For this purpose, Joel Migdal's work provides a useful point of departure. Spurning all linear theories, he argues for an "anthropology of the state" that investigates how the organizational and symbolic ties that link state and society promote distinctive patterns of political change. Migdal assumes neither that the state is a coherent entity that creates and enforcers preferences, nor that it is a prisoner of society's competing social forces. Instead, he argues that different levels of stateness affect the goals and strategies that regimes and oppositions pursue. Migdal suggests that political change depends on whether the balance of power between state and society produces "total transformation" of the second by the first, "state incorporation" of existing forces, "societal incorporation" of the state, or a total failure of the latter to penetrate the state.[8]

The above typological map elaborates upon Migdal's earlier analysis of "strong societies and weak states." Politics in many Third World countries, he argued, is structured by the presence of well entrenched religious, ethnic, or cultural groups.[9] Their use of organizational and symbolic resources limits the

---

[7] Theda Skocpol, "Bringing the State Back In: Strategies of Analysis in Current Research" in Peter B. Evans, Dietrich Rueschemeyer, and Theda Skocpol, eds., *Bringing the State Back In* (Cambridge: Cambridge University Press, 1985), 22.

[8] Joel S. Migdal, "The State in Society" in Joel S. Migdal, Atul Kholi, and Vivienne Shue, eds., *State Power and Social Forces, Domination and Transformation in the Third World* (Cambridge: Cambridge University Press, 1994), 7–36.

[9] Joel S. Migdal, *Strong Societies and Weak States: State-Society Relations and State Capabilities in the Third World* (Princeton: Princeton University Press, 1988).

kinds of strategies and techniques that weak states can employ to mobilize, control, or contain strong societies. Constrained by their societies, weak states are better at dominating than transforming, controlling than changing, surviving than innovating.

The notion of dissonant institutionalization that I shall now outline turns this argument on its head. Whereas Migdal holds that competing sociopolitical forces often constrain ruling elites, I see the prevalence of such forces as a spur not only to regime survival, but within limits, to regime innovation and controlled change. Migdal's "state incorporation" hints at this dynamic but is not equivalent to dissonant institutionalization. When state incorporation occurs, the state retains a measure of autonomy sufficient to achieve domination, but it is still compelled by societal forces to act in some ways and not in others. By contrast, dissonant institutionalization obtains when the state has abetted the institutionalization of contradictory visions of authority in organizations, parties, or groups that maintain a degree of autonomy or at the least some capacity to define preferences independently of the state. These groups can be structured along corporatist lines, but corporatism is one of many institutional mechanisms found in dissonant states.[10] What makes the concept of dissonant politics useful is that it highlights a dynamic that can unfold in traditional monarchies such as Morocco, in populist authoritarian regimes such as Egypt, or in revolutionary or postrevolutionary states such as Iran.

Dissonant politics pivots around the institutional and ideological space that distances contending societal organizations both from the state and from one another. The competition by the leaders of these organizations for popular support hinders the efforts of any one group to impose ideological hegemony, while relative autonomy and elite competition facilitate both the state's manipulation of competing elites and the latter's efforts to manipulate the state. Still, it is usually the state that prevails. By encouraging contending elites to constantly negotiate particular policy questions or to debate this or that symbolic issue, the state enhances its room for maneuver and thus benefits from the specter of institutionalized conflict.[11] Divide and rule and elite accommodation are thus two sides of the same coin. Some of the most dissonant states in the Middle East are ruled by monarchs whose staying power stems from their ability to play off traditional and modern groups. The result, as the cases of Morocco and Kuwait suggest, is a game in which negotiations over particular sociocultural issues (such as women's rights) give competing groups a sense that their positions count without allowing them to pose a serious threat to the ruling powers.[12]

---

[10] A notion of dissonant politics informs Robert Bianchi's *Unruly Corporatism, Associational Life in Twentieth-Century Egypt* (Oxford: Oxford University Press, 1989).

[11] See Lewis Coser, *The Functions of Social Conflict* (New York: The Free Press, 1956). It should be noted that Coser's analysis focused on Western, pluralistic democracies.

[12] On the Gulf states, see Michael Herb, *All in the Family: Absolutism, Revolution, and Democracy in the Middle Eastern Monarchies* (Albany: State University of New York Press, 1999). On Morocco, see Guilan Denoeux and Abdelslam Maghraoui, "King Hassan's Strategy of Political Dualism," *Middle East Policy 5* (January 1998): 104–30.

Dissonant politics is a product of many factors, three of which bear particular comment. First, it is an outgrowth of strategies of indirect rule through which colonial powers promoted indigenous political elites. Thus in Morocco the French not only tolerated Sufi (mystical) religious orders, Islamic reformist movements, and Westernized elites; they also supported a well respected monarch.[13] The king's role as master arbiter was enshrined in the 1962 Constitution, which sanctioned the politically useful myth that the "Commander of the Faithful" stood above the political fray.[14] Second, dissonant politics is a product of sharp socioeconomic and cultural discontinuities between modern elites and the wider population. Because modern elites govern societies in which traditional religious, tribal, or ethnic groups retain influence, the former have often had to accommodate the latter.[15] Finally, globalization has played a key role in promoting dissonant systems. Said Amir Arjomand addressed this point in a seminal study that shows how the diffusion of Western constitutional models encouraged modernizing elites in Islamic polities to imbibe both legal-rational and traditional notions of authority. The resulting "inconsistency of . . . principles and the appositeness of the relative weight then given to them in a particular constitution . . . set the parameters for the constitutional politics of the subsequent period."[16]

Over the last two decades this dissonant dynamic has been manifest in parliaments, the press, and even in the discourse of political elites. New media such as the Internet and the satellite dish have accelerated this process by beaming contending visions of community to a growing audience.[17] In turn, this dynamic has shaped the "multiple imaginations" of Islamist elites. Exposed to competing concepts of authority, some Islamic leaders have come to view ideological eclecticism as natural and even useful.[18] For a Khatami in Iran or an Abdurrahman Wahid in Indonesia, the challenge is not so much to produce a coherent synthesis of Islam and democracy, or pluralism and piety, as it is to find ways to make competing notions of political and religious community coexist.

[13] See Michel Le Gall, "The Historical Context" in I. William Zartman and William Mark Habeeb, eds., *Polity and Society in Contemporary North Africa* (Boulder: Westview Press, 1993), 3–18.

[14] J. Aveille, "Le Moroc se donne un monarchie constitutionelle," *Confluent* 27 (1963). Cited in Abdeslam Maghraoui, "Morocco: From Symbolic to Democratic Legitimacy?" (unpublished manuscript), 13.

[15] See Clifford Geertz, "The Integrative Revolution: Primordial Sentiments and Civil Politics in the New States" in Clifford Geertz, *The Interpretation of Cultures* (New York: Basic Books, 1973), 254–310.

[16] Said Amir Arjomand, "Constitutions and the Struggle for Political Order," *Archives of European Sociology* 33 (Winter/Spring 1992): 39.

[17] See Akbar S. Ahmed and Hastings Donnan, "Islam in the Age of Postmodernity" in S. Ahmed Akbar and Hastings Donnan, eds., *Islam, Globalization and Postmodernity* (London and New York: Routledge, 1994), 1–20. This dynamic is not entirely new. In *An Islamic Response to Imperialism, Political and Religious Writing of Sayyid Jamal ad-Din "al-Afghani"* (Berkeley: University of California Press, 1983), Nikki Keddi examined the efforts of this nineteenth-century Islamic reformer to address competing visions to different audiences.

[18] See Ronald Glassman, "Legitimacy and Manufactured Charisma," *Social Research* 42 (Winter 1975): 621.

Renegotiating and Redefining Dissonant Legacies

In dissonant systems, elites, institutions, and ideologies are in a state of constant competition and contention, but absent a system-threatening crisis this discordant dynamic is unlikely to produce a major renegotiation of the rules of the game. Such a crisis can be economic or ideological. While the first has been widely studied, the second merits close attention.[19] Controlled ideological dissonance can support an authoritarian system so long as rulers prevent disaffected elites from using symbolic fissures as a foundation for mass mobilization. This effort to "transform the institutional relations of society by exploiting ... contradictions" is blocked not merely by repression, but also by the unifying influence of charismatic leaders.[20] By virtue of their personal allure, they intentionally or inadvertently obscure symbolic anomalies.[21] But when charismatic leaders are discredited by economic or political crises, or when they die or fall prey to a coup, such momentous events can provoke sharp struggles over contending ideological legacies.

To grasp this phenomenon we must move beyond the deterministic and one-dimensional notion of "path dependency" that animates some new institutionalist analyses. The view that "once a critical choice has been made it cannot be taken back"[22] fails to account for the fact that different authoritarian states are more or less path dependent. Dissonant states create multiple institutional-ideological paths that in turn create unintended opportunities for path innovation. By housing competing visions of authority in diverse arenas such as the press, founding constitutions, parliaments, universities, or religious institutions, they create windows of opportunity that competing elites can exploit to discredit, redefine, or renegotiate the prevailing political order.

What are the likely consequences of such contests? First, by inhibiting efforts to impose ideological hegemony, states that are substantially dissonant—those that maintain considerable symbolic and institutional distance from society's competing sociocultural groups and promote a *multipolar* symbolic field—create more space for renegotiating the rules of the game. Conversely, states that are moderately dissonant—those that narrow the symbolic and institutional distance between state and society and constrain the degree of ideological and institutional dissonance by limiting competition to a bipolar ideological field—create less space for renegotiating the political/symbolic order. In short,

---

[19] See Stephan Haggard and Robert R. Kaufman, *The Political Economy of Democratic Transitions* (Princeton: Princeton University Press, 1995).

[20] Robert Friedland and Robert Alford, "Bringing Society Back In: Symbolic Practices and Institutional Contradictions" in Walter W. Powell and Paul J. DiMaggio, eds., *The New Institutionalism in Organizational Analysis* (Chicago: University of Chicago Press, 1991), 232.

[21] See Daniel Brumberg, *Reinventing Khomeini: The Struggle for Reform in Iran* (Chicago: University of Chicago Press, 2001). See also Michael Fischer, "Imam Khomeini: Four Levels of Understanding" in John Esposito, ed., *Voices of Resurgent Islam* (New York and Oxford: Oxford University Press, 1983), 150–74.

[22] Stephen D. Krasner, "Approaches to the State: Alternative Conceptions and Historical Dynamics," *Comparative Politics* 16 (January 1984): 223–46, 240.

the chances for a more dramatic renegotiation of the political field will be greater in the first case than in the second. Second, the particular institutional mechanisms that regimes use to manage dissonance also affect struggles to renegotiate the rules of the game. States that rule through centralized control organizations such as single party systems will be relatively more constrained than those that use corporatist, monarchical, or other institutions to distance themselves from the process of ideological or symbolic reproduction.

The above model suggests a counterintuitive dynamic: the more dissonant an institutional and ideological legacy, the more opportunities there are for "regime survival strategies" through which rulers encourage interelite accommodations that prevent a full transition to multiparty democracy.[23] In short, the phenomenon of "semi-autocratic regimes" is hardly an anomaly.[24] On the contrary, the extent to which it is manifest in the Islamic world can be explained theoretically—by reference to a shared set of institutional and symbolic structures. Yet there is no guarantee that survival strategies will succeed. Some dissonant states will create conditions advantageous to sustaining liberalized autocracy, while others might engender dynamics that eventually allow regimes and oppositions to negotiate a "contingent institutional compromise" or political pact.[25] What I want to emphasize, however, is the indeterminacy of dissonant systems. Although they create space for change, a comprehensive causal theory that correlates particular types of dissonant legacies with particular types of political reform must await a fuller analysis of dissonant politics in a myriad of states, including Bangladesh, Egypt, Kuwait, Lebanon, Morocco, Iran, and Indonesia. By focusing on the latter two cases, this article offers a modest yet crucial first step toward a comprehensive theory of dissonant politics.

Bipolar Dissonant Institutionalization in Iran

Iran's 1978–1979 Islamic revolution was led by an alliance between two overlapping socio-ideological forces. On the Islamist left was a disparate movement

---

[23] Daniel Brumberg, "Reform Strategies in the Arab World" in Rex Brynen, Baghat Korany, and Paul Noble, *Political Liberalization and Democratization in the Arab World, Vol. 1* (Boulder, CO: Lynne Rienner Publishers, 1995), 229–60; and Daniel Brumberg, "Survival Strategies vs. Democratic Bargains: The Politics of Economic Stabilization in Contemporary Egypt" in Henri Barkey, ed., *Economic Crisis and Political Response: The Politics of Economic Reform in the Middle East* (New York: St. Martins Press, 1992). Well before I wrote these two articles, Joel Midgal had used a similar term—"strategies of survival"—but in a much broader sense. As I became familiar with his work only much later, I was not able to incorporate a comparison of the similar and different ways we each conceive of "survival." See Migdal's *Strong Societies and Weak States*, 26–7.

[24] One of the few comparative studies of this phenomenon can be found in Martha Brill Olcott and Marina Ottaway, "The Challenge of Semi-Authoritarianism," Working Papers, (Washington, DC: The Carnegie Endowment for International Peace, 1999) (http://www.ceip.files/publications/wp7.asp). It is no coincidence that Iran and Indonesia are both primary cases in the working paper, given the extent to which regime-opposition accommodation and competition defined politics in both states.

[25] Adam Przeworski, "The Games of Transitions" in Scott Mainwaring, Guillermo McDonald, and J. Samuel Valenzuela, eds., *Issues in Democratic Consolidation: The New South American Democracies in Comparative Perspective* (Notre Dame: University of Notre Dame Press, 1992), 136.

of university students, professors, independent intellectuals, and some radical clerics, all of whom to various degrees had been exposed to Western notions of politics.[26] Their leader was Ali Shariati—a political essayist and aspiring Iranologist. During years of study in Paris, he had absorbed a multiple vision of revolutionary politics that combined Marxism, existentialism, and Shi'ite-Islamic utopianism. Although no democrat, Shariati advocated a radical, instrumentalist, and rationalist approach to Islam. He held that it was the mission of the lay intelligentsia to remold Islamic symbols into a total ideology that could mobilize the masses against the Western powers and their local allies.[27] While this nativist ideologization of Islam paradoxically echoed revolutionary and totalitarian traditions rooted in the West,[28] it was also inspired by the messianic symbols that animate Twelver Shi'ism, a branch of Islam holding that the Prophet Mohammad's message will only be fully revealed upon the return of the Mahdi or twelveth Imam. To the right of Shariati and his allies was a group of clerics who had little exposure to the West and who believed that they alone grasped Shi'ism's verities. Led by Khomeini, the "clerical right" borrowed many of Shariati's symbols and ideas while assailing Shariati's radical instrumentalism and his implicit affinity for Western notions of mass participation.[29]

During the 1960s and early 1970s, this alliance between Islamic left and clerical right gained a foothold in many religious seminaries and universities. That it did so owed much to the legal, moral, and charismatic authority that Shi'ism accorded to the leading interpreters of the law.[30] Because Shi'ites gave financial support to different "sources of emulation" (*maraje'-e taqlid*), sometimes referred to as "Grand Ayatollahs," contending visions of Shi'ism sunk institutional roots outside of the state. The support given by the British, Russians, and Americans to secular autocrats such as Shah Reza Pahlavi did little to undermine such pluralism. Thus, even though Khomeini effectively silenced the Grand Ayatollahs—all of whom opposed his theory of *velayat-e faqih* (Rule of the Jurist)—and repressed many leaders of the Islamist left, he did not completely dispense with the competing visions of authority he had inherited in 1979. Instead, Khomeini and his allies absorbed these visions into a system whose contours were laid out in the 1979 constitution.

This document provided for a *faqih* (ruling jurist) whose nearly unlimited powers derived from the people's embrace of Khomeini and his messianic mes-

---

[26] I use the term "left" because of the influence that Marxist ideology had on these Islamists, particularly Marxist notions of collective versus individual rights.

[27] Hamid Dabashi, *Theology of Discontent: The Ideological Foundation of the Islamic Revolution in Iran* (New York: New York University Press, 1993). See also Ali Shariati, *An Approach to the Understanding of Islam*, transl. Venus Kaivantash (Houston: Free Islamic Literatures, 1980).

[28] See Mehrzad Boroujerdi, *Iranian Intellectuals and the West: The Tormented Triumph of Nativism* (Syracuse: Syracuse University Press, 1996), 52–76.

[29] For an analysis of Khomeini's use of leftist terms, see Ervand Abrahamian, *Khomeinism, Essays on the Islamic Republic* (Berkeley: University of California Press, 1993).

[30] Shahrough Akhavi, *Religion and Politics in Contemporary Iran: Clergy-State Relations in the Pahlavi Period* (Albany: State University Press, 1980).

sage; a judiciary and Council of Guardians controlled by the conservative clergy; and a Majles (parliament) whose members were elected every five years.[31] Although the Constitution held that the Council of Guardians could veto any legislation it deemed "un-Islamic," the Majles played a crucial role by providing the central arena through which leaders of the Islamist left and the clerical right voiced ideologies and negotiated differences. Khomeini stood at the pinnacle of this institutional mess. His charismatic and constitutional authority gave him the means and right to referee Majles conflicts. By both encouraging and limiting such conflicts, he displayed his utopian vision of Islamic unity while enhancing his authority as the master arbiter. Thus, Khomeini himself became a vehicle of dissonant institutionalization. In his speeches and edicts, he communicated competing notions of authority, sometimes upholding his revolutionary notion of clerical rule, sometimes resorting to a more traditional approach that called for limiting the clerics' role in politics, sometimes taking refuge in mystical visions, while on other occasions singing the praises of the Majles as representative of a presumably united entity called the "people." Khomeini was a contradictory leader of a contradictory system, but his own charisma hid and thus perpetuated ideological dissonance.

Dissonant Politics: The Battle over the Revolution's Multidimensional Legacy

The death of Khomeini in July 1989 changed everything. Henceforth, the gates were open for a battle not only over his multiple legacy, but also over the contending visions of authority that had been institutionalized in the constitution and even in Khomeini's rhetoric. The clerical right immediately went on the offensive, as was demonstrated by the alliance that was forged between the new President Ali Akbar Hashemi Rafsanjani and Khomeini's heir, Ayatollah Khamanei. When these two men pushed for an economic reform program that sought to undermine the Islamist left's quasi-socialist policies, leaders of the left in the Majles attacked Rafsanjani directly while implicitly defying the authority of the new *faqih*, Ayatollah Khamanei. But note how this battle was fought: Islamic leftists invoked Khomeini's repeated insistence that "the center of all law and power is the Majles. It guides all and it should do so"[32] to defend the principle of popular sovereignty and constitutional rule, while the clerical rightists invoked Khomeini's notion of *velayat-i faqih* to bolster their claim that Khamanei's word was final and absolute.

Rafsanjani and Khamanei responded to the Islamist left's assaults by conducting a purge of the Majles in advance of the May 1992 elections. Invoking its right to supervise these elections, the Council of Guardians disqualified over

---

[31] Albert P. Blaustein and Gisber H. Flanz, "The Islamic Republic of Iran, 1979," *Constitutions of the Countries of the World* (Dobbs Ferry, NY: Oceana Publications, 1980). On the Majles, see Bahman Baktiari, *Parliamentary Politics in Revolutionary Iran* (Gainesville: University Press of Florida, 1996).

[32] *Foreign Broadcast Information Service, South Asia* [hereafter *FBIS-SAS*], 27 May 1980, 80–103.

1,000 radicals from running for office. In retrospect, it is clear that this purge set the stage for today's reform movement. Accused of being insufficiently Islamic, several prominent Islamist leftists began rethinking basic questions such as the relationship between mosque and state or the question of individual versus collective rights. That such revisionism unfolded on the floor of the Majles magnified its effect. After all, here were men with impeccable revolutionary credentials invoking, as one deputy put it, "Montesquieu and other political and social thinkers" to legitimate their assertion that the regime should "not violate the Constitution."[33] Moreover, Islamist leftists defended their constitutional rights over (and implicitly against) the traditional authority of the *faqih* by again invoking the very name of Khomeini, giving credence to criticisms that went far beyond mere politics. A key feature of the 1991 to 1992 Majles debates was the implicit defense of ideological pluralism that some deputies articulated.

Such maneuvers were not born out of pure principle. Islamist leftists had often invoked their constitutional rights to block the right's attacks. But the intensity of the Islamist left's criticisms of the regime's autocratic behavior and its focus on questions of individual freedoms as opposed to the collective (and thus qualified) freedoms that Islamic leftists had long advocated, suggested that by 1992 some Children of Revolution (as they were called) were moving from Islamic Bolshevism to Islamic Menshevism. This trend was an outgrowth of dissonant institutionalization; it stemmed from a redefinition from within one ideological path that had been shaped by the very elites who were now trying to redefine it. And it was precisely because they had charted this path that transforming it proved tricky. For apart from the other imposing path that Islamist leftists had to contend with—the clerical right's control of powerful institutions such as the Office of the *Faqih*, the Judiciary, and the Council of Guardians— Islamic leftists faced an imposing dilemma: how to advance notions of political participation, the rule of law, and rational political dialogue without appearing to betray the very revolutionary principles of Islamic government and cultural independence that Khomeini had championed.

Two Children of the Revolution played key roles in addressing this dilemma: Mohammad Khatami and Abdolkarim Soroush. Although the first was a cleric and the second a lay intellectual, both were Islamic leftists whose multiple political imaginations had been shaped by their exposures to Western political thought. Although they had occupied key positions in the ideological apparatus of the state, these leftists were eventually persecuted by the very state they had once defended. In August 1992, Khatami resigned his post as minister of Islamic Culture when the new Majles prepared to impeach him for failing to defend Islamic values. Soroush—an academic who had once been close to Shariati and who had helped to reorganize the universities during the first years of the revolution—was forced in 1996 to resign his post at Teheran University after

---

[33] *FBIS, Near East South Asia (NES)*, 92-098-S, 17 June 1992, from *Resalat*, 23 April 1992.

his writings provoked a violent response from regime hard-liners and their thugs in the paramilitary Hezbollah.

While there were significant differences between Khatami and Soroush, both men held that the most effective way to prevent young people from becoming disaffected from Islam was to get the clergy out of the business of imposing Islamic ideology.[34] Faith and politics had to be distanced to prevent the second from corrupting the first.[35] This implicitly reformationist stance allowed each to argue that religious freedom would secure rather than undermine religious authenticity—that Khomeini's quest for cultural independence would be served by more rather less pluralism. That such pluralism might invite Western influence was a dilemma that both men addressed, although in different ways. Khatami argued that when confronted by a global revolution in technology and communications, the only way to instill in the young a sense of dignity was to give them the critical and rational faculties to address the West. This goal, he argued, could not be attained by "building fences around people's consciousness."[36] Soroush echoed but went far beyond Khatami's thesis. Touching a raw nerve, he reminded his fellow Islamist leftists that much of the existential language they had used to vilify the West was hardly Islamic. "In their zeal for opposing the West," he noted, "they want to denounce modernism . . . with reasoning taken from foreigners themselves!"[37] Moreover, Soroush took the idea of "saving Islam by distancing cleric and state" much further than Khatami could, given that the latter was a cleric. Soroush did this not only by making the classic Weberian argument that religious knowledge was distinct from the scientific knowledge and thus could not provide a basis for modern politics; he also reached into Shi'ite mystical tradition to argue that God was a divine mystery whose "essences" could never be expressed in man-made ideologies.[38] By redefining the mystical aspects of Khomeini's (and Shariati's) ideology in ways that pointed toward individual rather than mass charismatic experience, Soroush tried to forge a vision of political reform that was both spiritually inspiring and politically rational.

The Limits of Path Innovation in Post-Khomeini Iran

The revisionist ideas advanced by Khatami and Soroush were echoed by a growing body of lay intellectuals and by several leading clerics such as Ayatol-

---

[34] See Soroush's controversial article on the clergy in *Kiyan*, April–May 1995, as translated in *FBIS-NES*, 95-241-S.

[35] Mohammad Khatami, *Hope and Challenge: The Iranian President Speaks* (Binghamton, NY: Institute of Global and Cultural Studies, 1997). "The West," Khatami wrote, "has . . . cast aside the deification of repressive thinking that had been imposed on the masses in the name of religion."

[36] Ibid., 47.

[37] Abdolkarmin Soroush, "Knowledge Seen as Basis of Modernism" *Kiyan*, 22 June–August 1994, in *FBIS-NES*, 95-109-S, 7 June 1995.

[38] See "Soroush on Meaning, Foundation," *Kiyan*, August–September, 1995, 4–13, in *FBIS-NES*, 96-022-S, 1 February 1996.

lah Mohammad Montazeri and his student Mohsen Kadivar. This lay-clerical alliance directed its message to the colleges and universities. By 1996, the two offered a mass arena through which the reformists could mobilize nearly one million students. Moreover, despite the state's efforts, it had failed to completely purge the universities of Western-trained academics, or to remove social science and humanities curricula, which included significant doses of Western political theory.[39] Thus, Khatami's victory in May 1997 was not fortuitous. On the contrary, he won 70 percent of the nearly 30 million votes cast because he articulated the disaffection of both the children and grandchildren of the revolution.

Despite this progress, the struggle that Khatami and his allies waged from the spring of 1997 through the spring of 2000 demonstrated that dissonant institutionalization was a double-edged sword. On the one hand, Khatami and his allies had reinterpreted a major path of the revolution to legitimate a pluralistic agenda. That they did so through, rather than against, Khomeini's eclectic vision showed that a state which had aspired to ideological hegemony had bequeathed a dissonant legacy. But that same state had also generated a competing institutional-ideological legacy that was quintessentially path dependent. This dependency took the form of powerful organizations and constituencies, which sought to defend the institutional and ideological prerogatives of the new *faqih*, Ayatollah Khamanei. A clerical elite that had invested political and social capital in powerful organizations such as the Council of Guardians, the Judiciary, and wealthy charitable foundations (for example, the Martyrs' Foundation) would not give up such sunk costs without a fight.

How would this battle be waged, and what would be its outcome? To answer these questions we must compare the constitutional powers of the *faqih* and the president. In 1989 those powers had been redefined in revisions of the constitution that in some ways undercut the Supreme Leader's authority while bolstering that of the president. By holding that the *faqih* no longer had to be a *marja* (religious source of emulation), the 1989 Constitution created the possibility that a popular cleric might emerge as a rival to the *faqih*. Moreover, by abolishing the post of prime minister, the 1989 constitution left the president as the sole national representative directly elected by popular mandate. The *faqih*, by contrast, was indirectly elected by a clerical body known as the Council of Experts. The Council's central role in choosing the Supreme Leader signaled that henceforth the *faqih's* legitimacy derived in the main from traditional authority and institutions.[40] In short, the 1989 constitution set up a poten-

---

[39] Azadeh Kian-Thiébaut, "Political and Social Transformations in Post-Islamist Iran," *Middle East Report* 29 (Fall 1999): 12–16.

[40] I write "in the main" because the *faqih's* authority, as defined in the 1989 constitution, also has legal-rational foundations. Among his qualifications, not only must he be a man of "scholarship, as required for performing the function of *mufti* in . . . fields of *fiqh* (Islamic jurisprudence); but he must also possess the "better jurisprudential and political perspicacity." By contrast, Article Five of the 1979 constitution stated that Khomeini had been "recognized and accepted by the majority of the people as . . . leader," thus giving ultimate legal sanction to the charismatic foundations of Khomeini's authority.

tial conflict between a president whose authority derived from modern, legal-rational procedures and principles and a *faqih* whose formal authority emanated from a traditional office and ideology. The potential for a "*faqih* versus president" conflict seems to have been anticipated in the l989 constitution. By expanding the institutional powers of the *faqih* over bodies such as the military and the police, it gave the Supreme Leader the means and right to limit the president's authority.[41] That this strengthening of patrimonialism occurred in tandem with increased democratization within one wing of the revolutionary family, and that this dynamic was partly abetted by the very same constitution that reinforced the *faqih's* formal powers is precisely the point: this dissonant arrangement helps to explain the contradictory political contest that unfolded during the three years following Khatami's May 1997 election.

Power Sharing/Power Struggle: Khamanei and Khatami

That contest can be summarized as one of fragile and limited power sharing at the zenith of the state and an open-ended power struggle within and between that state and society. Following his election, Khatami tried to increase his leverage by forming a cabinet that offered Islamic leftists significant posts and by encouraging a boisterous reformist press. The mission of the press was to compensate for a Majles that was still controlled by conservatives. An "Islamic" civil society, as Khatami called it, would mobilize the youth and thus help set the stage for a reformist victory during the winter 2000 Majles elections. Yet Khatami had to be careful; if this process proceeded too quickly, it would not only provoke a backlash from the conservative clerical elite judiciary and security establishment, but might also compel the *faqih* to turn against the president. Since such a development would probably result in the political demise of one or both of these leaders, Khatami and Khamanei had a shared incentive to restrain their militant allies and build an effective entente while at the same time maintaining their credibility as spokesmen for contending wings of the Islamic revolution.

This balancing act worked fairly well during the first two years of Khatami's presidency. While Khatami promoted the opposition press; called for a "dialogue of civilization"; and made speeches in favor of Majles "rights," freedom of opinion, and the rule of law; Khamanei attacked the West; issued periodic threats against the reform movement; and condoned the judiciary's periodic closures of opposition newspapers and the arrests of their editors. But when such acts encouraged their most militant followers to push the proverbial envelope, Khatami and Khamanei would draw together. For example, after a July 1999 attack by security forces on a dorm at Teheran University, Khatami called for restraint from the students while Khamanei praised the president and

---

[41] See Mohsen M. Milani, "The Transformation of the Velayat-e Faqih Institution: From Khomeini to Khamanei," *The Muslim World* 82 (July–October 1991): 175–90.

warned his hard-line allies that they should not take the law into their own hands.[42] For both Khomeini and Khatami, the peaceful coexistence of Iran's increasingly contentious forces had to be maintained.

Yet it soon became clear that this fragile entente had succeeded in part because Khamanei's conservative allies still controlled the Majles. Because they could be depended on to pass draconian legislation (such as a press law that sparked the July 1999 student riots at Teheran University), Khamanei's militant allies remained confident that they could block the reform movement. Thus, in the run up to the February 2000 Majles elections it was widely expected that the Council of Guardians would again disqualify a large number of reformists from running. Although the Council failed to do so (in part because the reformists had flooded the election arena with thousands of candidates), in the aftermath of the first round—during which the reformists won 180 out of 290 seats—the conservatives regrouped. Within two months all seventeen opposition newspapers were closed down, and the Council of Guardians reversed ten reformist victories on various pretexts. Moreover, given that by April the Council had still not validated the crucial Teheran results, where nearly every one of the thirty available seats had been won by the pro-reform Iran Participation Front (IPF), it seemed that the popular will might still be thwarted. It took Khamanei's direct intervention to assure that the second round of elections was held and that most of the Teheran seats were awarded to the IPF. While this dramatic act allowed the reformists to take control of the Majles in May 2000, it also reminded reformists that their fate hung on the *faqih's* words and good will. This point was driven home two months later, when Khamanei blocked the attempts of the Majles to revise the draconian press law and implicitly supported the arrest of many prominent editors and writers in the reform movement. In one form or another, dissonant politics had recreated itself, thus limiting the ability of Iran's reformists to move from ideological innovation to political power.

Indonesia: Recognizing and Institutionalizing Multipolar Diversity

"Indonesia," Fred von De Mehden writes, "is a nation of Muslims divided in their understanding of what is entailed in being an adherent to that faith."[43] By itself, this statement would not distinguish Indonesia's Sunni Muslims from Iran's Shi'ites, whose lay and clerical leaders also advanced contending visions of religion and politics. The key difference is that Indonesia's Islamists established *mass* organizations, which articulated contending visions outside the

---

[42] See Charles Kurzman, "Student Protests and the Stability of Gridlock in Khatami's Iran," (http://www.sba.widener.edu/zang/default.html.), 5 November 1998. The author was present during this speech by Khamanei.

[43] Quoted in Douglas E. Ramage, *Politics in Indonesia: Democracy, Islam and the Ideology of Tolerance* (London and New York: Routledge, 1995), 15.

gambit of the state. President Sukarno (who ruled from 1945 through 1965) and President Suharto (who ruled from 1966 to 1998) institutionalized the principle that domestic peace in Indonesia required a distancing of church and state, and state and society. This factor makes Indonesia a case of substantial, multipolar dissonance.

The distancing of culture and state that unfolded during the 1950s and 1960s was impelled by Indonesia's plural nature. Quite apart from the obvious and sometimes violent cleavages that divide Indonesia's Muslims—who constitute 90 percent of the country's 200 million citizens—from its Christian and Chinese minorities were divisions between Muslims. Indonesia has 300 ethnic groups and 250 distinct languages spread across some 3,000 islands.[44] Within this rich quilt, a key symbolic divide exists between Muslims who favor blending indigenous Javanese-Hindu and mystical or Sufi traditions with Islam, and those who spurn such syncreticism in favor of a unitary vision of Islam. In 1960 Clifford Geertz described this division in terms of *santri* (devout) versus *abangan* (nominal) Muslims. The authority of the *abangan*, he argued, stemmed from a pre-Islamic symbolic system whose patrimonialist ethos was deeply rooted in rural Java.[45] Although decades of urbanization and increased education have blurred the *santri/abangan* distinction, a sociocultural and ideological divide remains between traditionalist and modernist Muslims. Much of Indonesian politics was shaped by the efforts of Presidents Sukarno and Suharto—as well as their allies and opponents inside and outside the state—to institutionalize and manipulate these two visions of Islam.

These manipulative strategies were abetted by the legacy of Dutch colonialism. The Dutch reached a *modus vivendi* with the *kiai* (traditional clerics), which allowed the latter to maintain control over local bureaucratic and religious organizations so long as they accepted the authority of the secular government.[46] Although Indonesia's Japanese occupiers tried to unify Islamic organizations by creating the Masyumi party, the latter was always a loose alliance of competing groups, the most important of which were the *Nahdlatul Ulema* (The Renaissance of the Ulema or NU) and the *Muhammadiya* (followers of Mohammad). Created in 1926, the NU was led by a coalition of rural clerics from East and Central Java and urban politicians from Java's cities. The NU was traditionalist in that its leaders held that the *Sunna* (example) of the Prophet Mohammad as codified in the *mazhab* (four orthodox schools) of Sunni Islam provided *the* authoritative foundation for political life. But NU's vision was syncretic in that many of its rural adherents—some 30 million by the late 1970s—maintained heterodox Javanese-Hindu and quite possibly Sufi mystical prac-

---

[44] See Karl D. Jackson, "Bureaucratic Polity: A Theoretical Framework for the Analysis of Power and Communications in Indonesia" in Karl D. Jackson and Lucian W. Pye, eds., *Political Power and Communications in Indonesia* (Berkeley: University of California Press, 1978), 3–22.

[45] See Clifford Geertz, *The Religion of Java* (Chicago: University of Chicago Press, 1960).

[46] See Karel Steenbrink, *Dutch Colonialism and Indonesian Islam, Contacts and Conflicts 1596–1950*, transl. Jan Steenbrink and Henry Jansen (Amsterdam-Atlanta, GA: Rodopi, 1993).

tices. By contrast, *Muhammadiya*, established in 1906, was led by politically active clerics and lay Islamic thinkers who opposed the "non-Islamic" practices of NU's members. These men were influenced by the ideas of Mohammad Abduh, the turn of the century Egyptian Islamic reformer. Although a liberal, many of Abduh's disciples such as Rashid Rida were authoritarian. Like Iran's Shariati, Rida strove to transform Islam into a comprehensive mobilizing ideology that could compete with the "ideologies" of the West.[47] It was this reformist example that inspired *Muhammadiya's* leaders and earned the movement the label "modernist," an ambiguous term that obscured the movement's illiberalism.

Although *Muhammadiya* and NU were competitors, their differences were at times obscured by their competition with the secular-nationalist parties. Yet in as much as NU sought to prevent the state from becoming a vehicle of Islamization, its leaders often felt more comfortable supporting the ruling Indonesian Nationalist party (PNI) and its various successors and rivals, such as the Indonesian Democratic party (PDI) and Golkar—the official ruling party established in 1967. By mediating between *Muhammadiya* and the nationalist parties, NU helped sustain a multipolar ideological field that encouraged interelite competition, negotiations, and accommodations.

After Indonesia won independence in 1945, Sukarno attempted to accommodate (and control) this multipolar field by using several devices, one of which was an eclectic ideology known as "Pancasila."[48] A Sanskrit term meaning "five principles," the first principle of Pancasila was belief in God. While all Indonesians were expected to follow one of the monotheistic religions, it was understood that all religious practices would issue from society rather than the state. This principle was favored by the nationalists, communists, and the NU. The second principle, a just and civilized humanity, articulated the desire of socialists and nationalists (i.e., *abangan* Muslims) to align Indonesia with the international community. The third principle, Indonesian national unity, emphasized the desire of Sukarno and his allies in the nationalist and NU camps to forge a common identity that would coexist with other religious and ethnic identities. The fourth principle, an Indonesian style-democracy based upon the ideals of *musyawarah* and *mufakat* (consultation and consensus), addressed the sensibilities of both traditionalist and modernist Muslims. Derived from the *Quran* (Koran), these two terms symbolized a cooperative vision of political community in implicit opposition to what many Muslims deemed to be the conflictual foundations of Western liberal democracy. Pancasila's fifth principle, one dear to nationalists and communists, but which had widespread support, called for social justice.

---

[47] "Alfian," *Muhammadiyah: The Political Behavior of a Muslim Modernist Organization Under Dutch Colonialism* (Yogyakarta, Indonesia: Gadjah Mada University Press, 1989), 134–79.

[48] On Pancasila, see Ramage, *Politics in Indonesia*, 10–22.

It has been noted that Pancasila was not "meant to be internally consistent."[49] For Sukarno and his allies, it offered a symbolic compromise that Indonesians could interpret in various ways, providing they accepted the unifying principle that implicitly animated Pancasila, namely that no group could use the state to impose its culture, religion, or ideology on society. Thus, Pancasila served a function similar to that of the Iranian constitutions of 1979 and 1989 or to that of Khomeini's eclectic ideology. By inviting and institutionalizing contradictions, it created a medium of symbolic competition that could be harnessed to reinforce or renegotiate public order.

To sustain such order, Sukarno used two additional instruments. First, he deployed his charisma to both legitimate and control symbolic anomalies. Unlike Khomeini, who exhibited but could hardly tolerate contradictions, Sukarno thrived on them. "I have made myself the meeting place of all trends and ideologies," he declared. "I have blended . . . them until they finally became the present Sukarno."[50] Second, Sukarno created a presidential regime that gave the executive almost unlimited powers. Although this development was preceded by a chaotic experiment in multiparty politics, during the "Guided Democracy" of 1958 to 1965, the lower and upper houses of parliament—the Representative Council (DPR) and the Consultative Council (MPR)—were replaced by a body whose members were appointed by the president. Backed by the military, Sukarno created a "bureaucratic polity," whose essential features—a strong presidency, military control, and bureaucratic centralism—endured during the ensuing four and a half decades.[51]

The emasculation of the legislature meant that henceforth Indonesia's parliament would never provide an arena of controlled ideological contest comparable to that of Iran's Majles. Yet under Sukarno and Suharto, political parties did play a role in sustaining dissonant politics. In one incarnation or another, they articulated the "distinctive visions of polity" that contending sociocultural communities espoused by maintaining shifting degrees of institutional and ideological distance from the state.[52] Relative autonomy facilitated an elaborate game by which Indonesia's presidents and their allies tried to divide or coopt their opponents, while the latter tried to use state bodies such as the Ministry of Religion to advance their agendas. In the resulting confluence of party and elite politics it became "all too easy for rival claimants to power to conclude that the only rational way to engage in politics is to work behind the scenes, forging alliances with ascendant factions in the ruling elite and taking care not to push for broader political participation."[53]

---

[49] Mochtar Pabotinngi, "Indonesia: Historicizing the New Order's Legitimacy Dilemma" in Muthiah Alagappa, ed., *Political Legitimacy in Southeast Asia* (Stanford: Stanford University Press, 1995), 234.

[50] Ibid.

[51] DPR stands for Dewan Perwakilan Rakyat and MPR stands for Majelis Permusyawaratan Rakyat. On the workings of Indonesia's "bureaucratic polity" see Jackson, "Bureaucratic Polity," 2–22.

[52] R. William Liddle, "Participation and Political Parties" in Jackson and Pye, *Political Power*, 187.

[53] Robert W. Hefner, "Islam in an Era of Nation-States: Politics and Religious Renewal in Muslim Southeast Asia" in Robert W. Hefner and Patricia Horvatich eds., *Islam in an Era of Nation-States* (Honolulu: University of Hawaii Press, 1997), 12.

Conflict and Accommodation Under Sukarno

While we cannot analyze this game in detail, we must highlight how three of its central features eventually facilitated a transition to power sharing and democratic reform. First, the modernist and traditionalist Islamic parties competed to defend their constituencies and ideologies by using the state while at the same time trying to maintain distance from it; second, the ruling and opposition elites made various attempts to reappropriate the dissonant legacy bequeathed by Sukarno; and third, Suharto and his allies sought to divide or coopt opposition elites in a manner that enhanced the regime's autonomy and defused calls for political reform.

From the early 1960s until the late 1970s, Indonesia's leaders pursued a strategy designed to divide and coopt the opposition and to isolate Islamic leaders who espoused radical changes or the establishment of an Islamic state. NU leaders facilitated these efforts. While paying lip service to the notion of an Islamic state, they feared that establishing such a state would give their modernist rivals in *Muhammadiya* a vehicle through which to "purify" NU's eclectic view of Islam. During the 1950s Islamic separatist revolts reinforced the perception among NU leaders that an open democratic system would empower their modernist rivals. This concern led NU to quit the Masyumi Federation (in which *Muhammadiya* played a leading role) and to back Sukarno's Guided Democracy. In short, given the absence of credible alliance alternatives,[54] and animated by a conservative ideology that valorized the quest for political order, NU's clerics sought the protection of an authoritarian state.[55] The state paid NU back by awarding it's chairman control over the Ministry of Religion and by excluding NU's leaders from periodic reorganizations of the political parties. Still, the NU could not halt a descent into ideological and ethnic conflict to which Sukarno himself contributed by trying to imbue Pancasila with a Javanese and thus implicitly anti-Islamic interpretation.[56] Islamic leaders retaliated by assailing Pancasila, a dangerous development that prompted Sukarno to rely on the Indonesian Communist party (PKI). Such miscalculations set the stage for the September 1965 coup engineered by Suharto and a wing of the military.

Rationalizing Dissonant Politics: State/Society Dynamics Under Suharto

Suharto attempted to succeed where Sukarno had failed by repudiating the latter's quasi-socialist economic policies, by further centralizing the system of bu-

---

[54] In the 1955 elections, Masyumi obtained 57 seats (23 percent), NU, 45 seats (18.4. percent), the Indonesian Nationalist party (PNI), 27 seats (21 percent), and the Indonesian Communist party, 39 seats (16.4 percent). Since the NU spurned both the communists and Masyumi, it could offer the PNI a credible ally. See Liddle, "Participation and Political Parties," 174–75.

[55] Greg Fealy, "'Rowing in a Typhoon' Nahdlatul Ulama and the Decline of Parliamentary Democracy" in David Bourchier and John Legge, *Democracy in Indonesia, 1950s and 1990s* (Monash, Australia: Monash Papers on Southeast Asia No. 31, Centre of Southeast Asian Studies, Monash University, 1994), 88–97.

[56] Ramage, *Democracy, Politics in Indonesia*, 17.

reaucratic control, by enhancing the power of the military, and by purging both communist and Islamic militants. This purge was accomplished by a cynical maneuver: in 1965 and 1966, Sukarno's allies mobilized Islamic groups—particularly the student wing of the NU (*Ansar*)—in an anticommunist campaign. When the bloodletting ceased with some 500,000 dead, NU leaders were rewarded; whereas nearly every ministry was reduced in scope and power, the Ministry of Religion was expanded. Moreover, although Suharto revived the lower and upper houses of parliament, he imposed controls that not only assured the government of a majority, but also gave the regime almost unlimited powers to select candidates for both the ruling Golkar party and the opposition parties. In the run up to the 1971 elections, Suharto used these powers to conduct a purge of Islamists from which NU emerged virtually unscathed.

Yet while the state became more autocratic, dissonant politics endured as each faction within the ideologically eclectic elite tried to repackage the ideological legacies of the previous era. A key element in this contest was the battle to reappropriate Pancasila. In the late 1960s Suharto, as well several leading intellectuals and military officers, began advocating the view that Pancasila constituted an organic ideology that reflected the intrinsic personality of the Indonesian people. Retaliating against this apparent effort to impose Javanese-Hindu identity, the Islamic parties (including the NU) called for reintroducing a controversial section of the Jakarta Charter—a statement of principle that called upon Muslims to follow *Shariah* (Islamic law). Its insertion in the 1945 Constitution had been rejected by Sukarno. The attempt to reintroduce the Charter's *Shariah* section demonstrated that the recent banning of the Masyumi Party had not silenced the Islamic issue. Pressed by their followers, the leaders of *Muhammadiya* and NU had to join forces.[57] This development again put the NU in the awkward position of allying with its modernist foes. NU tried to skirt this dilemma by endorsing a compromise calling for Islamic parties to affirm that the "Jakarta Charter 'inspires' the 1945 Constitution . . . without attempting to further define or modify it."[58] But this solution pacified neither the government nor its radical Islamist opponents. As a result, NU found itself on the receiving end of hostility from both. In late 1971 the government ended NU's eighteen-year control of the Ministry of Religion by appointing an intellectual technocrat as minister.

Path Innovation in the NU: From Traditionalism to Liberalism?

These events had a transformatory effect on NU that was similar to changes that would unfold within Iran's Islamic left twenty years later. By the early 1970s, the politicization of NU's leadership had provoked a profound process of rethinking among a group of students and political activists. Known as the

---

[57] See Allan Samson, "Conceptions of Politics, Power, and Ideology in Contemporary Indonesian Islam" in Jackson and Pye, *Political Power*, 221–22.
[58] Ibid., 221.

"Generation of 66," they had expected to benefit from their implicit alliance with the New Order. Instead, they found that Muslims had been drawn into a morass of political conflict that was deflecting NU from promoting its cultural and ethical goals. Seeking to remedy this problem, several intellectual/political activists began to redefine NU's traditionalist ideology. In the ensuing decade, they showed that the symbolic-institutional path that had long played a central role in Indonesian's dissonant politics could be pushed in new directions.

This movement's chief theorist was Nurcholish Madjid, the former leader of the Islamic Student Association.[59] Madjid sought to create an inspiring alternative to the totalistic ideologies advanced by militant Islamists. The latter legitimated such ideologies by arguing that the doctrine of the transcendent unity of God (*tauhid*) demanded total political, social, and ideological unity. As *Muhammadiya* leader Amien Rais put it, because in Islam there can be "no differentiation between worldly and other-worldly," there can be no "contradictions." *Tauhid*, Rais insisted, demands "a society ... free from ... exploitation, feudalism and rejection of differentiation among class, race ... and so forth."[60] Fearing that this intolerant vision would sap Islam of its spiritual force, Madjid tried to discredit it by standing the concept of *tauhid* (and secularism) on its head. *Tauhid*, he held, was *not* about politics. On the contrary, because "absolute transcendence pertains *solely* to God," it should "give rise to an attitude of 'desacralization' towards that which is other than God, namely the world, its problems and values.... To sacralize anything other than God is, in reality, *shirk* [polytheism]." To make this case for desacralization Madjid turned to mystical ideas that were rooted deeply in Indonesian society. Invoking a central tenet of mysticism, he argued that "because God is the Ultimate Absolute ... beyond the ken of human comprehension," it was a sacrilege to assume that man could transform God's mysteries into mundane ideology. The remedy was to embrace a form of secularization that would strengthen Islamic piety by "temporalizing ... values which are ... worldly, and ... freeing the *umma* [Muslim community] from the tendency to spiritualize them."[61]

Madjid's choice of words may have been unfortunate. For most Muslim Indonesians, secularism connoted an attack on, rather than a defense of, religion. Yet if he did not anticipate this reaction, it was because Madjid was a man of multiple imaginations. While he celebrated the particularities of Indonesian Islam, his exposure to the ideas of American Protestant thinkers such as Harvey Cox led Madjid to make arguments in terms that most Indonesians could not

---

[59] Hefner, "Islamization and Democratization in Indonesia" in Hefner et al., eds., *Islam in an Era of Nation-States*, 75–127.

[60] Howard M. Federspeil, *Indonesia in Transition: Muslim Intellectuals and National Development* (Commack, NY: Nova Science Publishers, 1998), 75–6.

[61] From a talk given by Madjid in January 1970. See "Necessity of Renewing Islamic Thought and Reinvigorating Religious Understanding" in Charles Kurzman, ed., *Liberal Islam, A Sourcebook* (New York and Oxford: Oxford University Press, 1998), 286, 209. (Emphasis added.)

easily grasp.[62] Nevertheless, because his overall message found a receptive audience among NU's traditionalist followers, it began to stick. In the 1980s traditionalism and modernism were grafted to produce what one scholar called "neo-modernism."[63]

The man most responsible for institutionalizing this ideological shift was Madjid's colleague, Abdurrahman Wahid, also known as "Gus Dur." The grandson of NU's founder and son of its second leader, Wahid Yasyim, Wahid too was a man of multiple imaginations. After pursuing Islamic studies at Egypt's Al-Azhar University during the 1960s, he moved to Iraq where he studied Arabic literature and European philosophy at Baghdad University. He then lived in Western Europe for a time before returning to Indonesia. Wahid's affinity for Western European liberal thought, his gritty feel for the syncretic culture of Javanese Islam, and his intimate knowledge of NU's politics made him an ideal candidate for linking the ideas of Indonesia's liberal Muslim intelligentsia to NU's mass base.[64] But his decision to pursue this challenge was also motivated by Suharto's renewed campaign to impose a "Javanized" version of Pancasila. This campaign reached new heights in 1982, when the government proposed legislation requiring that all social and professional organizations adopt Pancasila as their sole guiding ideology (*asas tunggal*). When this policy provoked a vitriolic response from Muslim politicians and anti-Chinese riots in Jakarta in 1984, it appeared that irreparable harm had been done to Pancasila's ability to symbolize interconfessional compromise.

The dilemma facing Wahid was how to revive Pancasila's dissonant spirit without appearing to endorse Suharto's efforts to monopolize the ideological field. NU's 1984 Congress not only provided a chance not only to address this dilemma, but also to secure support for Wahid's neomodernist vision. Seizing upon the disenchantment of NU's clerics with the old guard of NU politicians, Wahid and his colleague Achmad Siddiq mounted a successful campaign to be elected general chairman and executive director of NU. They then convinced their followers to endorse two decisions: first, that NU would stop all participation in the state-controlled party system in order to focus its energies on promoting social and cultural reform on a grassroots level; and second, that NU would formally accept Pancasila and the 1945 Constitution as the final bases of state authority. But NU's leaders also stipulated that they were adopting Pan-

---

[62] Hefner, "Islamization and Democratization in Indonesia," 85. See also Madjid, "In Search of Islamic Roots for Modern Pluralism: The Indonesian Experiences" in Mark. R. Woodward, ed., *Toward a New Paradigm: Recent Developments in Indonesian Islamic Thought* (Tempe, AZ: Program for Southeast Asian Studies, 1997), 92.

[63] Greg Barton, "The Impact of Neo-Modernism on Indonesian Islamic Thought: The Emergence of a New Pluralism" in Bourchier and Legge, *Democracy in Indonesia*, 143–50.

[64] Greg Barton, "The Liberal, Progressive Roots of Abdurahman Wahid's Thought" in Greg Fealy and Greg Barton, eds., *Nahdlatul Ulama, Traditional Islam and Modernity* (Monash, Australia: Monash Asia Institute, 1998). This book is also available on the Internet at www.muslims.net/KMNU/pustaka/baku1/utama.html.

casila because it provided a framework in which *all* groups could pursue their religious faith. As Siddiq put it in a famous formula that echoed Madjid's mystical liberalism, in so far as Pancasila was a "philosophy created by human beings" whereas Islam was "a revelation," the former could provide the foundation for freely pursuing the latter.[65]

By design or default, Siddiq's formula served the interests of both the government and NU. In the ensuing two years, the government adopted his distinction between philosophy and revelation to convince other Islamic organizations that there was no contradiction between Islam and Pancasila. That Suharto decided at the same time to cease the campaign to Javanize Pancasila and to declare it instead an "open ideology" encouraged other Islamic leaders to renounce the notion of an Islamic state in favor of a society-based movement for "cultural Islam." As for NU, by withdrawing from a political arena that had been manipulated by the state, it was now free, in Wahid's words, to develop "an alternative view of Pancasila" that was both nonsectarian and democratic.[66]

NU: Between Autocratic State and Autocratic Islamists

Wahid and Siddiq pursued this goal with considerable success. Their efforts were facilitated by the growth of Indonesia's urban middle class, which provided a new cadre of activists, and by the creative ways in which Wahid introduced the use of *ijtihad* (free interpretation) of the Quran to enlist the support of maverick clerics. This push for a more liberal Islam was also abetted by a countervailing Islamic trend that took its cue from populist-fundamentalist Islamic movements in the Middle East.[67] Led in part by Rais, and partly housed in *Muhammadiya*, because this movement was based in the urban middle class, it competed with NU's attempts to broaden its following. Unlike NU, *Muhammadiya* had remained active in the political system through its affiliation with the United Development party (PPP), the sole Islamic party remaining after the 1973 reorganization of the party system. NU had quit the PPP in 1983—a move that caused great bitterness between the two because it undercut PPP's ability to compete in subsequent elections. This distrust also reflected the deep personal and ideological divide between Rais and Wahid. The latter denounced the former's xenophobic attacks on "Western civilization" and his verbal assaults on Indonesia's Christian and Chinese minorities, while Rais accused Wahid of "exaggerating differences among Muslims."[68]

One might assume that having benefited from NU's official endorsement of Pancasila as the sole basis of the state, the regime would now support Wahid

---

[65] Ramage, *Politics in Indonesia*, 54–5.

[66] Ibid., 56.

[67] On this dynamic, see Fred R. von de Mehden, *Two Worlds of Islam Interaction Between Southeast Asia and the Middle East* (Gainesville: University Of Florida Press, 1993).

[68] Adam Schwarz, *A Nation in Waiting: Indonesia in the 1990s* (Boulder, CO: Westview Press, 1994). Wahid also discussed these points with me during a 7 June 1999 interview.

rather than his Islamist rivals. But because Suharto remained committed to authoritarian rule, he was hardly inclined to back Wahid. Their relationship worsened in 1990, when Suharto endorsed the creation of the government-sponsored Indonesian Association of Muslim Intellectuals (ICMI). Chaired by Vice President B. J. Habibie, the ICMI's unstated purpose was to create a de-facto alliance between the regime and Islamists that gave the former control over the latter. But the entrance of Rais and other Islamists into the ICMI raised fears within NU that advocates of an illiberal Islamic vision might seize control of the state. These concerns were fed by radical Islamic groups such as the Indonesian Islamic Preaching Council, whose leaders readily admitted: "After 1990, Soeharto became more conducive to Muslim wishes so we supported him."[69] As for the ICMI, several of its members who came from the PPP and *Muhammadiya* openly stated that the "purpose of the ICMI is to establish a new Masyumi"—an organization that would control all Islamic movements.[70] Thus, when *Muhammadiya* endorsed Suharto for a fifth term, Wahid grew alarmed. Although the government had pressured NU to follow suit, during its 1992 congress NU refused to do so, choosing instead to reaffirm its commitment to Pancasila. Still, if during the ensuing six years the relationship between the two leaders had its ups and downs, Wahid avoided actions that would irrevocably antagonize Suharto—a strategy that echoed his commitment to power sharing and ideological inclusiveness.[71]

The 7 June 1999 Elections: Dissonant Politics and Power Sharing

Wahid may have succeeded in transforming NU into a more liberal organization, but as was the case with Iran's Islamic left, such path innovation took place in a highly constraining institutional and ideological context. Although there was no Council of Guardians in Indonesia, Wahid's efforts were hindered by the state's authoritarian institutions. Thus, for example, in 1994 the regime tried to unseat Wahid by supporting a rival candidate for the position of NU chairman. Yet Wahid and his allies enjoyed one advantage that Iran's Islamic leftists lacked: the NU could be rapidly transformed into an organized political party. Thus, when the economic and financial crisis that swept through Asia in 1998 provoked violent riots and the burning of Jakarta's China Town, Suharto resigned in May. After the new acting president, B. J. Habibie, promised to hold democratic elections, NU came out of its political hibernation by forming the National Awakening party (PKB).

---

[69] Interview of Ahmad Soemargono, August 1998, in Adam Schwarz, *A Nation in Waiting: Indonesia's Search for Stability*, rev. ed. (Boulder, CO: Westview Press, 2000), 26.

[70] Ramage, *Politics in Indonesia*, 93.

[71] In March 1991 Wahid, together with forty-four prominent intellectuals, established the Forum Democracy, an association that was largely made up of secular intellectuals. The Forum was created in part to provide a counterweight to the ICMI.

Joining the PKB in the 7 June 1999 Representative Council (DPR) elections were the following: the ruling Golkar party, whose leader was Habibie; the Struggling Democratic party of Indonesia (PDI-P), led by the avowedly secular Megawati Sukarnopoutra (who was Sukarno's daughter and thus very popular); PPP, the official Islamic party; and Amin Rais's National Mandate party (PAN), whose support came mostly from *Muhammadiya*. In addition, there were a myriad of smaller parties such as the Crescent Start and Justice parties, both of which were Islamist groupings whose ideologies echoed the more fundamentalist orientation of the PPP.

The above line-up reflected the two most important divisions in Indonesian politics: between secularists and Islamists on one side and Islamists and Islamists on the other. Given this dissonant legacy, it appeared that an effective challenge to Golkar required alliances that transcended the secular-Islamist divide. Yet this outcome was hardly preordained. Indeed, Suharto's previous courtship of Islamists suggested an alternative: a conservative alliance between Golkar and PPP (and perhaps PAN) that would block a PDI-P/PKB alliance. But such a combination would certainly provoke a harsh response from the military, which opposed Suharto's efforts to coopt Islamists. Given that the military had seventy-five preassigned seats in the Consultative Assembly (MPR) (which was slated to elect the president in the fall of 1999), its position could not be ignored. Moreover, all of the above actors had to consider the main force pushing for immediate and broad democratic reforms—the students. Their daily demonstrations in front of the MPR showed that they were ready to do battle with the police and military to thwart any effort to block or water down political reforms.

For the PKB, this messy political field offered opportunities. While it had never won more than 18.7 percent of the vote, NU's moderate credentials put the PKB in a position to chart a midway course between the secular PDI-P and the Islamic parties. Although a stroke had left Wahid half blind and weak, he tried to secure a "contingent institutional compromise" (or political pact) that would advance democratic reforms without ceding the field to exponents of radical or precipitous changes. Thus, in November 1998 Wahid convinced Megawati and Rais to sign a manifesto that called for a package of moderate reforms. When student leaders then rejected the changes proposed by the MPR (which included reducing the military's DPR seats to thirty-eight but left intact that much discredited system for indirectly electing the president), Wahid tried to defuse the situation by calling for a "national dialogue" between all the main players, including Suharto. Similarly, during the campaign PKB leaders declared that so long as Islam remained separate from politics, they wanted "all components in society [to] participate in government."[72] The broad appeal of this inclusivist approach may explain why Wahid's nemesis—Rais—then signed a vague communiqué in which he, Megawati, and PKB chairman Alwi Shihab

---

[72] "PKB Promises 'National Reconciliation' if Elected," *The Jakarta Post*, 9 May 1999, in *FBIS-East Asia*, 8 May 1999.

promised to "unite . . . to continue reform."[73] Since PAN's creation, Rais had worked hard to secure a more moderate and ecumenical image for himself and his party. But such efforts could not hide the close ties between PAN and *Muhammadiya*, many of whose members despised Megawati's secular policies. Trying to walk this tightrope, Rais then signed a separate alliance agreement with the PPP. This move only alienated Wahid and Megawati while encouraging *Muhammadiya's* supporters to vote for the PPP. As a result, PAN only won 7 percent of the vote, whereas the PDI-P prevailed with 34 percent, Golkar took 22 percent, PKB secured 13 percent, and PPP reached 11 percent.

The next order of business was for the 700-member MPR to elect a president. A body that met once a year, it consisted of the 462 recently elected DPR members, the DPR's thirty-eight appointed military officers, and 200 additional deputies chosen by a murky system of provincial and functional councils. Given Megawati's victory, she should have been the first choice for president, but two obstacles stood in her way. First, many Islamic leaders including some in PKB opposed electing a female president. The leaders of the PPP and PAN in particular feared that Megawati would pursue her father's anti-Islamic alliances and policies.[74] This fear was fed in part by Megawati's overtly secular orientation and also by what many Indonesians held was the over-representation of Chinese politicians in the PDI-P. Second, the existing election system gave Golkar's candidate, Habibie, an unfair advantage. The gerrymandered election system was not only designed to reward Golkar with more seats than was justified by its percentage of votes; it also gave Golkar disproportionate influence over choosing the MRP's 200 additional deputies. Thus, while Golkar won only 21 percent of the vote, it obtained 120 or 26 percent of the DPR's 468 elected seats. Along with the support from many of the 200 local and functional deputies, it was in a good position to forge a pro-Habibie alliance with Islamic parties, particularly the PPP, whose leaders were hardly advocates of liberal democratic reforms. Given that Habibie had continued to court Islamic leaders during the previous year, such a conservative alliance was not inconceivable.

But this was not to be. The military's pogrom in East Timor and the resulting insertion of United Nations troops in September 1999 forced Habibie to renounce his candidacy while it bolstered the authority of Golkar reformists who favored genuine democratic reform. Moreover, by discrediting the army, the East Timor debacle compelled the military to abstain from using its thirty-eight votes. Meanwhile, Rais secured the support of the major Islamic parties (known as the "Central Axis") for Wahid's candidacy, a development that Wahid actively encouraged. Rais's decision to back a man he so disliked is easily explained: at that moment Wahid was the only leader who could bring Indo-

---

[73] "No problem for Amien-Megawati Partnership," interview with Amien Rais, *Kompas Cberymedia* (www.compas.com/kompas-certak/9905/03English), 3 May 1999.

[74] The disproportionate role of Chinese in PDI-P's leadership ranks fed this fear. Although Wahid publicly supported Megawati, he privately feared that her candidacy would polarize the MPR and even the entire country. Interview with the author, 11 June 1999.

nesia's contending voices around one table. But Rais was not out of the game. Having previously engineered his election as Speaker of the DPR, he was well positioned to influence Wahid's future moves.[75] Thus the table was set. On 20 October 1999 Wahid was elected president and Megawati vice president. He then assembled a government that included politicians from Golkar, PAN, PPP, PDI-P, and PKB. With the possible exception of Lebanon, this consociational arrangement was unprecedented in the Islamic world.

Communal Violence Versus the Art and Ethos of Power Sharing

From the outset, Wahid's cabinet was beset by three problems: a severe economic crisis, escalating demands in the Outer Islands for independence or autonomy, and Muslim-Christian bloodletting in the Maluccas Islands, where some 2,000 people had died since August 1999.[76] The latter two fires were constantly stoked by the economic crisis: demands for autonomy in Aceh (located on the northern tip of Sumatra), West Papua (previously known as Irian Jaya), and Riau echoed long-standing perceptions that Java had exploited the mineral and agricultural wealth of the Outer Islands.[77] Separatist sentiments were further inflamed by communal loyalties. For decades Aceh's Muslims, who were far more orthodox than those of Java, had struggled for autonomy from Jakarta. As for West Papau, some two-thirds of its population were Christian Melanesians who resented Muslim-Javanese domination. Yet, however vexing these two problems were, it was intercommunal bloodletting in the Maluccas Islands that presented Wahid with an immediate political problem. By inflaming Muslim public opinion in Java itself, the violence put pressure on the main Islamic parties to adopt a more sectarian stance towards the Christian and Chinese minorities.

Amien Rais of PAN and Hamzah Haz of PPP exploited such pressures. As leaders of the Central Axis parties that had backed Wahid, they apparently expected the new, and seemingly enfeebled president to do their bidding. Wahid disappointed them. He not only refused to blame Christians for the killings in the Moluccas; in the ensuing months he proposed several controversial ideas, such as lifting the thirty-four-year-old ban on the Communist party. The December 1999 resignation from the cabinet of PPP leader Hamzah Haz, Coordi-

[75] See Sangweon Suh and Jose Tesoro, "Maneuvering to the Top Amid Chaos," (http://www.conn.com/AsiaNow/asiaweek/magazine/99/1029/cover.1/html.), 29 October 1999.

[76] During the 1998 East Asian financial crisis real GDP fell by 20 percent in 18 months as the economy contracted by some 13 percent. In 1999 the economy remained stagnant, with average annual incomes holding at about $600.00. See "Survey Indonesia, Gus Dur's Second Chance," (http://www.economist.com/editorial/freeforall/20000708/su4532.html), 8 July 2000.

[77] Aceh has natural gas, Riau oil, East Kalimantan oil and timber, and Irian Jaya copper, gold, and timber. As Adam Schwarz has noted, in both Irian Jaya and Aceh, "the wealth produced per inhabitant ... is among the highest in the Indonesia. But in both provinces income and consumption per person ... fall much lower in the national ranking." See Schwarz, *A Nation in Waiting* [1994 ed.], 63.

nating Minister of People's Welfare and Poverty Alleviation, underscored the growing gap between Wahid and the Islamic parties. After Haz was replaced by Basri Hasanuddin, who had no ties to PPP, Haz declared that without PPP's help, there was "no way" that Wahid "could have been elected president."[78] Haz's allies were more direct. One PPP leader insisted that "Gus Dur's move is for the purpose of destroying PPP," while Rais warned his rivals not to "provoke the Central Axis into a fight, otherwise we would certainly retaliate."[79]

That retaliation came a month later, when at a Jakarta rally marking the end of Ramadan, Haz suggested to an audience of some 80,000 that the Central Axis parties should reconsider their support for Wahid. Rais agreed. After disclosing that PPP, PAN, the Crescent Star, and Justice parties had signed a pact that called for uniting the four parties into one single party in advance of the 2004 elections, Rais turned to the situation in the Moluccas Islands. "Thus far," he warned, "Muslims have been quiet patient, but even that has limits." The president, he demanded, had to resolve the fighting "in one or two weeks," or otherwise the Muslims might be "wiped out." Amien and Haz then endorsed a proposal made by several leading clerics that unless the government quickly halted the violence, a *jihad* would be launched against Christians.[80]

Haz and Rais surely knew that even the slightest hint of carrying out this threat would provoke a coup. While Wahid's decision in January 2000 to retire General Wiranto—and thus remove him from the cabinet—made such a move less likely, the military retained the means to intervene. That it failed to do so may be attributed not only to Wahid's bold actions (which were wisely applauded by the United States), but also to the fact that despite their differences, the Central Axis parties had little choice but to cooperate with Wahid and Megawati. Wahid himself often undermined such cooperation by making unilateral decisions that dismayed cabinet members from both secular and religious parties. For their part, the Islamic parties continued to make life difficult for Wahid. Thus in April 2000, after Wahid again suggested that the ban on the Communist party be lifted, Rais briefly threatened to initiate impeachment proceedings against the president. Several months later, PPP leaders backed a controversial proposal (which *both* Rais and Wahid rejected) to reintroduce the portion of the Jakarta Charter that called for the application of Islamic law.

However disconcerting, such developments have unfolded in a multipolar symbolic-institutional field that has made it hard for any one faction to impose

---

[78] "Why Only That One," *Gatra*, Number 4/VI, 11 December 1999 (http://www.gatranews.net/_english/VI/4/NAS3-4.html), 3 March 2000.

[79] "The Honeymoon Will Soon Be Over," *Gatra*, Number 4/VI, 11 December 1999 (http://www.gatranews.net/−english/VI/4/NAS1-4.html), 8 March 2000.

[80] *Suara Merdeka*, 17 January 2000 and 13 January 2000. (http://www.suaramerdeka.org/harian/0001/11/eng/2/html and 0001/13/eng2.html), 9 March 2000. Wahid bitterly denounced the call for *jihad*, as did other leaders of PKB. Moreover, Muslim leaders repeatedly insisted that the call for *jihad* meant merely that Muslims should wage a political struggle to defend their rights. Nevertheless, such a call was obviously irresponsible and dangerous.

its will. Despite the push to introduce the Jakarta Charter's *Shariah* section, the leaders of PDI-P, PKB, and PAN continued to support the principle of keeping religion and state at arms length. Thus, it is unlikely that Indonesia will follow the sad example of Algeria, where the effort by militant Islamists to use democracy as a vehicle for imposing a counter-hegemonic project provoked a military coup and civil war. In Indonesia, political liberalization and power sharing are not Trojan horses for radical Islamization; rather they express a legacy of dissonant politics whose enduring logic is manifest in a politics of confrontation, brinkmanship, and negotiation among forces that have long advocated contending visions of community.

In July 2001, Wahid was forced out of office by the parliament. Megawati was then elected president, and Hamzah Haz vice-president. Given the latter's previous support for a more fundamentalist line, it is far from clear that this new chapter in power-sharing can succeed absent a critical role for the NU and its party, the PKB. Wahid may have made many efforts, but he was one of the few politicians who could mediate between secularists and Islamists. In time he may be missed.

Conclusion: Dissonant Versus Harmonic Politics

In this article I have used the concepts of multiple "paths" and "imaginations" to illuminate patterns of political change and negotiation that are not readily revealed by conventional analyses of regime transitions. But this has merely been a first step. Further studies of other dissonant states, such as Lebanon and Kuwait, must now be undertaken. If analyses of other dissonant states substantiate the central hypothesis—namely, that the institutionalization of multiple symbolic-institutional paths not only creates the space for regime-opposition accommodations, but also encourages ideological innovation within Islamic movements—then we will be on our way to forging a comprehensive middle-range theory of dissonant politics.

Three important lessons for the future study of comparative politics in general, and dissonant "Islamic" politics in particular, are suggested by this study. First, dissonant politics generates patterns of political change which do not move forward (or backwards) along one clear line. The notion that transitions involve the negotiation of a "bargained equilibrium" that allows political leaders to either move forward to democracy, or back to a more coherent and stable form of authoritarianism, does not readily apply to dissonant states.[81] Yet if their politics are messy and indeterminate, dissonant states are hardly unique or "exceptional." The seamless transition—from authoritarian crisis, to political liberalization, and finally to competitive democracy—that many scholars once hoped would become a universal trend has not materialized. In a world

---

[81] See Adam Przeworski, *Democracy and the Market: Political and Economic Reforms in Eastern Europe and Latin America* (Cambridge: Cambridge University Press, 1991), 59.

in which there is no end of history, accounting for different political systems and the different types of transitions they generate remains a key challenge for students of comparative politics.

Second, while the multiple legacies bequeathed by dissonant states are never static, they are not the mere handmaidens of a wider economic logic that can be arbitrarily molded by political entrepreneurs. In Indonesia, the ongoing economic crisis has certainly weakened the urban middle class and and discredited President Wahid, thus facilitating the efforts of the PPP to mobilize support for a more sectarian vision of Islam. By contrast, in Iran economic crisis has strengthened support for the Khordad Front, although efforts to impose economic reforms may provoke a backlash against the reformists. Yet while the ideological legacies inherited by the leaders of Iran and Indonesia have been affected by socioeconomic conditions, these leaders have discovered that the political logic that animates these legacies cannot be completely reinvented. President Khatami, for example, has redefined the ideology of the Islamic left in a more liberal direction. But he cannot easily expunge from this ideology the calculated nativism that gave it such force. Similarly, while President Wahid has tried to push the long-standing practice of elite competition in a more pluralistic direction, the well ingrained but destructive habit of viewing politics as a game of political one upmanship has endured.[82] In short, in both Indonesia and Iran, we have vivid examples of the shared scripts and routines that have received attention from new institutionalist scholars. What I have done is to show how such scripts and habits can be studied through a dynamic comparative lens that does not reduce them to reified structures that predetermine political outcomes.

Third, this article implicitly challenges the idea that the democratization in the Islamic polities hinges on forging a culturally authentic interpretation of democracy, one that will reflect a long-standing consensus as to what it means to be a Muslim. This notion not only exaggerates the extent to which such a consensus actually exists, but also underrates the impact of globalization in shaping the ideologies and programs of leaders such as Khatami, Soroush, and Wahid. These postmodern Islamists do not advocate a coherent synthesis of religion and politics. Instead, they offer ideological amalgams of contending symbols and traditions, some of which are indigenous, while others have been absorbed from the West. This does *not* mean that local cultural traditions are necessarily antagonistic to democracy. On the contrary, liberals such as Soroush and Wahid have turned to local forms of Islamic mysticism to defend pluralism. But their goal has not been to democratize Islam, but rather to get it out of politics. Indeed, the paradoxical fact is that Soroush and Wahid have invoked religious traditionalism and mystical spiritualism as symbolic bulwarks against the modernist ideologies of populists such as Iran's Shariati and Indonesia's Rais, both of whose world views were largely shaped during their years of graduate studies in Western universities.

[82] As Rais put it in May 1998, "I am going to play my own game . . . can play a good [game] with Gus Dur and Mega. . . ." See "Amien Rais on Abdurrahman-Wahid Megawati Coalition," *Kupan Pos Pupang*, 14 July 1998 in *FBIS East Asia*, 24 July 1998.

This is not to say that the amalgams espoused by Wahid, Soroush, or Khatami must necessarily promote pluralism. By their very nature, such hybrids invite competing and even contradictory rationalizations for political action. The multiple imagination of Wahid, for example, contains both a modern notion of authority that speaks to the aspirations of the urban middle class and a traditional ethos that speaks to the patrimonialist worldview of rural, Javanese Muslims. While the grafting of these two logics has often encouraged pluralism, it has at times pulled Wahid in an autocratic direction. For example, his tendency to unilaterally issue orders to his ministers—a habit that reflects the patrimonialist ethos of a *kiai* (rural religious teacher)[83]—may be welcomed by his traditional followers, but it is resented by his more modern colleagues in secular and Muslim political parties.

Wahid's autocratic habits eventually led to a confrontation with the Majles in spring of 2001 when, following two financial scandals that touched his administration, he refused the DPR's calls for a full accounting of his actions. Antagonized by a president whose judgment may have been impaired by the effects of a stroke, Wahid's opponents initiated impeachment procedures even though the 1989 constitution stipulates that the president is not accountable to either house or parliament. That Wahid's competitors, including Megawati herself, were ready to manipulate constitutional procedures to attain power, and that Wahid in turn was prepared to block such efforts by threatening to impose a state of emergency, reminds us that dissonant political sysems are always double-edged swords. Their institutions—and the leaders they bequeath—encourage bargaining, competition, and even ideological pluralism, but they also promote political habits that can be deeply sectarian and often authoritarian.

The varied and often fragile outcomes that arise from this dissonant logic may be a far cry from competitive democracy, but they are preferable to the stifling politics that predominates in harmonic states. These states institutionalize a vision of authority and a dominant political practice that is the very antithesis of dissonant politics. Rather than promote multiple paths, they institutionalize path dependence by absorbing competing Islamic institutions and ideas and by championing the notion that the state is the sole vehicle by which the Islamic community can realize its shared identity and history. This dynamic not only narrows the space for path innovation and regime-opposition accommodation; by its very nature, it also invites counter-hegemonic movements whose ultimate goal is to compel the state to reassert its mission as the vehicle of cultural conformity. Faced by such counter-hegemonic movements and lacking alliance partners who can mobilize organized support for genuine power sharing, the leaders of harmonic states are likely to face two bad choices: to crush their competitors, or absorb the latter's message by encouraging greater Islamization.

Nearly all leaders have grappled with the paradoxical consequences that ensue when harmonic states are so successful at stifling alternatives that re-

---

[83] See "In Search of Magic Power From Kiai," *Gatra*, Number 39, VI, 12 August 2000. (http://www.gatra.com/-VI/39/LPT2-39.html).

formers are easily convinced that sticking to old paths makes more sense than creating new ones. The leaders of Saudi Arabia, Egypt, and Malaysia have all contended with the beguiling legacy of harmonic institutionalization by repressing Islamic competitors while trying to control or monopolize the Islamic sphere. As for Algeria, its sad experience demonstrates how difficult it is to forge new institutional and ideological paths *ex post facto*. When in 1988 the former president of Algeria, Chadli Benjedid, initiated dramatic political reforms, he soon faced a mass movement whose crusade for a unified Islamic state echoed the National Liberation Front's (FLN) own hegemonic project. By insisting that the state recapture its historical mission as the *sole* vehicle by which the Algerian people expressed its authentic identity, the Islamic Salvation Front (FIS) acted as the "son" of the FLN.[84] Moreover, Benjedid's efforts to promote an Islamic alternative to the FIS also failed, in large measure because the alternative—the Hamas party—had little popular support and did not provide a genuinely pluralistic alternative to the counter-hegemonic ideology of the FIS.[85] Under such polarized conditions, which played right into the hands of hardliners in the military, hopes for political accommodation were doomed almost from the start.[86]

This unhappy outcome has little to do with Islam or the legacy of "Arab" or "Islamic" authoritarianism. The Arab nationalist ideologies propounded by Egypt's Nasser, or the leaders of the Ba'ath Party in Syria, were as much influenced by the West as they were by Islamic ideals. In short, symbolic contradictions are hardly absent in harmonic states. What counts is whether such contradictions are explicitly recognized and how they are institutionalized. Many harmonic states are as divided by ethno-religious identities or ideologies as other Third World societies. Yet, there is all the difference in the world between Syria or Iraq, states that—in Iliya Harik's evocative words—suffered "the imposition of uniformity on a pluralistic reality" by ethnic minorities who used the ecumenical language of Arab nationalism to defend particularistic interests; and Lebanon or Indonesia, states whose leaders allowed competing sociocultural groups to sink institutional roots in society at some distance from the state.[87] Whether by design or default, this dissonant pattern created possibilities for ideological innovations and accommodations that were not readily available to the leaders of harmonic states.*

---

[84] See Lahouari Addi, "L'utopie Islamiste," *L'impasse du Populisme, L'Algerie et la Democratie* (Paris: Editions La Découverte, 1994), 143–65.

[85] See Hilmi Mahmud Qa'ud, *Al-Nizam al-Askari fi al-Jaza'ir* [The Military Apparatus in Algeria] (Cairo: Dar al-Itisam, 1993), 59.

[86] See Abed Charef, *Algerie Le Grand Dérapage* (Editions de l'aube, 1994). The Hamas party in Algeria had no relationship to Hamas in Palestine.

[87] Iliya Harik, "The Ethnic Revolution and Political Integration in the Middle East," *International Journal of Middle East Studies* 3 (July 1972): 310.

* The author would like to thank the United States Institute of Peace, under whose auspices much of the Indonesia section was written.

Part IV:
LOOKING TO THE FUTURE

Al Qaeda, Military Commissions, and American Self-Defense

RUTH WEDGWOOD

The toppling of the World Trade Center towers on September 11 broadcast live to the world that radical Islam must be taken seriously. This was a holocaust, forcing us to witness the planned deaths of 3,000 people and to imagine their anguish and suffering. Anyone could have been there. The rampage struck at the financial center of the world, at a city that symbolizes cultural diversity and inclusion, and perhaps not by chance, at the city that became home to so many European Jews fleeing from fascism.

This has been a decade in coming. After abandoning his family's construction empire in Saudi Arabia and fighting the Soviets in Afghanistan, Osama bin Laden had the foul imagination to conceive of a holding company for globalized terror. His ease with corporate forms has allowed him to provide financing, training, and materiel to Islamic insurgents around the world, and to escalate the destructive range of their work. In most political confrontations, there is an unspoken norm of proportionality, a customary law of violence, even an expected pattern of terrorist tactics. The techniques of terrorism are a way to get on television, to drain the good feeling out of life and demoralize resistance, to undermine the credibility of a regime that cannot offer protection. But at the hands of ordinary insurgents, the deaths of innocents usually are sought in numbers of five, ten, or one hundred. Al Qaeda's jihad against Judaism, Christianity, and the West has chosen to move the decimal point and increase the scale of destruction by several orders of magnitude with no apparent hesitation. Though one must speak with reticence and care about the past, bin Laden's imagination resembles that of Hitler, scaling up from pogrom to extermination.

RUTH WEDGWOOD is professor of law at Yale and Johns Hopkins universities and a former federal prosecutor in the Southern District of New York. She has served on the secretary of state's advisory committee on international law and as an independent expert for the International Criminal Tribunal for the former Yugoslavia in The Hague.

When George W. Bush spoke of bin Laden as the "evil one," even a sophisticate could accept the reference.

Al Qaeda's heedlessness poses an unprecedented threat, because the usual rules of deterrence have no evident application. In military defense, as in criminal law, we ordinarily assume that an adversary can be dissuaded by increasing the cost of his action. The stability of the nuclear era, dangerous as it was, depended on deterrence—the notorious "mutually assured destructive capability" of two state adversaries who wished to have their people and polity survive. A nonstate actor such as al Qaeda has no population or territory held in thrall, and its cult of martyrdom sees death as unimportant. Thus, the daunting task is to anticipate and intercept specific operations, aided perhaps by disruption of al Qaeda's infrastructure. Al Qaeda's interest in weapons of mass destruction makes this a high stakes game.

Al Qaeda in the 1990s

Bin Laden and al Qaeda were viewed as an escalating threat in American policy circles over the last decade. The United States was occupied with other problems, to be sure, and these were more than enough to tax the limited attention of a president who never warmed to foreign policy. It was worthwhile trying to quell the civil wars in Bosnia and Rwanda, and important to counter North Korea's bellicose gestures toward Seoul and Tokyo. The United States was tending the confrontation between the Chinese and Taiwanese in their hot standoff across the straits. It had to think through the post-cold war evolution of Europe and to craft a new relationship with Russia after communism. Terror by nonstate actors was nothing new. The 1984 attack on the Marine barracks in Lebanon killed over 200 personnel.

But there was the nagging sense in some parts of Washington that bin Laden and al Qaeda were different and dangerous. Their program of activity has been steady, paced, and increasingly effective in its destruction. American soldiers on their way to Somalia were killed in Aden by al Qaeda in 1992. In the famous episode of "Black Hawk Down," eighteen army rangers were killed in a shoot-out in 1993 on the streets of Mogadishu by Somali fighters trained by al Qaeda. The loss of two Black Hawk helicopters and mistreatment of the corpse of an American soldier, dragged through the alleys of the Somali capital, brought about the abrupt withdrawal of American forces, on the mistaken ground that "peacekeeping" was the culprit. Bin Laden may have been emboldened to suppose that the United States would leave the region altogether.

Jihad on American soil began in early 1993 with the truck bombing of the World Trade Center in New York City. The explosion shattered the lower levels of the complex and knocked out its utility systems. Thousands of civilians evacuated the building down smoky stairwells. Six office workers died. But several conspirators were quickly traced and arrested, and this good fortune and good police work may have added to the dangerous conceit that the United States could thwart terror networks by criminal law enforcement alone.

World Trade Center conspirator Ramsey Ahmad Youssef returned to the Philippines to stage-manage the plans of al Qaeda's growing regional network. Al Qaeda's southeast Asian division, in cooperation with the radical Filipino terror group, Abu Sayyaf, hoped to assassinate President Bill Clinton on a visit to Manila in 1994, to assassinate the pope, and to bomb two United Airlines jets en route to Hong Kong. The midair bombings were to be simultaneous, a marked feature of al Qaeda's aesthetics of violence. Other ongoing plans included a diabolical version of a Busbee Berklee water ballet, staging the destruction of eleven American jetliners crossing the Pacific as they prepared to land at American airports. The bombing operation was near launch when a fire broke out in Youssef's Manila apartment; authorities responded and stumbled on the plans. Ramsey Youssef was later arrested by American agents in Karachi. The Asian group carried out the successful bombing of a Philippines airliner bound for Tokyo. Throughout, bin Laden and al Qaeda continued to show a talent for friendly takeovers, contacting local Islamic groups and offering the money and plans to multiply their capabilities. Nor did the network abandon ambitions for attacks in the United States. A plan was hatched to fly a small aircraft laden with explosives into the Central Intelligence Agency headquarters. Another plan was underway to bomb the Holland and Lincoln Tunnels in New York City and to blow up the United Nations. This was interrupted only when an informant was infiltrated into the group.

Bin Laden's terror bombings continued in the Middle East. In 1995, the U.S. training center for the Saudi National Guard near Riyadh was truck-bombed, killing five Americans. In June 1996 (five weeks after bin Laden was expelled from Sudan and was forced to regroup in Afghanistan) he sent another TNT-packed truck to the Khobar Towers military barracks in Saudi Arabia. American sentries lacked an adequate alarm system to empty the dormitory in time. Ten American soldiers were killed and many were wounded. The Saudis awarded the contract for reconstruction to a firm owned by bin Laden's brothers. The Saudis beheaded four prime suspects without allowing the FBI to debrief them.

In 1998, with practiced logistics and coordination, bin Laden commissioned catastrophic attacks on American embassies in East Africa. Truck bomb explosions toppled the embassy buildings in Nairobi and Dar es Saleem, killing 224 people, including fourteen Americans, and wounding 4,500. In a sense, at this moment bin Laden crossed an escalatory threshold. FBI agents were again dispatched to look for usable evidence, but Washington finally resorted to the use of military force. Two volleys of Tomahawk land attack missiles were launched from American naval vessels against sites in Afghanistan and Sudan. One target was al Qaeda's training camp near Khost, Afghanistan. The second was the al Shifa pharmaceutical factory in Khartoum, Sudan, serving as an alleged transfer point for chemical weapons. The press scoffed that this was a wag-the-dog diversion from the Monica Lewinsky-Bill Clinton scandal and assumed the al Shifa plant was an ill chosen target.[1]

FBI director Louis Freeh also chipped away at the decision, complaining in a unique account of the national chain of command that he was not consulted on targeting. Some critics argued that any response should wait until the end of the criminal investigation, even when other American embassies were under threat from the al Qaeda network. Others suggested that Washington should share its available intelligence with the UN Security Council. The UN role was further complicated by the decision of senior staff of the Hague chemical weapons monitoring secretariat to publicly air their skepticism about U.S. methodology in target assessment, perhaps in an attempt to distance their own inspection activities from the American use of force.

The White House lacked the courage of its own convictions in the execution of the air strikes. The prime target was a scheduled meeting of bin Laden's senior lieutenants (and perhaps bin Laden himself) in a camp near Khost. But the Tomahawk launch was delayed for several hours, until 7:30 p.m. Sudan time and 10 p.m. Afghan time, in order to avoid any chance of collateral damage in the strike against the secondary target in Khartoum. By then, the meeting of bin Laden's lieutenants in Khost was over. Military value must be weighed against collateral danger to civilians. But the White House could not have supposed the military mission was worth much except as symbolism with this fatal delay in execution. One could have abandoned the Khartoum target altogether, in favor of decapitating al Qaeda's command and control.[2]

In October 2000, bin Laden struck again, using a skiff loaded with explosives to blow a hole in an American destroyer at harbor in Aden, nearly sinking the ship. The Federal Bureau of Investigation was again dispatched to investigate—perhaps because the United States doubted the authorship, perhaps because criminal investigation allows it to do something. But the Yemeni government quickly put the lid on what the agents could ask, and they were withdrawn. The United States passed through the millennium celebrations without incident, but an Algerian caught at the Canadian border confessed that the explosives in his car were designed for an attack at the Los Angeles airport.

The Attacks of September 11, 2001

On September 11, 2001, everything changed. A country of 250 million people, returning from its summer vacation, was turned upside down by the inconceiv-

---

[1] The rationale for the al Shifa target was further obscured when senior members of Clinton's cabinet boggled background facts in their public statements. The administration belatedly pointed to intercepted telephone links between the al Shifa owner and the director of the Iraqi chemical weapons program, but the press cycle had passed. Washington attempted to freeze the assets of the al Shifa plant owner but later abandoned the suit, and this was read by the press as an admission of mistaken targeting. It did not occur to any reporters that pretrial discovery in the civil suit might compromise ongoing surveillance activities. See Ruth Wedgwood, "Responding to Terrorism: The Strikes Against bin Laden," *Yale Journal of International Law* 24 (Summer 1999): 599.

[2] Ibid.

able destruction of two of the nation's tallest buildings. As many as 28,000 people are employed in the World Trade Center at the beginning of the workday, and the surprise is that more were not killed. Some law enforcement veterans remembered the warning issued by Ramsey Youssef when he was captured after the 1993 bombing: it had been their intention, he said, to topple the buildings entirely.

Like many other travelers, I was on a plane to Washington at the time. It was diverted to the Baltimore airport amid reports that one hijacked plane had hit the Pentagon and that another plane was still circling near Washington. (This was the plane that crashed in Pennsylvania.) The hijackers' plan to hit the White House or the Capitol as a fourth target has been corroborated by debriefings of personnel captured in Afghanistan.

The next several days were extraordinarily tense. Bin Laden had boasted to his circle of a Hiroshima-style event, and September 11 raised the fear that the metaphor might be literal. The evacuation of the President from Washington was not unreasonable under the circumstances. Bin Laden's keen interest in acquiring a nuclear device had been reported for years, and his escalation of violence lessened any confidence that he would step back from its use. The documents captured in Afghanistan have given no greater comfort about his ambition, although it appears that he still lacks a working bomb. On the supply side, there is limited cause for confidence. Roald Sagdeev, the famed Russian physicist, says it is unlikely that Moscow would have shared control of any so-called suitcase bombs with regional commands. Encrypted decoupling links could defeat any attempt to excavate the arming code with modern computing capability. But other observers, including former CIA Director James Woolsey and former UN weapons inspector Richard Butler, as well as Russian sources, have estimated that there are a dozen or more suitcase bombs unaccounted for. Russia also had hundreds of nuclear artillery shells prepared for a war in Europe. With the Russian economy in tatters, an unemployed scientist, technician, or guard might be tempted by the unspeakable. In addition, Saddam Hussein was thought to be six months away from atomic weapons capability at the time UN inspectors withdrew from Iraq in December 1998.

Al Qaeda's interest in developing chemical and biological weapons has also been corroborated in the aftermath of the American campaign in Afghanistan. Documents found on hard drives and schematics drawn on blackboards in al Qaeda's Afghan offices suggest that the network remains actively interested in developing weapons of mass destruction. During the 1990s, Iraq began to explore a policy of subcontracting abroad for the production of forbidden weapons to avoid the UN inspectors. A representative of Saddam Hussein's son Qusayy reportedly met with al Qaeda representatives in 1998 to explore a joint interest in chemical weapons.[3]

---

[3] "Sudanese Factory Was Working with Iraq on VX Nerve Agent, U.S. Intelligence Says; Assessment Based in Part on Intercepted Phone Calls," *Baltimore Sun*, 26 August 1998.

Finally, little comfort can be taken from new discoveries about the structure of al Qaeda's compartmentalized network. Arrests and searches conducted by foreign authorities have revealed that al Qaeda cells are placed throughout Europe and Asia in cities such as Milan and Hamburg, Singapore and Manila with plans to attack American embassies and other targets in locations as farflung as Singapore and Sarajevo. The al Qaeda training manual found in a London apartment carefully instructs new recruits in the skills of terrorism. The manual, placed in the court record at the East African embassy bombings trial (as government exhibit 1677-T), decries Islam's "wasted generation that pursued everything that is western and produced rulers, ministers, leaders, physicians, engineers, businessmen, politicians, journalists, and information specialists." It celebrates "missions" such as "assassinating enemy personnel as well as foreign tourists," and "blasting and destroying the embassies and attacking vital economic centers" and "the bridges leading into and out of the cities." It notes the need in such special operations for "tranquility and calm personality that allows coping with psychological traumas such as those of the operation of bloodshed, mass murder."

At length, the manual instructs new members in countersurveillance, encryption, the preparation of safe houses, and the choice of escape routes after an assassination. The jihad's "undercover members" are to avoid any outward appearance of "Islamic orientation." The jihadist should not frequent mosques. He should avoid open devotions to the prophet, shave his beard, wear gold, and even listen to music in order to blend into the secular society of the West. The hijackers of September 11 who passed through security in the Boston airport looked like ordinary travelers.

September 11 is evident proof that attacks on civilians are within al Qaeda's theory of conflict. Bin Laden's 1998 fatwa declared that members of al Qaeda should target Americans and Jews, and his interviews since then have stated that even "taxpayers" are fair targets. What then should one do?

U.S. MILITARY RESPONSE AND LEGISLATIVE MEASURES

The Bush administration's first strategy was to disrupt al Qaeda by military means, using air power and limited ground forces to attack the network's logistics and training centers in Afghanistan. Overthrowing the Taliban faction was also a signal lesson to complicit Muslim regimes that might be tempted to shelter al Qaeda. The response was approved by the United Nations Security Council[4] and NATO,[5] as a campaign of self-defense against armed attack. The flight of al Qaeda leadership over the mountains into neighboring territories in Pakistan and Iran has been a disappointment. But the military action has also provided a portfolio of documentary evidence to assist in the tracking of al Qaeda

---

[4] UN S.C. Res. 1368, 12 September 2001; S.C. Res. 1373, 28 September 2001.
[5] Statement by the North Atlantic Council, 12 September 2001, in Press Release 124.

network members in other countries, and corroborates beyond doubt the terror group's troublesome interest in weapons of mass destruction.

The public debate in North America and Europe has concerned what measures should supplement this initial campaign of military force—whether terrorism should still be countered through the ordinary means of criminal law or through some significant shift in enforcement methods. It is interesting to note that the modern international guarantees of human rights openly anticipate the possibility of social threats that are hard to meet. The International Covenant on Civil and Political Rights, the European Convention on Human Rights, and the American Convention speak openly of possible emergencies, perhaps because these legal instruments were designed for countries that are more familiar with such hazards than is the continentally protected American republic. Each document is quite frank in asserting that in a situation of emergency, a state may be bound to take measures that would be inappropriate in peacetime. In an acknowledged emergency, a government can derogate from listed rights, so long as the modification is proportionate and necessary, excepting only a few fundamental norms guaranteeing physical integrity of the body and protection against racial discrimination. This is much more open-ended than the American Constitution, where any necessary latitude for wartime travails is to be read into the rights themselves or (if you are Abraham Lincoln) handled through the radical measure of suspending habeas corpus.

In the response to September 11, the first contentious measure was approved by Congress in the so-called Patriot Act, which allows a crucial sharing of information between the intelligence and criminal justice agencies.[6] Over the last twenty-five years, in the aftermath of the Church and Pike congressional hearings, Washington created a wide firebreak between intelligence and law enforcement. This was to be a visible protection for the American ideal of privacy. Government scrutiny of ordinary citizens and resident aliens within the United States was limited to criminal acts established by demonstrable facts, where reasonable or probable cause was already in hand to indicate the law had been violated. This often meant the FBI was reactive, waiting for problems to present themselves, rather than going out searching. Any scrutiny based on acts of speech or political views was forbidden, even though incendiary advocacy of violence might sometimes give way to violent action. The FBI was largely unable to share grand jury information or criminal wiretap information with intelligence agencies as a matter of law and agency culture. Even foreign counterintelligence wiretaps conducted by the FBI often were not shared with the CIA. In turn, the intelligence agencies were reluctant to engage with the criminal justice agencies for fear that the linkage might appear to be a backdoor around the privacy rules of law enforcement.

This bureaucratic lobotomy had an obvious cost. Only the CIA can operate clandestinely offshore. FBI legates depend on the foreign host's say-so and per-

---

[6] The Uniting and Strengthening America by Providing Appropriate Tools to Intercept and Obstruct Terrorism Act of 2001 (USA Patriot Act), P.L. 107-05, 115 Stat. 2721, at section 203.

mission. Only the FBI can operate stateside. Yet al Qaeda moves onshore and offshore in real time, with operatives flying between Europe, Asia, and North America. The necessary synthesis of circumstantial evidence was profoundly difficult in the circumstances. Despite the cautions from the past, it may take a network to catch a network. For a limited term, the Patriot Act permits the FBI to share grand jury information and Title III wiretap information with intelligence agencies investigating catastrophic terrorism; it must keep a record for later court review. In addition, the FBI has been instructed to share data from its foreign counterintelligence wiretaps. The intelligence agencies are now mandated to share their offshore investigative findings with the FBI.

The second major change in overcoming the "two-brain" government is a liberalized test for foreign counterintelligence wiretaps. Under the president's foreign affairs power, the constitutional right to monitor foreign adversaries (and even friends) has not depended on a showing of crime. Rather, the sleuthing of foreign intentions has only required the identification of a foreign government or agency relationship. Such surveillance within the United States is regulated by a judicial panel under the Foreign Intelligence Surveillance Act (FISA).[7] But in the past, the Justice Department was fearful of seeking a FISA tap when there was a realistic chance of criminal prosecution as well. The statutory test required that the singular purpose of the wiretap must be intelligence alone. This has now been changed by statute to permit a FISA tap where intelligence is a "significant" purpose.[8] Both criminal justice prosecutions and intelligence interception will be appropriate responses to a terrorist threat, and this statutory change avoids the unwonted pressure to pretend that one purpose is uppermost. It avoids the dilemma that would otherwise push agencies to forgo interdiction of a scheme because there was a felt interest in prosecution as well. To be sure, the limitations stemmed from the mishaps of the 1950s and 1960s—seeming to avoid any dilution of standards for government surveillance in a libertarian society. But if anything, the lesson was learned too well. We have been hobbled in gathering, pooling, and evaluating the necessary information on terrorist networks, cells, and their members—a task often requiring the examination of such minutiae as apartment leases, hotel registrations, check endorsements, wire transfers, travel itineraries, as well as intercepted electronic messages and conversations.

A third controverted measure was the Congress's authorization for the arrest of noncitizens "reasonably believed" to be involved with terrorism and the power to hold them for a period of seven days, before they were charged with a crime or immigration violation. This was perhaps the most illiberal of the government's measures. But it may count for something that Congress specifically delegated the authority in light of the emergency. As Justice Robert Jackson noted in the Steel Seizure Case in 1952,[9] the President's emergency power is at

---

[7] 50 N.Y.S. 1801 et. seq.
[8] USA Patriot Act, section 218.
[9] *Youngstown Sheet & Tube Co. v. Sawyer*, 343 U.S. 579 (1952), Jackson, J., concurring.

its height when he acts pursuant to Congress's instructions. Congress has the constitutional power to take far-reaching measures in wartime, including the suspension of habeas corpus (a measure widely indulged in during the Civil War when Lincoln was concerned that Confederate sympathizers in Maryland might cut off the nation's capital from the rest of the North). Another standard of comparison lies in the traditional prerogative of states in wartime to intern enemy aliens. This harsh power can reach even those enemy aliens who openly disdain their own foreign government. In Great Britain, shortly after September 11, Prime Minister Tony Blair successfully proposed to the Parliament that he should have the power to order the indefinite detention of aliens suspected of connection to the al Qaeda network.

Initially, approximately 1,100 aliens were taken into custody under the powers of Section 236A of the Patriot Act.[10] This was the only exercise of the emergency seven-day detention power, and was near in time to September 11. By late November 2001, 55 defendants were still held on criminal charges, and approximately 548 on immigration charges. Some material witnesses were also detained, but the number is not recorded because of grand jury secrecy.[11]

The administration's mustered defense turns on the urgency of throwing al Qaeda off balance. One did not know whether other attacks were in the works. There was little sense of luxury in resorting to patient grand jury investigations when greater mass catastrophe seemed a real threat. Oddly, accurate judgment could be hobbled by success. No violent attacks have been mounted within the United States since September 11, other than the disputed post office mailing of anthrax letters and the attempt to down an airplane with a powerfully packed shoe-bomb.[12] A critic may suppose that this proves the measures were unnecessary. But the absence of attacks may also indicate the opposite.

A fourth deeply controverted measure is the Bureau of Prisons order that permits the rare monitoring of attorney-client conversations within federal prisons.[13] Legal consultations between a lawyer and his client are sacrosanct under almost all circumstances. But statements that advance the commission of a crime are not protected under the Sixth Amendment or under the rules of

---

[10] USA Patriot Act, supra note 6, at section 236A.

[11] See *Attorney General Ashcroft Provides Total Number of Federal Criminal Charges and INS Detainees*, 27 November 2001, available at www.usdoj.gov/ag/speeches/2001/agcrisisremarks11_27.htm.

[12] Nonetheless, al Qaeda's activity has continued with the truck-bombing of a synagogue in Tunisia, plans to bomb the Duomo in Milan and the marketplace in Strasbourg, France (venue of the European Court of Human Rights). The unhappy youth of the French suburbs have been named as the source of attacks against synagogues and other Jewish facilities, but foreign collaboration is not improbable. The violence in Israel may give pause in light of bin Laden's October 2001 reiteration that "We are in a decisive battle with the Jews and those who support them. . . . The killing of Jews and Americans is one of the greatest duties." See transcript of bin Laden's October 2001 interview with Al-Jazeera television, posted on www.CNN.com, 5 February 2002, available at http://www.cnn.com/2002/WORLD/asiapsf/south/02/05/binladen.transcript/index.html, 5 July 2002.

[13] *National Security: Prevention of Acts of Violence and Terrorism*, 28 Code of Federal Regulations, Parts 500 and 501, 66 Federal Register 55061, 31 October 2001.

legal ethics. An attorney is entitled to reveal a confidence where the disclosure is necessary to avoid the death of an innocent person. Attorneys are sometimes asked to carry messages for their clients, including convicted felons, who try to run their networks from jail. An attorney may not even realize the significance of what he is asked to transmit. This is a price we have been willing to pay for the sake of privacy and confidence in ordinary criminal schemes where only a handful of lives are at stake. Al Qaeda operations are aimed at massive casualties, and the moral and constitutional calculus becomes more perplexing. The view that all terrorism inquiries belong in the federal courts and the wish for full and free choice of defense lawyers ratchets up this dilemma.

The way that similar problems have been treated in the past is to have a strict segregation between an intelligence monitoring team and a trial team. This kind of firewall protection has been used before in cases where a defense attorney may have occasion to talk to officials of a foreign government office monitored under the Foreign Intelligence Surveillance Act. There is an attempt to "minimize" (not listen to or record) any privileged conversation. Any inadvertent knowledge of defense strategy is kept from the trial team. This has worked well and without scandal in past national security prosecutions, and it is perhaps the unfamiliarity of the arrangement that elicited such vehement initial comment by people who seemed unfamiliar with the judge's role. If any information is ever to be turned over, it can be done only with the permission of a federal judge.

But the greatest attention has been directed to the President's order on military commissions as mode of trial against the al Qaeda and Taliban leadership. Perhaps because the first implementing order was issued under the pressure of time and emergency,[14] critics initially treated it as an occasion to express accumulated fears that catastrophic terrorism might lessen the commitment to American liberties. One may wish to see the commission proposal as a response instead to the evident limits of federal court prosecutions.

U.S. strategy throughout the 1990s was to conduct criminal investigations through the grand jury and attempt to gather the necessary evidence for trial before a petit jury. Criminal charges in the 1993 Trade Center bombing and the embassies bombings were brought in the federal district court in lower Manhattan, and prosecutors in the Southern District of New York (under the leadership of U.S. Attorney Mary Jo White) had an impressive record of obtaining convictions. But the limits of criminal inquiries were evident when the World Trade Center toppled five blocks from the courthouse in the September 11 ca-

---

[14] Military Order Regarding Detention, Treatment, and Trial of Certain Non-Citizens in the War Against Terrorism, available at www.whitehouse.gov/news/releases/2001/11/20011113-27.html, 5 July 2002. But see *Procedures for Trials by Military Commissions of Non-United States Citizens in the War Against Terrorism*, Department of Defense Military Commission Order No. 1, 21 March 2002, available at www.defenselink.mil/news/Mar2002/d20020321ord.pdf, July 2002.

tastrophe.[15] Every criminal case has in a sense represented an intelligence failure, for it means the United States failed to intercept an ongoing plan.

Remaining Concerns

There are several specific concerns with the capacities of federal courts. First is protecting intelligence information, especially in the middle of an ongoing conflict. Against an impenetrable network, a criminal conviction may well depend on the use of intelligence information obtained from exquisitely sensitive sources. The need for electronic intercepts and other delicate information will be especially acute in trials against the leadership and logicians, the organizers and entrepreneurs who dispatch the suicidal operatives to the bombing sites. A compartmentalized network schooled to avoid detection is not likely to generate many witnesses to its inner workings, hence requiring this broader availability of sources. Yet anything considered against the defendant must be put into the public trial record in a federal court, where it is available for review by al Qaeda as well as more benign court watchers. The Classified Information Procedures Act passed in 1980 permits some greater ability to gauge the extent of prejudice to ongoing intelligence work and compromise of classified information likely to occur in the course of a trial.[16] It may permit the substitution of a generic description for a specific particle of intelligence. But ultimately, the particulars to be used against the defendant must be made known to him and to the world at large. In the case of electronic surveillance, this can be extremely troublesome for keeping track of a terrorist network's ongoing plans. Bin Laden and al Qaeda are sophisticates in avoiding ongoing surveillance by changing telephone systems on regular occasions and switching to emails and couriers. To lose track of an open wire even for a few weeks could have serious consequences.

The second problem is the tightly woven exclusion of probative evidence in traditional federal trials, limiting what can be placed before a jury for evaluation. There is an historical distrust of juries in the Anglo-American tradition with sharp limits on what they are permitted to consider, excluding many forms of evidence used in everyday life. One wants to be rigorous in estimating what is sufficient proof of a criminal act for purposes of punishment and sanction—the *weight* of proof, commonly thought of as proof beyond a reasonable doubt. But restrictions on the *admissibility* of evidence are another matter and are far less exclusionary in European trials, international courts, and civil courts. In an American criminal jury trial, only eyewitness testimony and first-hand speech by the defendant can be considered, with very few exceptions. Authentication

---

[15] See Ruth Wedgwood, "Cause for Alarm: Legal Action Can Bring Victories, But Preventing Terrorism Calls for Tougher Tactics," *Washington Post*, 3 June 2001.

[16] Classified Information Procedures Act, P.L. 96-456, 96th Cong., 94 Stat. 2025, 18 U.S.C. Appendix, as amended by P.L. 100-690, Title 7, sec. 7020(G), 18 November 1988, 102 Stat. 4396.

requirements are rigorous for physical evidence, and search and seizure law is enforced by keeping avowedly reliable evidence away from the view of the jury.

Hearsay can lack desirable indicia of reliability, since the speaker is not available for cross-examination on his accuracy of perception, his possible motive to lie, and his memory. But one can also imagine examples where the indicia of reliability seem strong. Take, for example, Osama bin Laden's reported call to his mother before September 11, warning her that he could not call for awhile. If, hypothetically, bin Laden's mother told her best friend, the friend would not be permitted to testify to the conversation, even where she was the only available witness. First-hand evidence is clearly to be preferred, but there may be instances where hearsay is probative, especially where corroborated by other sources of evidence.

So, too, in a federal district court trial, if evidence was obtained through a legally defective search, it must be excluded from evidence. This has nothing to do with its probative quality, but rather with maintaining a peacetime incentive system for appropriate police behavior. Yet in the case of extraordinary threat, with a group such as al Qaeda, admitting evidence based on its probative quality may seem more attractive.

There are also rather technical authentication requirements that surround the introduction of evidence in federal trials. This often involves proving chain of custody, producing a custodian of records to testify how records were kept, and showing that the condition of an object has not changed. In the harried circumstances of a cave search, it will not be possible to maintain crime scene standards. Indeed, one of the most interesting discoveries concerning al Qaeda would face high hurdles for admission in federal court. A *Wall Street Journal* reporter assigned to cover the Afghan war broke his computer and needed a new laptop hard drive. He ventured into the marketplace in Kabul and discovered two hard drives for sale that had apparently been looted from al Qaeda offices, replete with al Qaeda memos, including reports on scouting targets.[17] One would hate to deprive a fact-finder of so rich a source of information.

In creating these limits on inquiry and probative power, we may have tied our hands beyond easy amendment except by constitutional change. Many restrictions on hearsay have been placed into the Sixth Amendment in its so-called confrontation clause. The open record of all portions of a criminal trial has been placed within the guarantee of an open and public trial in the Sixth Amendment. The exclusionary rule has been placed within the Fourth Amendment. The constitutionalizing of criminal procedure was designed to reform state criminal justice systems that could only be reached through the due process clause of the Fourteenth Amendment. But the upshot is that after September 11, there is little ability to change the modality of trial within the civilian court system except after serious conversation on the limits of constitutional change in wartime.

---

[17] See Alan Cullison and Andrew Higgins, "How al Qaeda Agent Scouted Attack Sites in Israel and Egypt," *Wall Street Journal*, 16 January 2002.

The third felt concern has been trial security. In ordinary matters, the safety of the jury, judge, and witnesses is assumed. But in the trial of al Qaeda, there is cause for great caution. The federal judges who presided over al Qaeda cases are under round-the-clock protection by rotating teams of federal marshals after concerted threats to their safety. Jurors do not have similar teams of marshals for lifetime protection, and jury anonymity is a thin shield for a citizen summoned for mandatory service. The threats have not been all talk. German tourists killed at Luxor in 1997 were mistaken for Americans, and their bodies were found with a note railing at the trial judge in New York. The Pan Am 103 bombing trial was held at Camp Zeist, a mothballed American military base outside of The Hague. Even with Colonel Muammar el-Qadaffi's consent to the trial, the United Nations preferred to pick up the defendants in a UN transport plane that didn't need to linger in Tripoli for refueling. An al Qaeda embassy bombing defendant has used the occasion of his lawyer's visit to wield a filed-off pocket comb as a knife, stabbing and crippling a jailhouse guard in order to take over the floor of the detention facility.[18] The willingness of al Qaeda to target innocent civilians gives no comfort that they would respect the etiquette of courtroom safety.

MILITARY COMMISSIONS AND TRIBUNALS

It was reasonable to consider other options for trying al Qaeda and Taliban fighters captured in Afghanistan. The President's decision to authorize military commissions follows the tradition of Nuremberg and the law of war itself.[19] The trial of the Nazi leadership in 1945 was conducted in a mixed military tribunal, with rules of evidence and cross-examination quite different from what is familiar in federal court. In the aftermath of World War II, 2,500 commission trials were convened in Europe and the Far East to try people accused of atrocities, including the Tokyo trials. Military courts are so much the venue of international humanitarian law and the law of armed conflict that the 1949 Third Geneva Convention on Prisoners of War demands military trials in preference to civilian, unless the particular legal system also tries its own soldiers in civilian court.[20]

---

[18] See *United States v. Mamdouh Mahmud Salim*, 151 F. Supp. 2nd 281 (S.D.N.Y. 2001).

[19] On the early history of American military commissions, see William Winthrop, *Military Law and Precedents* (Washington, DC: W.H. Morrison, 1886); and William Birkhimer, *Military Government and Martial Law* (3rd ed., Kansas City, MO: F. Hudson, 1914). On the history of commissions generally, see also A. Wigfall Green, "The Military Commission," *American Journal of International Law* 832 (1948); and *Madsen v. Kinsella*, 343 U.S. 341 (1952).

[20] See Geneva Convention Relative to the Treatment of Prisoners of War, 12 August 1949, 6 U.S.T. 3316, 75 U.N.T.S. 135, Article 84, "A prisoner of war shall be tried only by a military court, unless the existing laws of the Detaining Power expressly permit the civil courts to try a member of the armed forces of the Detaining Power in respect of the particular offence alleged to have been committed by the prisoner of war."

What has distracted us, perhaps, is that in the 1990s, the Security Council created two civilian tribunals of limited jurisdiction to try the atrocities of the civil wars in the former Yugoslavia and in Rwanda. These tribunals have had some successes but have not been able to handle any volume of cases. In addition, the protection of sensitive intelligence information in an international institution is daunting, to say the least; and only one American judge, at most, would sit in such a venue. These two ad hoc arrangements have not been the typical method of trial for a body of law that is created, after all, through the state practice of responsible militaries as well as through the views of humanitarian organizations. So, too, the treaty-based International Criminal Court, which the United States has declined to join, will have jurisdiction only over future offenses committed after it comes into force in July 2002 and is equally problematic as a place to deposit sensitive operational intelligence in an ongoing conflict against catastrophic terrorism.[21]

The claim that the president has violated the principle of separation of powers is hard to square with Congress's repeated endorsement of a "common law" jurisdiction for military commissions in time of war and armed conflict. Judge Advocate General Enoch Crowder addressed the point in 1912 testimony concerning military courts-martial and new "articles of war" (equivalent to the Uniform Code of Military Justice). General Crowder noted that "There will be more instances in the future than in the past when the jurisdiction of courts-martial will overlap that of the war courts." He went on, "the question would arise whether Congress having vested jurisdiction by statute [in courts-martial] the common law of war jurisdiction was not ousted. I wish to make it perfectly plain ... that in such cases the jurisdiction of the war court is concurrent."[22]

Congress's regulation of the court-martial system has been accompanied each time by acknowledgment that military commissions are still appropriate for prosecuting offenses against the law of war committed by adversaries. Article 15 of the 1920 Articles of War stated, for example, that "The provisions of these articles conferring jurisdiction upon courts-martial shall not be construed as depriving military commissions ... of concurrent jurisdiction in respect of offenders or offenses that by statute *or by the law of war* may be triable by such military commissions...."[23] Similar language was included in the more famous Uniform Code of Military Justice in 1950, replacing the Articles of War.[24] In the 1996 War Crimes Act, newly permitting concurrent jurisdiction over certain

---

[21] See Ruth Wedgwood, "The International Criminal Court: An American View," *European Journal of International Law* 10 (1999): 93.

[22] Statement of Major General Enoch H. Crowder, judge advocate general, on Revision of the Articles of War, Hearings before the Committee on Military Affairs, U.S. Senate, 62nd Cong., 2nd sess., 1912, 35.

[23] Article 15 of the Articles of War, in Chapter 227, P.L. No. 242, 66th Cong., 2nd sess., 1920.

[24] See 10 U.S.C. 361, cited in the preambular language of President George W. Bush's 13 November 2001 order.

war crimes in the district courts, the legislative conference report again acknowledged the longstanding legitimacy of commissions.[25]

The U.S. Supreme Court reviewed the role of military commissions in several cases arising in World War II: the prosecutions of German saboteurs who landed on Long Island and Florida,[26] Germans in China who had passed information to the Japanese even after Germany's surrender,[27] and Japanese General Yamashita, whose forces abused civilians and prisoners in the Philippines.[28] As Justice Robert H. Jackson recounted in *Johnson v. Eisentrager*, "[W]e have held . . . that the military commission is a lawful tribunal to adjudge enemy offenses against the laws of war."[29] The trials look more vulnerable now. For example, the defense counsel in the German saboteurs case had a conflict of interest that we would not now tolerate. But civil trials of that era also often appear deficient to our eyes, and the matter depends on the quality of the designed procedures.

The procedures announced by the Secretary of Defense Donald Rumsfeld on 21 March 2002 include most guarantees familiar to lay observers.[30] Defendants would be presumed innocent, guaranteed the right against self-incrimination, protected against adverse comment for their exercise of that right, and guaranteed timely notice of charges. Defendants could choose among military defense counsel and could hire their own civilian counsel. The trial would be open to the press except in discrete moments when classified or sensitive intelligence was to be presented. The burden of proof would remain on the government and defendants would be free to call any witnesses in their defense. Convictions would require proof beyond a reasonable doubt, and the death penalty could be imposed only by a unanimous verdict. Appeal could be taken to an independent appellate panel on which civilians could serve, with the power to reverse and remand a conviction. The concessions to circumstance are that the presiding panel could consider any evidence that would appear to be probative to a reasonable person. And for exquisitely sensitive intelligence particles, the defendant might have to rely on his military defense counsel for their rebuttal and challenge.

These are not the procedures of a railroad proceeding that some in the press and civil liberties community had feared. Upon publication of the procedures, the public conversation over the tribunals largely abated.[31] The proof of fairness

---

[25] War Crimes Act of 1996, Report of the Committee on the Judiciary, U.S. House of Representatives, H.Rep. 104-698, 104th Cong., 2nd sess., 24 July 1996.

[26] *Ex parte Quirin*, 317 U.S. 1 (1942).

[27] *Johnson v. Eisentrager*, 339 U.S. 763 (1950).

[28] *In re Yamashita*, 327 U.S. 1 (1945).

[29] *Johnson v. Eisentrager*, 339 U.S. at 786.

[30] See *Procedures for Trials by Military Commissions of Certain Non-United States Citizens in the War Against Terrorism*, Department of Defense Military Commission Order No. 1, 21 March 2002, available at www.defenselink.mil/Mar2002/d2002032/ord.pdf, 5 July 2002.

[31] Several Washington veterans were asked individually by Secretary Rumsfeld to advise him on the desirable form of the procedures. The statement endorsing the fairness of the procedures appears in the Appendix.

lies in the actual application, of course. The first prosecutions against alleged members of al Qaeda have proceeded in civilian courts. The so-called American Taliban, John Walker Lindh, was excluded from the reach of the President's order by virtue of his nationality. British citizen Richard Reid and French citizen Zaccarias Moussaoui were indicted before the military commission rules were available. The ambitious defense motions in those civilian cases may frame expectations of what a trial looks like; one lawyer has creatively argued there is a Second Amendment right to bear arms applicable in Afghanistan, a First Amendment right to associate with the Taliban, and a form of "combat immunity" for a "mere foot soldier" recruited to the Afghan front lines.[32]

In real life, there may be little information about the individual actions of combatants captured in Afghanistan. If the evidence does not rise to the quality of criminal proof, it would be a mistake to convene a criminal proceeding of any kind. This will leave the United States and its allies with the dilemma of potentially detaining captured combatants qua combatants. Such internment is a traditional prerogative of wartime: a nation state can capture and continue to detain enemy combatants until a war's active hostilities are over to prevent the soldiers from returning to the fight. But in the paradoxical world of al Qaeda's terrorism, there are fewer legal guideposts. Neither al Qaeda nor the Taliban chooses to wear a military uniform, and no one has ever defined an alternative standard of proof of combatant status. In terrorism sponsored by nonstate actors, there is no government able to demobilize young men embarked on a violent jihad, and the conflict has no evident end. One may be put to drawing analogies from elsewhere in the law, including the emergency powers recognized in international human rights law and the peacetime law of civil commitment with periodic review of the status of battlefield combatants and the necessity for their detention.

The basic norms of the law remain the same—to preserve liberty except where there is a grave danger to others posed by violent behavior, and to limit measures to what is necessary and proportionate. In a world where terrorist action flirts with catastrophic weapons, the competing paradigms of crime and war may provide no more than analogies. Fitting the law to this unwanted new world thus will require tact, judgment, and the weight of a heavy heart.

Appendix

Trying al Qaeda's War Crimes, 25 March 2002

by Griffin B. Bell, William T. Coleman, Lloyd N. Cutler, Martin Hoffman, Bernard D. Meltzer, Newton N. Minow, Terrence O'Donnell, William H. Webster, and Ruth Wedgwood*

No war can be won without overcoming unexpected challenges. This is true of the fateful struggle between civilized nations and the al Qaeda terror network.

---

[32] See (E.D. Va. Crim. No. 02-37-A), Memorandum Opinion, 11 July 2002.

* Griffin B. Bell served as the attorney general of the United States under President Jimmy Carter. William T. Coleman served as secretary of transportation under President Gerald Ford. Lloyd N. Cut-

Six months ago, members of al Qaeda hijacked four passenger aircraft and turned the planes into weapons of mass destruction against the United States, singling out the World Trade Center and Pentagon for deadly attack. Three thousand innocent people, predominantly civilians, died in the attacks, and our nation still mourns the loss.

Allied military action in Afghanistan has now successfully routed al Qaeda from its center of operations. Alleged al Qaeda and Taliban personnel have been captured and several hundred have been transferred to facilities supervised by the United States at Guantanamo, Cuba.

International law and the law of war permit the detention of al Qaeda combatants under humane conditions until the conflict is over. Premature release would permit them wrongfully to return to al Qaeda's worldwide activities of murder and mayhem.

The most culpable should be put on trial for violations of the law of war. On November 13, President Bush authorized military commissions as a venue for such trials. Last Thursday, the Secretary of Defense announced the rules of procedure that will govern such military commissions. We endorse those rules as a fair and realistic framework for adjudicating al Qaeda's crimes. This framework is consistent with America's belief in the rule of law.

The trials of alleged al Qaeda members pose several unique challenges. First, it may be essential to present intelligence intercepts as proof at trial. Yet fugitive members of al Qaeda will seize upon any disclosure of American or allied intelligence methods to continue their murderous work. One needs a way to present proof without educating al Qaeda about the sources, methods, and results of intelligence collection and surveillance. This protection is not available in federal district court.

Second, without sacrificing our standards for what constitutes sufficient proof of a crime, all sources of probative evidence should be admissible in the trial of al Qaeda suspects. Al Qaeda has become skilled at running a secretive and compartmentalized network. Fewer witnesses may be available to describe its activities than in an ordinary criminal case. The consideration of all probative forms of evidence has been permitted in other tribunals that have dealt with grave war crimes, including the international military tribunal at Nuremberg. Evidence admitted into the trial record will be evaluated and weighed, but at least the evidence should be heard.

Third, the demonstrated and persistent ruthlessness of al Qaeda in threatening the participants in previous terrorist trials may make it prudent to hold trials in a setting where appropriate security can be provided.

Deliberate attacks upon civilians constitute war crimes of the most serious kind. Military commissions have been used for the trial of war crimes since the beginning of the American Republic. Their use has been approved by the United States Supreme

---

ler served as the White House counsel under Presidents Jimmy Carter and Bill Clinton. Martin Hoffman served as general counsel of the Department of Defense and secretary of the Army under President Gerald Ford. Bernard D. Meltzer is a professor of law at the University of Chicago and was a Nuremberg prosecutor. Newton N. Minow served as chairman of the Federal Communications Commission under President John F. Kennedy. William H. Webster, a former judge of the U.S. Court of Appeals for the Eighth Circuit, served as director of the Federal Bureau of Investigation under Presidents Jimmy Carter and Ronald Reagan, and as director of Central Intelligence under Presidents Ronald Reagan and George H. W. Bush. Terrence O'Donnell served as general counsel of the Department of Defense under President George H. W. Bush. Ruth Wedgwood is a professor of international and constitutional law at Yale and Johns Hopkins and a former federal prosecutor.

Court on at least three occasions, against defendants accused of the crimes of sabotage and atrocity. The use of commissions has been endorsed by the Congress in the passage of the Articles of War in 1920, the Uniform Code of Military Justice in 1950, and most recently, in the passage of the War Crimes Act of 1996.

The completed rules for military commission trials have taken careful account of Congressional suggestions. The safeguards assure a defendant of the presumption of innocence, the privilege against self-incrimination, the timely notice of charges, the right to cross-examine and to present defense witnesses, and proof beyond a reasonable doubt. The accused will be provided with military defense counsel, and can retain any civilian counsel eligible for a security clearance. Trials will be open, and can be attended by members of the press, except in limited circumstances where sensitive information is presented. The defendant's military counsel will have access even to classified information, in order to protect the defendant's interests, and bears the solemn duty to provide effective assistance of counsel and a zealous defense of the accused.

Trial panels will vary in size, with three to seven fact-assessors. Any finding of guilt must be concurred in by at least two-thirds of a panel. Because the death penalty is an especially serious matter, even in crimes so horrific as the September 11 attacks, any capital sentence must be approved unanimously by a seven-member panel.

There will also be a second review panel to assess the completed trial proceedings. This appellate panel (on which specially commissioned civilians may serve) has the power, acting by a majority, to return the case for further proceedings where a material error of law has occurred. The commission rules may also be amended in the future as circumstances may warrant.

These standards are consistent with the norms of international humanitarian law as well as American law and legal traditions. Though al Qaeda fighters and Taliban leaders are not lawful combatants, due to their demonstrated failure to abide by the laws of war, the implementing rules will provide to all suspects a full and fair trial.

We have each offered our advice individually to the Secretary of Defense on the appropriate form and substance of the rules for the proposed military commissions. The public discussion and Congressional views on procedures have also been helpful. Although some of us might have treated some details differently, we are all convinced that the completed rules, under consideration for four months, will provide a balanced framework for fair trials. The rules for military commissions—framed within the circumstances of open societal discussion—merit the confidence of America, her allies abroad, and other nations who would choose to elevate the rule of law over the chaos of terrorism.

The regulations mandate each military commission to provide a "full and fair" trial. Success will ultimately depend on the work of the dedicated judges, prosecutors and defense lawyers, in whom we have great confidence. In a very real sense, the qualities of the American legal system will be on display before the world. The ideals of a law-dedicated culture stand in stark contrast to the nihilistic aims of al Qaeda's global network of terror and violence.

An Interim Assessment of September 11: What Has Changed and What Has Not?

ROBERT JERVIS

I do not think any of us has a definitive understanding of the causes and consequences of the terrorist attacks of September 11; I know that I do not. These events are so recent that we lack information as well as time for thought and discussion. Emotions also remain raw, and we have little general knowledge to draw on because our grasp of terrorism is even less secure than it is of other important social phenomena such as poverty, ethnic conflict, and wars. Terrorism grounded in religion poses special problems for modern social science, which has paid little attention to religion, perhaps because most social scientists find this subject uninteresting if not embarrassing. These obstacles help explain if not excuse why most of my arguments will be negative ones. It is easier to dispute some commonly held views than to say what is right. I will argue that the threat of terrorism is not as new as is often claimed, that terrorism reinforces state power more than it undermines it or exemplifies the decreasing importance of states, that the claims for reducing terrorism by getting at its root causes are largely tendentious, that the world is not likely to unite against terrorism. Contrary to what I believed at first, September 11 has occasioned major changes in Russian and, even more, U.S. foreign policy and may usher in a period of assertive American hegemony.

What is New?

When we are confronted with something as unsettling as the terrorist attacks, our first reaction is to see them as unprecedented, and indeed the world had never seen a terrorist attack that killed so many people. But terrorism itself is not new. A precise definition may be impossible, but some stab at one is un-

---

ROBERT JERVIS is the Adlai E. Stevenson Professor of International Politics at Columbia University. His most recent book is *System Effects: Complexity in Politics and Social Life*.

avoidable: the use of violence for political or social purposes that is not publicly authorized by leaders of recognized political units, including acts that are sponsored and supported by states, but not publicly avowed.

It is not surprising that terrorism is ancient, because individuals have never been fully bound to established states and terror is needed by the weak who lack other instruments. Terrorism, although not easy to mount, is much easier than fielding a full-scale military apparatus; a great deal of disruption is possible with relatively little force. Whether the goal is revenge, the hope to inflict enough pain to get the adversary to change its behavior, or the desire to call attention to one's cause, terror may be the only tool that might prove effective.

This is not to claim that September 11 represented nothing new, however. The form and scale of the attack obviously were enabled by modern technology. Airplanes could not be turned into weapons until recently; since people now live and work packed together, many can be killed in one blow; since modern societies are highly interconnected, they can be disrupted by limited destruction. The advantages that medical science has given the world are matched by the speed with which infectious diseases can be spread through air travel.

Modern societies may also be uniquely psychologically vulnerable. The density of personal networks multiplies the number of people who lost a relative or close friend or know someone who did. Everyone I know in New York fits into the latter category if not the former. The rapid flow of information means that everyone immediately learns about any terrorist attack and follows it as it unfolds. Furthermore, because everyone gets this information, it dominates not only the thoughts of separated individuals but social conversation and so is incorporated into popular consciousness and culture. This effect is magnified by the availability of videos, which by their vividness make a deep and lasting impression.

Not only do terrorist attacks resonate more deeply through society than was the case in the past, but they are more shocking because we are no longer accustomed to war, violent domestic disturbances, and raging epidemics. People in the advanced democracies now see themselves, their relatives, and their friends live long and relatively tranquil lives. Terrorism was less shocking when it was only one of many forms of violent death that could be expected. Now it stands out, which helps explain why people so overreact. The fear of anthrax is much greater than concern about influenza, although the latter will kill thousands of times more Americans that the former and the chance of a massive anthrax attack is slight; people cancel flights to drive, at a greatly increased chance of dying.

Similar processes explain the economic impact of September 11. The attacks came at a time when the U.S. economy was slipping, and the direct effect through damage to the airline and tourist industries was significant. But this cannot explain most of the subsequent economic downturn. Consumer confidence is crucial and is susceptible to significant psychological magnification. Not only is confidence inherently subjective, being an estimate of how well the economy is likely to do in the future, but it is highly interdependent in the sense that each person's confidence is in part based on her or his estimate of how confident others are. Positive feedbacks and bandwagon effects then are likely. These should not be dismissed as irrational: since the fate of the economy depends on how much people will buy, and this in turn is strongly influenced by their predictions of their future economic fortunes, I should be less confident if I think others are. So when shocks like terrorism are very widely felt and the level of consumer confidence is known to the general public, the economic health of the society is highly vulnerable. The chief economist of the International Monetary Fund noted that after September 11, most of the world economies suffered badly, not only because they reflected the downturn in the United States; but "One reason we have become more synchronized is because we're all watching CNN."[1]

The obvious irony is that American society is now more vulnerable than the military. Although the military action in Afghanistan may have significantly reduced the threat of terrorism against the United States, at least in the short run, it cannot perform the standard function of defense. In the classical model, the armed forces literally stand between the population and the enemy. The development of air power and, even more, nuclear weapons reduced if not destroyed this conception, erecting in its place the edifice of deterrence. Fulfilling this mission required retaliatory forces to be as invulnerable as possible, buried deep beneath the soil or the oceans, and standard conceptions of the stability of a mutually deterrent relationship called for the civilian population to be unprotected so that neither side would be tempted to attack. No theories mandate civilian vulnerability to terrorism, but civilian targets are easier to destroy than are military ones, and civilian life is easier to disrupt than is the military. This might not be problematic if deterrence held, but terrorists have little to lose.[2]

We should remember, however, that short of an attack by a lethal and infectious disease such as smallpox, no terrorist can inflict nearly as much damage as warfare.[3] Even a mere decade after the end of the cold war, it is easy to forget that we used to live with the possibility of unimaginable devastation. Interestingly enough, in the earlier years of the cold war, American leaders doubted

---

[1] Quoted in Joseph Kahn, "The World's Economies Slide Together Into Recession," *New York Times*, 25 November 2001.

[2] The Bush administration's rejection of deterrence seems to go beyond terrorism, however. Even before September 11, the President advocated the deployment of missile defense because "rogue" states could not be deterred and the call for overthrowing Saddam Hussein rests on the premise that threats are insufficient to keep his behavior within acceptable bounds. Bush's commencement speech at West Point revealed his skepticism about deterrence: "Remarks by the President at 2002 Graduation Exercise of the United States Military Academy," White House Press Release, 1 June 2002, 2–3. A recent academic critique of deterrence that shares the administration's perspective is Keith Payne, *The Fallacies of Cold War Deterrence and a New Direction* (Lexington: University Press of Kentucky, 2001).

[3] Of course, terrorists might employ a nuclear device, but these are likely to be very small in number and relatively small in lethality. They hardly compare to the destruction that either superpower could have brought on the other.

that the country could live with such a prospect over a prolonged period of time.[4] In fact, the country did adjust without sacrificing many of its deepest values, and this gives some hope for our ability to cope with the psychological burdens imposed by the new threats.

THE DECLINE OF STATES?

At first glance, terrorism in general and September 11 in particular would seem to epitomize the declining relevance of states. Putting aside state-sponsored terrorism, these attacks are violence by private actors who are seeking public ends, which is just what states are supposed to stamp out. They represent the failure of states to protect their own citizens, which is their primary purpose. A world characterized by extensive terrorism is one in which states are not the most important actors.

September 11 also represents the declining importance of states in two other ways. First, terrorist groups are transnational, united not by their national citizenship or even the desire to form a state, but by religious and ideological beliefs. Although most of the hijackers were Saudis, letters found in al Qaeda headquarters in Kabul indicate that its members came from at least twenty countries.[5] Were this a peaceful enterprise, we would celebrate it as showing the ability of people from different countries, social classes, and experiences to work together. Second, the attack demonstrates the importance of globalization. Not only did the hijackers come from many countries, but they traveled throughout the world and depended on the efficient movement of information and money. Their motives and goals also epitomize globalization. They are seeking not the expansion or retraction of national power, let alone territory, but the stanching of the global flow of corrupting ideas and the protection if not expansion of the realm in which proper forms of Islam dominate.

There is something to these arguments, but in other ways September 11 shows the crucial role of states. To start with, al Qaeda gained much if its capabilities through its close ties to, if not its capture of, the Afghan government. It could not have operated as it did without the acquiescence and the sponsorship of the state government. Extensive training of terrorists would have been impossible; semipermanent headquarters could not have been established; the maintenance of a far-flung network would have been extremely difficult. In a way, the United States has ratified and reinforced the links between terrorists and states by making it clear that it will now hold the latter accountable for any acts of terror emanating from their territory.[6]

[4] Gregory Mitrovich, *Undermining the Kremlin: America's Strategy to Subvert the Soviet Bloc, 1947–1956* (Ithaca, NY: Cornell University Press, 2000).

[5] David Rhoad, "On Paper Scraps, Talk of Judgment Day and Words To Friends At Home," *New York Times*, 24 November 2001.

[6] It can be argued that this stance, and the attack against Afghanistan, will weaken states by ignoring their sovereignty and perhaps opening the door to other modifications of this cornerstone of the state system. But sovereignty always has been complex, flexible, and pragmatic. See Stephen Krasner, *Sovereignty: Organized Hypocrisy* (Princeton: Princeton University Press, 1999).

The targets of September 11 also included major elements of state power. The Pentagon was attacked, and the White House probably was the target of the plane that crashed in Pennsylvania. The response further showed the continued centrality of states. Most strikingly, American public opinion and even traditionally antistate conservatives immediately looked to the organs of the government for order and protection. The national guard was sent to New York City and airports; federal moneys poured into affected locales; airport security personnel was federalized; the federal government was granted greatly increased powers of investigation and prosecution, despite the doubts of the relatively isolated group of civil libertarians. In a time of crisis, Americans turned not to their churches, multinational corporations, or the UN, but to the national government. For better or for worse, one of the long-run consequences of September 11 is almost certain to be a larger and more powerful state apparatus.

Internationally as well, states were the dominant actors in the response. The United States put together a coalition of states, and when dealing with countries like Pakistan, Uzbekistan, and Tajikistan, did so in a way that increased the power of those states over their own societies by providing resources and expertise. Although the coalition is not an ordinary alliance, being more ad hoc and flexible, an alliance of states it nevertheless is. It also uses traditional diplomatic, economic, and military instruments. The technology is modern, and the intelligence network represents a form of globalization, but there is little in the fundamental nature of the activities that would surprise an observer of the past centuries.

We Must Get at the Root Causes of Terrorism: We Must Understand Why We Are Hated

It has become a truism, especially among liberals, that while attacking al Qaeda is necessary, it is not sufficient. Even if the campaign is successful, terrorism will recur unless the United States and its allies deal with the conditions that produced it. Central among these are grinding poverty in the Third World, great and increasing inequality within and among nations, corrupt and unresponsive governments, and American policies that too often range it alongside of the forces of injustice and oppression. In some ways, this argument is deeply attractive. We all want to make this a better world, and few would disagree with the proposition that poverty and oppression cause enormous misery around the world.

This perspective is misleading as an explanation for terrorism or a prescription for dealing with it, however. It is difficult to say exactly what the root causes of terrorism are. Poverty and lack of liberties do not appear on the list of grievances articulated by terrorist leaders, and neither the al Qaeda leadership nor the hijackers were poor. Of course, leaders of almost all political causes are drawn from the upper and middle classes of society; perhaps they would not have chosen their cause had their societies been richer and more egalitarian.

But rich societies produce their own terrorists and many poor societies do not, and it is hard to argue that poverty is either a necessary of a sufficient cause of terrorism. There is one specific thing that the United States could do that in all probability will have a good effect, however: it could provide funds for education and press Muslim governments to do likewise; as it stands now, parents often send their children to madrassas because no other education is available.

To see the absence of liberal arrangements as the root cause of terrorism is even more perverse. Tolerance for diversity, respect for human rights as the West defines them, free and diverse mass media, vigorous political competition, and equality for women is not the vision of the good society held by the terrorists and their supporters. The very notion of elevating the rights of individuals and the ability to choose one's way of life is anathema to them. Traditions, real or imagined, community values as they interpret them, and life regulated by Muslim clerics who read the Koran the way Taliban leaders did are their avowed objectives. Perhaps if their countries were remodeled along Western lines, terrorism would eventually subside. But resistance, including terrorism, would almost certainly increase during the transition, which could last for generations.[7]

Even if poverty, inequality, and oppression were the root causes of terrorism, there is little reason to think that we could deal with them effectively. Many of us believe that the United States should provide higher levels of economic assistance to the Third World and lower tariff barriers to their goods, but we cannot point to solid evidence to support the argument that doing so would make much difference. For all our studies, we are far from a complete understanding of what produces democracy, a well-functioning civil society, and respect for human rights. It is even less clear that the relevant variables can be much affected by outside interventions. It can be argued that one of the main barriers to democracy in Islamic countries is the lack of a separation between church and state and an absence of the idea that even in a religiously homogeneous society the direct political influence of theological leaders should be limited. It is hard to see what outsiders could do to effect such a separation, however.

Somewhat parallel to the call for attacking the root causes of terrorism is the plea to understand why the perpetrators undertook such dreadful acts. There are many barriers to understanding, starting with the fact that the terrorists come from different cultural and religious backgrounds than we do. Even if we can trust the translations of their statements, they metaphorically as well as literally speak a different language. Furthermore, there are political and psychological inhibitions to understanding why one is hated, since this may lead to asking whether there is some validity to the grievances. This is why a few

---

[7] This is why Samuel Huntington's *The Clash of Civilizations and the Remaking of World Order* (New York: Simon and Schuster, 1996), far from proclaiming the superiority of the West and calling for the westernization of the world, asks for toleration of different cultures and decries Western attempts to force its values and way of life on others. To interfere in other cultures is a recipe for greatly increasing conflict to no good end.

hotheads initially attacked such pleas, seeing them as excusing the terrorists. I do not think this is fair. Understanding and even empathy is not inconsistent with the strongest possible condemnation.

Once we put aside these superficial objections, the need for understanding is almost self-evident. Intellectuals seek understanding for its own sake; policy makers need understanding to establish an appropriate policy. But it is worth noting that the second proposition is not without its problems. Sometimes understanding a problem can push solutions beyond reach. One important historical case is British policy following the fall of France in May 1940. Almost alone among top British decision makers, Winston Churchill adamantly opposed opening peace talks with Germany, but he reached (or at least justified) his conclusion on the basis of wildly incorrect information and misleading analysis.[8] More generally, Albert Hirschman has shown that many important human endeavors are made possible only by what he calls the "hiding hand."[9] We start many ventures because we greatly underestimate the hindrances and are fortunate to fully understand them only when we have invested so much time and effort that is seems better to push on rather than try something else. Had we understood the magnitude of the task at the start, we never would have undertaken it, as many advanced graduate students come to appreciate. Collective action problems may also be harder to solve if they are understood. Many voluntary associations and related efforts succeed because few members understand that each individual's contribution is too small to make a noticeable difference. Thus it is not surprising that when I ask my students to play a form of a collective action game in class, the level of successful cooperation falls from the introductory class to the advanced undergraduate class to the graduate classes. Sometimes a lot of learning is even more dangerous than a little.

Putting aside this possibility, the worthy cause of understanding why the United States is hated may lead in directions unanticipated by those who call loudest for the effort. Bin Laden appears to hate the United States both for what it is and what it has done. The United States exemplifies consumerism, individual choice, and a relatively high degree of sexual permissiveness and equality. By being so powerful around the world, it cannot but be a threat to cultures that are built on very different values. The terrorists and others who share these concerns are not being paranoid to fear that fundamentalist Islam will be under great pressure from corrosive Western values as long as the latter have global reach.

---

[8] P. M. H. Bell, *A Certain Eventuality: Britain and the Fall of France* (Farnborough, UK: Saxon House, 1974); David Reynolds, "Churchill and the British 'Decision' to Fight on in 1940: Right Policy, Wrong Reasons" in Richard Langhorne, ed., *Diplomacy and Intelligence During the Second World War* (New York: Cambridge University Press, 1985), 147–67. A recent, more popular treatment is John Lukacs, *Five Days in London: May 1940* (New Haven: Yale University Press, 1999).

[9] Albert Hirschman, *Development Projects Observed* (Washington, DC: Brookings Institution, 1967), 9–34.

Of course, the United States has not been passive, and the terrorists see a number of horrific policies. Foremost among them is the stationing of troops in Saudi Arabia and the support for a corrupt Saudi regime. Thus it is no accident that most of the hijackers were Saudis. The grievance that is second in prominence is the American attacks on Iraq. But it is not clear whether this position is much more than an attempt to cater to the beliefs of the followers; Saddam Hussein's regime, although repressive, has not propagated fundamentalist Islam. Bin Laden also berates the United States for its support of Israel, although this position received stress only after September 11 and also may be designed to garner support from the widest possible Arab audience. Furthermore, bin Laden's opposition is to the existence of Israel and the American support for the Jewish state, not to the settlements or Israeli sovereignty over parts of Jerusalem.

What this means is that there are no conceivable changes in the United States and American policy that could reduce al Qaeda's hatred. Powerful states are always hated, even if they exercise their power relatively benignly.[10] Perhaps the United States might reduce the terrorists' hatred by withdrawing its troops from Saudi Arabia. Whether this would do any good at this point is far from clear, however, and probably would increase the chance of another Iraqi attack on Kuwait.

The much larger group throughout the Islamic world that has some sympathy for the September 11 attacks and that sees bin Laden as at least in part a hero and is glad to see the United States humbled by the attacks, is of course harder to analyze, being much more disparate. Much of the rage is attributable to their own governments, which are unable to provide a decent life for their people while sponsoring mass media that blame most of their ills on the United States. Democracy, reform, and more diverse media might have good effect here, especially if they were coupled with economic growth that led to improved lives for society's lower strata. But whether such an outcome could be produced by a different United States policy is questionable.

Turning to foreign policy, following a more "moderate" policy toward Iraq and lifting the embargo would meet one of the grievances. But doing so might not reduce suffering within Iraq, because the oil-for-food program already provides sufficient funds to provide food and medicine for the people of Iraq, and it is unclear that a change in American policy would lead to a change in Saddam's priorities. If the United States were to withdraw its protective umbrella over the northern areas, the regime would reestablish control, with the resulting repression and flow of refugees. If the terrorists were motivated by compassion for the Kurds, this could increase terrorism.

U.S. support for Israel is perhaps highest on the list of grievances in the Muslim world. Over the long run, the Arab-Israeli dispute and the American

---

[10] See Richard K. Betts, "The Soft Underbelly of American Primacy," *Political Science Quarterly* 117 (Spring 2002).

role in it may play a large role in cultivating the next generation of terrorists, even if it has not generated the current one. But in the short run, it is hard to tell what difference United States policy would make, and the United States was not without enemies when it was actively promoting a settlement that would have given the PLO a state, most of the West Bank, and East Jerusalem. It is also interesting that those who believe that the United States could diminish Arab hatred toward it by pressing for an Israeli withdrawal also believe that this policy is moral and would bring peace between Israel and its neighbors. Here, as with policy toward Iraq, those who call for a tougher stance toward Israel (or toward the PLO) held these views on 10 September. It would be more impressive if those advocating a different American policy in the Middle East argued that while the old policy had been appropriate previously and was morally well-grounded, the new circumstances require a courting of important groups in the Middle East even at Israel's expense. I think that if the shoe had been on the other foot and circumstances had arisen that could lead people to call for greater American support for an unyielding Israeli policy, calls to do so would be rejected by liberals on the grounds that it would be wrong to make people in the Middle East pay for a policy that served American interests elsewhere.

More reasonable is the argument that the roots of much terrorism lie in the intolerance and hatred preached in many mosques and taught in madrases, often supported by Saudi money. While those who reject social constructivism should be slow to give too much credit to the power of socialization and should ask why these messages find a receptive audience, al Qaeda surely would have had fewer recruits had these voices been quieter or were alternative views expressed clearly by other religious and political leaders. But for many countries, tolerating or sponsoring religious extremism is more attractive than domestic reform, and it is far from clear how much the United States can do to change this landscape.

The call to understand why people hate us, while intellectually sound, is largely motivated by political agendas unrelated to September 11. There are many reasons to object to the Bush administration's policy in the Middle East. I myself think it has been badly misguided, but it is disingenuous to claim that such a conclusion follows from an understanding of the motives of any course of action that can be rationalized on the grounds that it will reduce terrorism. Thus a member of the Kuwaiti parliament urged that his country adopt Sharia on the grounds that if this were done, "there would be no terrorism."[11]

---

[11] Quoted in Douglas Jehl, "Democracy's Uneasy Steps in Islamic World," *New York Times*, 23 November 2001. Also see Serge Schmemann, "U.N. Gets a Litany of Antiterror Plans," ibid., 12 January 2002; and Neil MacFarquhar, "Syria Repackages Its Repression of Muslim Militants as Antiterror Lesson," ibid., 14 January 2002.

It's a War

In his speech to a joint session of Congress after the attack, President George W. Bush declared that the United States was waging a war against terrorism, and it used military force to overthrow the government of Afghanistan. But this was not a "normal" war, and the very label is contentious and questionable.[12] To start with, the overthrow of the Afghan government was not the ultimate goal of the effort but only a means to combat terrorism. The point was not to change Afghan external policy or reduce the power of that regime or country, as it would have been in most wars. Rather, Afghanistan was attacked in order to install a new government that would eliminate the terrorists; had it been possible to attack the terrorists directly, this would have been done and the Afghan authorities, even though repellent to many American values, would have been left in place.

If this is a war, the obvious question is what its objectives are. The normal answer would be to get the adversary to withdraw from disputed territory, to make it impossible for that country to follow obnoxious policies, or to replace a government that was deemed a menace by its very existence. But these conceptions of victory seem inappropriate here, and there are no clear replacements. So it is not surprising that the administration has never issued a definitive statement of its war aims. Secretaries Colin Powell and Donald Rumsfeld have said that the war will be won when Americans feel secure again, an objective that sounds more like psychotherapy than international politics. This is not to say that it is an inappropriate formulation when dealing with terrorism, however. By its nature, terror seeks to utilize political and psychological leverage in order to produce political effects that are disproportionate to the military force deployed. To the extent that it is more than mere revenge (a motive not to be underestimated, as I will discuss later), it seeks change through inducing fear, and generally fear that is a magnified rather than a true reflection of what else could follow. So reducing fear and making Americans feel secure should be a crucial focus of American policy. But it is an unusual reason to wage a war.

Making Americans feel secure is presumably related to destroying al Qaeda and the Taliban regime that was linked to it. But as Bush has said on numerous occasions, Afghanistan and the terrorists located there are only the first target of the American efforts. With whom exactly are we at war? Who else is to be attacked? What constitutes terrorism? How do we distinguish terrorism from insurgency, let alone fighters for freedom? Will we keep fighting until terrorism disappears or will we be content with the lesser objective of reducing terrorism to manageable levels? What constitutes harboring terrorism, a crime which Bush has equated with terrorism itself? Questions like these can never be answered with complete clarity, and fortunately a coherent response is not necessary for a sensible policy. Indeed, under most circumstances the questions are

[12] See Michael Howard, "What's in a Name? How to Fight Terrorism," *Foreign Affairs* 81 (January-February 2002): 8–13.

not even asked, because satisfactory answers will not be forthcoming. But if one calls for a war, it becomes harder to avoid them, and the messy pragmatism, ambiguity, and inconsistency that are normal facts of policy life become more troublesome.

The most obvious question, which may be answered by the time this article appears in print, is whether the United States should attack Iraq. A significant group has long felt that the first Bush administration made a mistake by not finishing off Saddam Hussein after the Gulf War, although the difficulties in doing so are rarely examined. These people have been quick to see ambiguous evidence as indicating close links between Iraq and al Qaeda, just as opponents of this policy have been quick to provide other interpretations of the evidence. They have argued that Saddam is rapidly developing weapons of mass destruction.[13] Even if these points are granted, the obvious question is whether Saddam can be deterred from using these weapons. Saying that we are at war, however, distracts us from asking this or implies that deterrence has broken down and that the use rather than the threat of force is necessary.

The label "war" implies the primary use of military force. Other instruments like diplomacy and intelligence may be used, but they are in service of the deployment of armed force. I believe this conceptual frame is unfortunate when it comes to dealing with terrorism. Here diplomacy, the international criminal justice system, and especially intelligence are primary. With good information, almost everything can be done to reduce terrorism; without it, very little is possible. Force and the threat of force play a vital role both in helping to generate information and in the final elimination of terrorist targets, but intelligence and international information-sharing is central. If they are sacrificed in order to gain military advantage, the policy will suffer. Thinking of this as war then gets us thinking in the wrong terms.

Others have seen the advantages of taking the United States at its word and justifying their behavior in terms of fighting terrorism. In addition to the Russian rhetoric in its conflict in Chechnya, a leader of Hamas said that no one expected the United States to refrain from violence in response to the September 11 attack, "so why do you expect me to react peacefully to occupation?"[14] In parallel, Israeli Prime Minister Ariel Sharon argues: "You in America are in a war against terror. We in Israel are in a war against terror. It's the same

---

[13] In his press conference of 26 November, Bush equated the seeking of weapons of mass destruction to "terrorize nations" with terrorism. In this context, it is worth asking why there has been no call to target Iran, a country that has sponsored more terrorism than Iraq, is closer to gaining nuclear weapons, and is more anti-Israeli and almost as anti-American. The obvious reply is that there is a greater chance of peaceful change in that country than in Iraq, but I suspect that at least as important is the strength of the anti-Saddam faction within the U.S. elite, which realizes that military action against Iran would undercut the possibility of moving against Iraq.

[14] Quoted in James Bennett, "Israeli Soldier Killed in Gaza, Nablus Mourns a Hamas Leader," *New York Times*, 25 November 2001.

war."[15] One of his advisers explained that "the Palestinian Authority has an obligation to no longer harbor or give shelter to international terrorist organizations" like Hamas.[16] The Indians have equated 13 December (the date of the attack on their parliament) with September 11, an interpretation the United States has largely endorsed. All sorts of domestic oppression are also being claimed as counter-terrorism. Thus the Mugabe government in Zimbabwe claimed that critical reporters "are assisting terrorists.... We would like them to know that we agree with President Bush that anyone who in any way finances, harbors or defends terrorists is himself a terrorist. We, too, will not make any difference between terrorists and their friends or supporters."[17]

The United States initially responded that war was not against terrorism in general, but only against "terrorism with a global reach," as Bush put it in his speech of 20 September. This modifier nicely got the United States out of one dilemma, but opened the door to several others. If the war were to be against all terrorism, defeat would be inevitable and the collateral damage would be enormous. Even on the unreasonable assumption that such an effort would receive widespread support abroad, it would engender enormous opposition as well. In December 2001, bloody suicide attacks against Israel and the Indian parliament led the United States to broaden its definition, pushing Arafat and Musharraf to eliminate the groups responsible. Despite further broadening, the focus and consistency of the American effort remains to be seen.

To say that we are at war only with a subset of terrorists raises the question of in whose interest the war is being waged. The United States seeks worldwide support on the grounds that al Qaeda and related groups are seeking weapons of mass destruction, which "would be a threat to every nation and, eventually, to civilization itself."[18] But terrorists, even with nuclear weapons, do not target the entire globe. Instead, they attack sites in and representatives of particular states. As a Russian diplomat said to me shortly after Bush's speech, "Ah, a global reach—that means terrorists who can attack the United States." Terrorists in Sri Lanka, for example, do not seem to qualify. Neither, I suspect, would the IRA if it were to resume violence in Northern Ireland. (This is fortunate, because an attack on areas supporting these terrorists would require military action in New York's Lower East Side and Boston's South End.) Would renewed Algerian terrorism in France be "global"? I suspect the answer would turn on the extent of French support for American efforts. Politically and

---

[15] Quoted in William Safire, "Israel or Arafat," ibid., 3 December 2001; also see the remarks quoted in James Bennet, "Israelis Storm Village in the West Bank," ibid., 25 October 2001; Bennet, "15 Israelis Die in Bus Attack," ibid., 3 December 2001.

[16] Quoted in Bennet, "New Clashes in Gaza; Hamas to Limit Suicide Attacks," ibid., 22 December 2001.

[17] Rachel L. Swarns, "West's Envoys Unhappy, Find Zimbabwe Unhelpful," ibid., 24 November 2001; also see Tony Hawkins, "Harare to Hold Talks Today on Sanctions Threat," *Financial Times*, 17 December 2001.

[18] Quoted in "President's Words: 'Lift This Dark Threat,'" *New York Times*, 7 November 2001.

rhetorically convenient in the short run, Bush's answer to the question of what terrorists we are at war with may prove more troublesome over the long run, at minimum in highlighting American hypocrisy. It might have been more straightforward and honorable to declare that it was only terrorists who could menace American assets and allies that were our target.[19]

Framing the conflict as war also implies that we must be prepared to sacrifice many values in order to prevail. In a normal war, this would mean that men would be called to the colors and those at home would expect to endure economic privation and even enemy bombardment. But none of this is required here. Logic might suggest that our leaders would tell people that they must accept further acts of terrorism in order to win the struggle, but instead we are being urged to fly and shop.[20]

Greater sacrifices are being required in the area of civil liberties. The claim that we must accept intrusions and restrictions that were previously intolerable is justified not by detailed claims that the value of the information produced will outweigh the cost to our privacy and liberty but rather by blanket assertions that war requires measures that were previously unacceptable. Similarly, careful arguments for bringing terrorists before military tribunals are short-circuited by statements that this is what is done during wartime. As Bush declared: "The United States is under attack. And at war, the president needs to have the capacity to protect the national security interests and the safety of the American people."[21]

The Terrorism is Senseless

The attacks of September 11 seem not only inhumane but senseless. It is hard to see what objective bin Laden thought he could reach. I doubt that he really

[19] See David Sanger, "As the Battlefield Changes, So Does the War Itself," ibid., 23 December 2001; Serge Schmemann, "Caution: This Weapon May Backfire," ibid., 30 December 2001. Perhaps because of the apparent success of the operation in Afghanistan, in early 2002 American rhetoric and some of its actions expanded to encompass terrorism in general. This is consistent with indications that Bush will seek to exploit and reinforce American hegemony. As he said in his press conference in response to criticisms of U.S. unilateralism levied by the French foreign minister: people around the world "understand . . . that history has given us a unique opportunity to defend freedom. And we're going to seize the moment, and do it." See "President Bush, Prime Minister Koizumi Hold Press Conference," White House Press Release, 18 February 2002. The clearest rationale for such a stance was the draft Defence Policy Guidance for Fiscal Years 1994–1999 that was written by Paul Wolfowitz when he was in Bush senior's Pentagon. The document was toned down after it was leaked to the press: *New York Times*, 8 March 1992 and 24 May 1992.

[20] For a good statement of the sacrifices that Bush might ask of Americans, see Thomas Friedman, "Ask Not What . . . ," ibid., 9 December 2001.

[21] Quoted in Elisabeth Bumiller and Katharine Q. Seelye, "Bush Defends Wartime Call for Tribunals," ibid., 15 December 2001. More recently, "President Bush has issued an executive order barring union representation at United States attorneys' offices and at four other agencies in the Justice Department . . . out of concern that union contracts could restrict the ability of workers in the Justice Department to protect Americans and national security." Steven Greenhouse, "Bush, Citing Security, Bans Some Unions at Justice Dept.," ibid., 16 January 2002.

expected to change American support for Saudi Arabia and Israel or its opposition to Iraq. His actions also seem self-defeating, because they endangered his life, al Qaeda, and the Taliban regime.

But actions that are horrible are not necessarily irrational. Bin Laden and his colleagues may have been motivated first of all by the desire for revenge and what they saw as justice. The United States had committed great crimes and had to be punished. Even if the attacks could not set the world aright, they would at least make the United States pay a price for its awful deeds. We—or at least academics—often underestimate the importance of revenge. Emotional, primitive, unamenable to analysis, it does not seem to belong in a civilized country. But it does. In everyday life we often try to inflict small punishments on others who have harmed us, not because we think it will change them, but because we think this is appropriate. The centerpiece of U.S. strategic policy during the cold war was the threat to massively retaliate against a Soviet attack on the United States. Putting aside arcane war-fighting scenarios of interest to a few theorists, the attack to which the United States was seen as responding would have been one that utterly destroyed it. Retaliation could have reached no meaningful goal and would have been motivated entirely by revenge. No one doubted the credibility of this threat, however.

Bin Laden may also have had an instrumental purpose. His focus may have been less on the United States and the short run than on the Islamic world over a longer period. He could have reasoned that a dramatic action would put his movement and ideology at the center of attention. He could expect to multiply the strength of his cause even if he was to die in the effort. As E. E. Schattschneider showed, the outcome of a conflict is often determined by the number and kind of people who are mobilized to join in it.[22] Bin Laden may also have expected the attack to serve as a provocation that would lead the United States to strike out in a way that would rally support for him. Although September 11 cannot be seen as a "clash of civilizations," he may have hoped to generate one.

THE UNITED STATES MUST NOT WALK AWAY FROM AFGHANISTAN AGAIN

It is often argued that the Taliban and bin Laden are a product of previous American actions in supporting the resistance to Soviet rule and then ignoring the country when the cold war ended. The first claim is largely correct, although the implied counterfactual may not be. That is, it can be argued that even without American aid the *mujahedeen* eventually would have forced the Soviet Union to withdraw.

However this may be, it is certainly true that the United States lost interest in Afghanistan after the end of the cold war. The lesson is obvious: the United

---

[22] E. E. Schattschneider, *The Semi-Sovereign People* (New York: Holt, Rinehart, and Winston, 1960).

States and others now must stay fully engaged. The implicit counterfactual here is that if the United States had remained involved, a more benign Afghan regime could have developed. While I share this view, we cannot be sure and should not overestimate what outsiders can do. Coalition building is extremely difficult for outsiders; nation building may be impossible. Both our knowledge and the relevant resources are sharply limited. In the short run, violence can be suppressed and some laws reestablished. Outside organizations are not without instruments they can deploy, especially money and technical assistance; but these instruments are not magic bullets and many of the consequences are unintended. A host of questions arise. Should we try to work through local leaders who can control their own areas and then cooperate with counterparts from different groups? Should we seek central power-sharing arrangements that aim at stability, the limitation of power of the local warlords, and reduced political competition? Should we instead push for new political groupings that crosscut older rivalries? It is neither clear whether outsiders could implement such arrangements nor whether they would produce the desired effects. Even food aid can backfire in several ways, for example by providing a resource that fuels violence, bolstering only those factions that are able to work with the aid groups, and discouraging farmers from returning to their fields.

None of this is to say that the United States and its allies should abandon Afghanistan, but we should not conclude that the previous abandonment created today's misery or have high expectations for what we can achieve. As one observer said about the dreary results of a variety of international efforts in Somalia: "Total benign neglect is problematic, but total engagement and obsession is problematic as well."[23]

A New World?

If is often said that "everything has changed after September 11," "this is the end of the post-cold war era," and "the world will never be the same." I now believe that there is more to this than I initially thought. While I remain skeptical that the world will unite against terrorism, fundamental shifts in U.S. foreign policy appear to be underway.[24]

One claim is that terrorism is such a scourge that the nations of the world will unite against it, just as most countries pull together if they are attacked. The Bush administration argues that this is what should happen, seeing the conflict as one of civilization against evil which must trump all differences. So the

---

[23] Quoted in Mark Turner, "Somalia Provides Lesson in Non-Interference," *Financial Times*, 19 November 2001.

[24] For a discussion of other drastic changes in world politics that are recent but pre-date September 11, most importantly the fact that war among the leading powers is now unthinkable, see John Mueller, *Retreat from Doomsday: The Obsolescence of Major War* (New York: Basic Books, 1989); and Robert Jervis, "Theories of War in an Era of Leading Power Peace," *American Political Science Review* 96 (March 2002): 1–15.

United States tells India and Pakistan to stand down and join the common coalition and urges Israel and the PLO to subordinate their dispute to the common cause. The expectation that the world will fall into line is not entirely unreasonable. In the past, nations put aside old conflicts when faced by an even more pressing common enemy, as Britain and the USSR finally did in their struggle against Nazi Germany. But I doubt that most countries see terrorism as posing a threat of this magnitude, although a serious biological or nuclear attack might change this. At this point, however, it is hard to argue that India has more reason to fear al Qaeda than Pakistan, nor are most other countries in the world more concerned about this network than they are by neighbors or local threats.[25]

Even if few countries support al Qaeda, many use forms of terror to advance their own goals. If the struggle were against terrorism rather than anti-American terrorism, these countries would have to forgo many of their most valued objects. And if the enemy is anti-American terror, there is even less reason for countries to unite against it, although the United States does have powerful incentives to deploy.

Thus it is not surprising that many countries have taken advantage of the new opportunities offered by September 11. Sudan has accepted the American "get out of jail free" card by offering intelligence cooperation in return for being removed from the list of countries that sponsor terrorism. Pakistan was transformed from a nuclear-powered troublemaker and an enemy of the new American potential ally in the region, India, to a pillar of stability meriting extensive aid and a forgiveness of past sins. Uzbekistan's lack of democracy and violations of human rights were put aside to gain necessary bases.

More importantly, the changes in Russian foreign policy and Russian-American relations since September 11 have been dramatic and unexpected by many analysts, myself included.[26] Russia has embraced a high degree of cooperation with the United States, largely on American terms. It not only endorsed the American response in Afghanistan, but facilitated it by not opposing an American military presence in Central Asia, an area previously seen as a Russian sphere of influence. Even more startlingly, Putin accepted the American renunciation of the ABM treaty and an arms reduction agreement that closely followed American preferences. It also appears that in return for a greater role in NATO, Putin has dropped his opposition to further eastward expansion of that organization. While points of friction remain, most obviously over Iran and

---

[25] The conflict between India and Pakistan over the alignment of the new Afghan regime influenced ·ruggle over the regime's composition and the American efforts to build a broad-based coalition. ·a's moves on the diplomatic front, see Edward Luce: "India Moves Quickly to Build Kabul *ncial Times*, 13 December 2001.
 k many American leaders by surprise: see, for example, Condoleezza Rice, "Promoting ·est," *Foreign Affairs* 79 (January/February 2000): 45–62. "This is a different Putin," ·g of the agreement making Russia a partial member of NATO. Quoted in David ·ly Welcomes Russia as a Partner," *New York Times*, 29 May 2002.

Iraq, Putin has chosen to bandwagon with the United States rather than balance against it. The latter policy was widely expected and might have succeeded, because on many issues Russia was not isolated. Had Putin maintained his opposition to the American renunciation of the ABM agreement, he could have recruited many European countries to his side. But he apparently calculated that the chances of success were not great and its value was limited. What he needed was American support for his regime, full acceptance into the ranks of Western countries, and help in rebuilding the Russian economy. For these goals, American support was necessary.

This choice has significantly altered world politics. Although it would go too far to say that Russia will now be treated like any other European country or to be certain that the new course will be maintained, especially if it does not yield visible benefits, the range and extent of Russian-American cooperation has greatly increased, the prospects for the integration of Russia into many Western projects has brightened, and the chances of major political conflicts between the United States and Russia have decreased. What cannot be readily determined, however, is the role that the common interest in fighting terrorism has played in bringing about this change. It seems unlikely that terrorism is Putin's main concern; while his desire for American support in Chechnya cannot be ignored, essentially he saw antiterrorism as a convenient opportunity for a general reorientation of Russian policy. Granting the United States a degree of dominance was a significant price, but one worth paying to gain American acceptance and economic assistance.

Probably more temporary is the change in U.S.-PRC relations. Before September 11, the Bush administration said that China was the greatest menace to world peace. This discussion has ceased, and for its part the PRC has been quick to point out that it staunchly opposes terrorism throughout the world, especially in the Muslim province of Xinjiang. But I doubt that this common interest will prove sufficient to override the conflict over Taiwan and other issues.

The most important change has been in American foreign policy, which is now on a different course both from what it was under Clinton and the direction that had been established by Bush before September 11. Although Clinton's foreign policy was far from consistent, it displayed a serious degree of multilateralism, meaningful consultation with allies, concern with preventing humanitarian disasters, and support for peacekeeping operations. Bush took a different stance in his campaign and his first year in office. He and his colleagues argued that the United States often had to act on its own, that military force should be used only to protect vital interests, and that the burden of humanitarian interventions should be left to others. The Defense Department and its ideological allies were pushing to withdraw American peacekeepers from Bosnia, Kosovo, and Sinai, and no one in the government thought the United States should engage in nation building.

Policy after September 11 continued and extended some of these elements but altered several others. Unilateralism continued and perhaps increased. Of course, some assistance from others was necessary in Afghanistan. British special forces were useful, and bases in Pakistan and Uzbekistan and cooperation from other countries in the region was essential. But this should not be mistaken for a joint venture. In order to gain support, the United States agreed to overlook the lack of democracy and human rights in its new friends and to provide them with significant financial assistance. But it did not bend its policy to meet their preferences. Indeed, in stressing that the United States was now building coalitions in the plural rather than an alliance, American leaders made it clear that they would forgo the participation of any particular country rather than compromise. Looking to the future, if the United States refrains from invading Iraq, it will be because of opposition from America's military, not its allies.

There has been no willingness to cater to world public opinion or to pay much heed to cries of outrage from European countries as the United States interprets its interest and the interest of the world in its own way. Thus the Bush administration walked away from the Kyoto protocol, the International Criminal Court, and the Comprehensive Nuclear Test-Ban Treaty rather than try to work within these frameworks and modify them. The United States also ignored European criticisms of its Middle Eastern policy. On a smaller scale, it forced out the heads of the Organization for the Prohibition of Chemical Weapons and the Intergovernmental Panel on Climate Change. In response to this kind of behavior, European diplomats can only say: "Big partners should consult with smaller partners."[27] The operative word is "should."

The administration has defended each of its actions, but has not explained its general stance. I think the most principled, persuasive, and perhaps correct defense is built around the familiar argument about the difficulty in procuring public goods. As long as leadership is truly shared, very little will happen, because no one actor will be willing to shoulder the costs and the responsibilities. "We are trying to lead the world," is how one administration official put it when the United States blocked language in a UN declaration on child health that might be read as condoning abortion.[28] This is not entirely hypocritical: many of the countries that endorsed the Kyoto protocol had grave reservations about it, but were unwilling to stand up to strongly committed domestic groups. True consultation is likely to produce inaction. This was true in 1993, when Clinton

---

[27] Quoted in Steven Erlanger, "Bush's Move On ABM Pact Gives Pause to Europeans," ibid., 13 December 2001; also see Suzanne Daley, "Many in Europe Voice Worry that U.S. Will Not Consult Them," ibid., 31 January 2002; Erlanger, "Protests, and Friends Too, Await Bush in Europe," ibid., 22 May 2002. For the view that I wish were correct that the United States has bound itself to being responsive to its allies, see G. John Ikenberry, "After September 11: America's Grand Strategy and International Order in the Age of Terror," *Survival* 43 (Winter 2001-2002): 19-34; Ikenberry, *After Victory: Institutions, Strategic Restraint, and the Rebuilding of Order After Major War* (Princeton: Princeton University Press, 2001); John Gerard Ruggie, *Winning the Peace: America and the New World Order* (New York: Columbia University Press, 1996).

[28] Quoted in Somini Sengupta, "U.N. Forum Stalls on Sex Education and Abortion Rights," *New York Times*, 10 May 2002.

favored the policy of "lift and strike" in Yugoslavia—lifting the arms embargo against Bosnia and striking Serbian forces—but was unwilling to move on his own. Instead, he sent Secretary of State Warren Christopher to ascertain European views. This multilateral and democratic procedure did not work, because the Europeans did not want to be put on the spot, and in the face of apparent American indecision refused to endorse such a strong policy. If the United States had informed the Europeans rather than consulted them, they probably would have gone along; what critics call unilateralism is in fact effective leadership. This is shown by the apparent willingness of the Europeans to put aside their fears and hesitations and assent to an American invasion of Iraq once the United States, rather than ask their opinions, showed that it was committed to the policy. Faced with an American decision to move ahead with or without their support, the Europeans would be emboldened; and given the choice between having an invasion proceed despite their opposition or acquiescing and maintaining a common front, they would choose the latter. The displayed willingness to move unilaterally then not only avoids paralysis, but is necessary to produce unity.

I believe that the basic ideas can be traced back to a blueprint for American security policy drafted by Paul Wolfowitz when he was undersecretary of defense for policy in the first Bush administration.[29] Once leaked, the document was disavowed, because it was too aggressive and coherent, but there is a great deal to be said for it. The key argument was that its interests and those of world freedom and stability required the United States to maintain and enhance its dominant position and prevent the rise of any peer competitor. This would mean not only sustaining such a high level of military spending that no other country or group of countries could think of challenging it, but also using force on behalf of others so they would not need to develop potent military establishments of their own. The implicit claim is that the United States cannot afford to return to traditional multipolar balance of power politics, which would inevitably turn dangerous and destructive. As Bush explained in his commencement address at West Point, "America has, and intends to keep, military strengths beyond challenge—thereby making the destabilizing arms races of other eras pointless, and limiting rivalries to trade and other pursuits of peace."[30]

To these views Bush has added a conception of what the war on terrorism requires that is so expansive as to require full-blown hegemony, if not an empire. Bush and his colleagues have decided to "seize the unipolar moment," in the phrase that Charles Krauthammer used when he urged the president's father to solidify American dominance after the fall of the Soviet Union.[31] This

---

[29] Ibid., 8 March and 24 May 1992. A fuller unclassified version is Zalmay Khalilzad, *From Containment to Global Leadership? America and the World After the Cold War* (Santa Monica, CA: RAND, 1995).

[30] "Remarks by the President at 2002 Graduation Exercise," 4.

[31] Charles Krauthammer, "The Unipolar Moment," *Foreign Affairs: America and the World, 1990-1991* 70 (No. 1): 23–33. For a critical recent analysis, see James Chace, "Imperial America and the Common Interest," *World Policy* 19 (Spring 2002): 1–9.

is not exactly the way Bush has put it, but his own words are not so different. In February 2002 he responded to a reporter's question about the predictable French criticism of his policy by saying that "history has given us a unique opportunity to defend freedom. And we're going to seize the moment, and do it."[32] One month later he declared, "we're resolved to fight the war on terror; this isn't a short-term strategy for us. . . . We understand history has called us into action, and we are not going to miss that opportunity to make the world more peaceful and more free.[33] These unscripted remarks are blunter but not greatly different from those in formal addresses such as the State of the Union: "History has called America and our allies to action, and it is both our responsibility and our privilege to fight freedom's fight."

American goals have grown steadily since September 11. At first, the war was limited to terrorists "with a global reach." But after the unexpected rapid success of the war in Afghanistan,[34] this modifier was dropped. Not only did administration rhetoric shift to seeing terrorism in general as a menace to civilization and "the new totalitarian threat,"[35] but the United States launched military efforts in the Philippines that can hardly be justified in terms of destroying al Qaeda. Furthermore, the administration has linked terrorism to the "axis of evil," arguing that the latter regimes are not only menaces on their own terms but must be combated lest they give weapons of mass destruction to terrorists. This position implies that the United States has little choice but to become the world's policeman. Terrorism has merged with a variety of disruptive behavior and regimes, all of which must be contained if not overthrown if the United States is to be secure.

Although not developed in as much detail, Bush and his colleagues seem to believe that this is a time of opportunity as well as danger: the combination of great American power and world outrage over terrorism presents what are likely to be unique circumstances that could permit the development of a better world. With American assistance—and threats—countries now will crush extremist movements, increase cooperation with each other, and give greater scope to the rule of law. A week after September 11, Bush is reported to have told one of his closest advisers: "We have an opportunity to restructure the world toward freedom, and we have to get it right." He expounded this theme in a formal speech marking the six-month anniversary of the attack: "When the terrorists are disrupted and scattered and discredited, . . . we will see then that

[32] "President Bush, Prime Minister Koizumi Hold Press Conference," White House Press Release, 18 February 2002, 6.

[33] "President, Vice President Discuss the Middle East," White House Press Release, 21 March 2002, 2.

[34] It should be noted, however, that the success in overthrowing the Taliban was not matched by success in rooting out al Qaeda.

[35] "President Thanks World Coalition for Anti-Terrorism Efforts," White House Press Release, 11 March 2002; David Sanger, "In Reichstag, Bush Condemns Terror as New Despotism," *New York Times*, 24 May 2002. Also see "Remarks by President at 2002 Graduation Exercise," 3.

the old and serious disputes can be settled within the bounds of reason, and goodwill, and mutual security. I see a peaceful world beyond the war on terror, and with courage and unity, we are building that world together."[36]

As this and other rhetoric indicate, Bush sees the U.S. engaged in a conflict between good and evil. While such a world view is consistent with the American political tradition,[37] it also owes something to Bush's outlook as a born-again Christian. There is reason to believe that just as his coming to Christ gave meaning to his previously aimless and dissolute personal life, so the war on terrorism has become not only the defining characteristic of his foreign policy, but also his sacred mission.[38]

Although for some government officials the war on terrorism permits the sort of highly assertive American foreign policy that they had favored from the start, for others, probably including Bush, it represents a true change. Whether it will last depends in part on events in the future, such as whether the United States chooses to invade Iraq and what the fate of such a move will be, the existence and nature of coming terrorist attacks, and the domestic political fortunes of the Bush administration. The structural conditions for American hegemony were produced by the size and vitality of the American economy, the lack of political unity within Europe, and the collapse of the Soviet Union. But it took both September 11 and the particular outlook of the Bush administration to put the United States on its current path. Although this trajectory may not be maintained, it is consistent both with the general tendency for states to expand their objectives as their power increases and with the American propensity to become fully involved in world politics only when it believes that it faces great threats or great opportunities.

For many of us, not a day will pass in which we will not think of September 11. Nevertheless, it may not change the world as much as it now appears. It is striking how much the diverse lessons of this event reinforce what the learner already believed. With the significant exceptions of many of the calls for increased domestic security and sacrifices of civil liberties, the measures that various groups advocate, from building missile defense, to shunning missile defense, to greater support of Ariel Sharon's policies, to greater opposition to them, to greater multilateralism, to increased economic assistance to the poor, to freer world trade, to shielding weak groups from the foreign competition, to

---

[36] Quoted in Frank Bruni, "For President, a Mission and a Role in History," *New York Times*, 22 September 2001; "President Thanks World Coalition for Anti-Terrorism Efforts," 3–4; also see "Remarks by the President at 2002 Graduation Exercise," 4–5.

[37] See, for example, George Kennan, *American Diplomacy, 1900-1965* (Chicago: University of Chicago Press, 1951); Robert Devine, *Perpetual War for Perpetual Peace* (College Station: Texas A & M University Press, 2000); for a related argument, see Frank Ninkovich, *Modernity and Power: A History of the Domino Theory in the 20th Century* (Chicago: University of Chicago Press, 1994).

[38] For a perceptive analysis, see Bruni, "For President, a Mission and a Role in History."

tax cuts at home all correspond to what the advocates had wanted earlier.[39] It is yet possible that the shock we have all felt will be translated into greater agreement and effective measures to deal with the world's ills, but I suspect that differences in diagnosis, values, and interests will continue to characterize how we understand terrorism and conduct world politics. If Bush continues to move the United States into a position of assertive hegemony, it will be interesting to see how the world reacts and whether American public opinion will provide the necessary support.*

---

[39] The most plausible argument that September 11 has strengthened the case for missile defense has not been widely made: it would increase the credibility of the threat to attack states that both possess weapons of mass destruction and harbor terrorists.

* This article has been slightly updated since the version that appeared in the Spring 2002 issue of *Political Science Quarterly*.